MARLOWE'S LITERARY SCEPTICISM

THE ARDEN SHAKESPEARE LIBRARY

MARLOWE'S LITERARY SCEPTICISM

Politic Religion and Post-Reformation Polemic

CHLOE KATHLEEN PREEDY

The Arden Shakespeare India
An imprint of Bloomsbury Publishing Plc

BLOOMSBURY
NEW DELHI • LONDON • OXFORD • NEW YORK • SYDNEY

First published in India 2018
First published in 2012 by The Arden Shakespeare

The Arden Shakespeare India
An imprint of Bloomsbury Publishing Plc
Bloomsbury is a registered trade mark of Bloomsbury Publishing PLC

This edition published with permission from Bloomsbury Publishing Plc,
50 Bedford Square, London, WC1B3DP, UK

British Library Cataloguing-in-Publication Data
A catalogue record for this book is available from the British Library.

Library of Congress Cataloging-in-Publication Data
A catalogue record for this book is available from the Library of Congress.

ISBN 978 93 8786 343 9
10 9 8 7 6 5 4 3 2
For sale in the Indian subcontinent only

Bloomsbury Publishing India Pvt. Ltd
Second Floor, Building No. 4
DDA Complex LSC, Pocket C – 6 & 7
Vasant Kunj, New Delhi 110070
www.bloomsbury.com

Digitally Printed and bound in India by Replika Press Pvt. Ltd.

CONTENTS

A NOTE ON TEXTS

Except where otherwise indicated, the following editions have been used for quotations from Marlowe's works:

Dido Queen of Carthage, in *'Dido Queen of Carthage' and 'The Massacre at Paris'*, ed. H.J. Oliver. The Revels Plays (London, 1968).

Doctor Faustus: A- and B-texts (*1604, 1616*), ed. David Bevington and Eric Rasmussen. The Revels Plays (Manchester and New York, 1993).

Edward the Second, ed. Martin Wiggins and Robert Lindsey, 2nd edition. New Mermaids (London, 1997).

Tamburlaine, Parts One and Two, ed. Anthony B. Dawson, 2nd edition. New Mermaids (London, 1997).

The Collected Poems of Christopher Marlowe, ed. Patrick Cheney and Brian J. Striar (New York and Oxford, 2006).

The Jew of Malta, ed. James R. Siemon, 2nd edition. New Mermaids (London, 1994).

The Massacre at Paris, in *'Dido Queen of Carthage' and 'The Massacre at Paris'*, ed. H. J. Oliver. The Revels Plays (London, 1968).

Quotations from Shakespeare's works, including *Sir Thomas More*, are taken from the most recent available Arden edition unless otherwise stated. All quotations from plays written by other early modern dramatists come from the most recent available New Mermaids edition, unless otherwise specified.

In quoting from early modern manuscripts and printed books the original spelling and punctuation has been retained except in the case of initial capitals in quotations, which have been silently normalised, as have u/v and i/j variations. The italicisation of proper names has been removed in accordance with modern usage, the abbreviations '&', 'w^{ch}', 'y^{e}' and 'M^{ies}' have been silently expanded, and 'n' and 'm' have been silently added where appropriate. Any other expansions or alterations are shown in square brackets. Unless specified otherwise, the publication information provided for early modern printed books is based on the appropriate entry in the *English Short Title Catalogue*, as given in the Select Bibliography.

ILLUSTRATIONS

Woodcut from the title page of the 1616 B-text edition of *Doctor Faustus.* Christopher Marlowe, *The tragicall history of the life and death of Doctor Faustus* (London, 1618; STC 10713). Page 33.

Dido Queen of Carthage, 3.4: Aeneas (Mark Bonnar) and Dido (Anastasia Hille) pledge their love to each other. National Theatre production, London, 2009, dir. James MacDonald. Photo by Johan Persson. Page 105.

ABBREVIATIONS

Baines, 'Note'	Richard Baines, 'A note containing the opinion of on[e] Christopher Marly', MSS BL Harleian 6848, in Park Honan, *Christopher Marlowe: Poet and Spy* (Oxford, 2005), p. 374.
EFB	*The English Faust Book: A critical edition based on the text of 1592*, ed. John Henry Jones (Cambridge, 1994).
ELH	*English Literary History*
ELR	*English Literary Renaissance*
'Execution' and 'Defense', ed. Kingdom	*'The Execution of Justice in England' by William Cecil and 'A True, Sincere and Modest Defense of English Catholics' by William Allen*, ed. Robert M. Kingdom (Ithaca, 1965)
Kyd, 'Unsigned Note'	Thomas Kyd, 'Unsigned Note to Puckering', BL Harleian MS 6849, in Park Honan, *Christopher Marlowe: Poet and Spy* (Oxford, 2005), p. 381.
MLR	*Modern Language Review*
Nashe, *Works*	*The Works of Thomas Nashe*, 3 vols, ed. R.B. McKerrow and F.P. Wilson (Oxford, 1958)
OED	*Oxford English Dictionary Online*
Peele, *Works*	*The Dramatic Works of George Peele* (New Haven and London, 1961)
PMLA	*Publications of the Modern Language Association of America*
RenQ	*Renaissance Quarterly*
RES	*Review of English Studies*
RSC	Royal Shakespeare Company
SEL	*Studies in English Literature*

ACKNOWLEDGEMENTS

One of the lovely things about writing this book is that it has provided an opportunity to thank some of the people who have been instrumental in supporting my research for the past five years. The book itself is dedicated to Professor Bill Sherman, a wonderful PhD supervisor and mentor without whom this project would never have got off the ground in the first place: I am immensely grateful for the unfailingly helpful advice, generous support and friendly assistance that Bill has given me over the last few years. The book itself developed out of the research I conducted as a PhD student at the University of York, and I owe a great debt of gratitude to the entire CREMS community for their assistance during this period. My PhD itself was funded by a doctoral award from the Arts and Humanities Research Council, and I am extremely grateful for the opportunity this funding provided for me to pursue my research. Valuable support and encouragement was offered during the early stages by Dr Pat Palmer, Professor John Roe and Dr Geoffrey Wall in the York English Department; Professor Bill Sheils and Professor Stuart Carroll kindly took time to discuss the confessional politics of sixteenth-century France with me; and Dr Helen Smith and Dr Abigail Shinn's work on conversion narratives helped to refine my understanding of confessional terminology in European literature. I owe a particular debt of gratitude to the examiners of my thesis, Professor Lisa Hopkins and Dr Richard Rowland, for the incisive advice they offered on how to extend my research further and for all the subsequent aid they have offered.

During the final stages of writing this book I moved to the Faculty of English at the University of Cambridge, and my colleagues here and at Lucy Cavendish College have proved equally supportive and helpful. I am especially grateful to Professor Helen Cooper for her valuable advice, and would also like to thank Professor John Kerrigan, Professor Janet Todd, Dr Isobel Maddison and Dr Maria Purves in particular for their kind words of encouragement. The staff at the various libraries I have visited have also been extremely helpful, and I would particularly like to thank the staff of the York Borthwick Institute, the British Library and Newnham College Library. Finally, some of the research on false conversion in *The Jew of Malta* that I discuss in Chapter Two was included in my article 'Bringing the House Down: Religion and the Household in Marlowe's *Jew of Malta*', *Renaissance Studies* 26 (2012) I am grateful to the editors for the use of this material.

On a more personal note, I cannot begin to express how grateful I am for all the encouragement and assistance I have received from my friends and family while writing this book. My parents in particular have been unfailingly supportive over the years, and I am extremely grateful to them for everything. Special thanks are also owed to Dr Varsha Panjwani and Sophie Battell, both for their kind assistance with editing and re-drafting during the early stages of this project and for their enthusiastic encouragement throughout. Jenny Baldwin, Dr Amritesh Singh, Katie Webb and Dr Rachel Willie have also been extremely generous with their time and advice, and again have my deepest thanks.

PREFACE

In his 1597 collection of cautionary tales, *The Theatre of Gods Judgements*, the moralist Thomas Beard delivered a memorable epitaph upon the Elizabethan poet and playwright Christopher Marlowe:

> Not inferiour to any of the former in Atheisme & impiety, and equall to all in maner of punishment was one of our own nation, of fresh and late memory, called Marlin, by profession a scholler, brought up from his youth in the Universitie of Cambridge, but by practice a play-maker, and a Poet of scurrilitie.

Beard goes on to describe how the young playwright denied the power of God, blasphemed the Trinity, and affirmed 'our Saviour to be but a deceiver . . . and all religion but a device of pollicie'.[1] Though virulently expressed, these charges were not new; during his own lifetime, Marlowe had acquired a reputation as a proselytising atheist. The various charges of blasphemy and disbelief voiced by his contemporaries, Beard among them, still colour modern responses; indeed, the image of Marlowe the atheist has been eagerly embraced by twentieth- and twenty-first-century scholars. Elevating Marlowe as the epitome of Elizabethan atheism, literary critics and intellectual historians have often placed his reported statements within a teleological framework that looks forward to modern secularism: Marlowe, as atheist, is recast in contemporary terms.

So, was Marlowe the Elizabethan Richard Dawkins? Perhaps not – but he is certainly a significant figure in the history of disbelief. Marlowe had a sigificant impact on the subsequent expression of religious doubt in seventeenth-century England, though his influence was both more specific and more diffuse than modern allusions to Marlowe as an atheist might suggest. Marlowe was not a philosopher or a theologian, but rather a poet and a playwright, and it is in his literary writings that he engaged with questions of religious belief. These fictional texts are not polemical manifestos for atheism. Instead, Marlowe's plays and poems invite their spectators and readers to question the nature of belief by depicting numerous episodes in which religion is exploited for secular ends. Beard's accusation that Marlowe termed all religion 'a device of pollicie' is indeed particularly telling here: in Elizabethan England, where the term 'policy' often denoted a self-interested or pragmatic secularism, the type of religious fraud that Marlowe portrays in his writings was commonly known as 'politic religion'.

Marlowe's interest in the secular appropriation of religious language and imagery can be traced in part to the classical treatises of disbelief he encountered at school and university, in which religion is exposed as a human fiction designed to keep men in awe, and perhaps more strongly to the sixteenth-century theorists who expressed such politic ideas in their own writings; Marlowe's contemporaries sometimes attributed his alleged atheism to Machiavelli's influence. On the other hand, Marlowe's literary engagement with religious fraud consistently reflects and responds to a specifically Elizabethan experience of confessional conflict. In fact, virtually all the religious issues explored in his poems and plays can be traced back to the anxieties expressed and accusations exchanged in post-Reformation religious polemic. While Marlowe's works are often set in classical or exotic locations, and feature as many pagan, Islamic and Jewish characters as Christian believers, the religious themes they deal with had an urgent contemporary significance; from regicide to equivocation, Marlowe's writings present instances of religious deceit that were only too familiar to his sixteenth-century readers and spectators.

The historically specific nature of Marlowe's interest in religion is important, since early modern atheism was by no means the same thing as twenty-first-century atheism; for this reason, we should be careful not to align Marlowe too closely with modern disbelief. When Marlowe's contemporaries termed him an atheist, they might have meant that he denied God's power to intervene on earth or the immortality of the soul; they might also have been using the term in a more generalised sense to denounce a blasphemer, suggest a lack of commitment to the English Protestant Church, or even vilify a professional rival. To term Marlowe an atheist nowadays is thus potentially misleading, because to modern readers it suggests a much narrower definition than the playwright's early modern accusers recognised. Moreover, in modern usage 'atheism' often denotes disbelief in *any* religious system or god, but this universality threatens to obscure one of the most striking and original features of Marlowe's politic religion: its cross-confessional reach. To show characters appropriating religious rhetoric for secular or even self-interested ends was far from unusual in the Elizabethan theatre; Marlowe's innovation was that, in his plays and poems, such deceit is not limited to those who are vilified as misbelievers. Instead, the politic appropriation of religion becomes a near-universal phenomenon in Marlowe's writings, associated with every confession and faith from Islam to Judaism, Catholicism to Protestantism.

Marlowe's cross-confessional representation of politic religion was inspired and shaped by the conflicting claims to religious authority that he encountered in post-Reformation polemic. Like many of his contemporaries, Marlowe had access to tracts written from a variety of confessional perspectives; cumulatively, the reciprocal accusations exchanged in such tracts suggested that every sixteenth-century faith was tainted with politic fraud. The religious doubts Marlowe expressed in his writings thus relate intriguingly to the sixteenth- and seventeenth-century tradition of sceptical thinking. While the modern term 'scepticism' often loosely indicates doubt about the truths of Christianity and other faiths, sixteenth-century scepticism was based on the classical philosophical tradition outlined by Sextus Empiricus and Diogenes Laertes, which denied that a particular truth could ever be proved in evidentiary terms. As Richard Popkin demonstrated in his groundbreaking study of *The History of Scepticism*, this position was by no means synonymous with disbelief.[2] The early modern discourse of scepticism certainly had religious implications, suggesting as it did the impossibility of ever 'proving' a spiritual truth, but authors from Erasmus to Montaigne argued that this outlook was compatible with a Christian emphasis on justification through faith alone. Even the stern theologian Philippe de Mornay, denouncing the foolishness of those who experienced any religious doubt, acknowledged that the 'kinde of Philosophers called Scepticks (that is to say Dowters) . . . did rather suspend their Judgement concerning the Godhead, then call it in question'.[3]

Marlowe, however, expressed doubts about the inherent truth of any religious position in response to the conflicting accusations of post-Reformation polemic. William Hamlin has shown that sceptical thinkers used a rhetoric of opposed voices and competing values to demonstrate the impossibility of proving a truth,[4] and Marlowe was especially sensitive to the competing ideologies of confessional polemic; as each faction discredited the claims of their opponents, only to be denounced in their turn, the provenance of any religious truth became a particularly charged question. Marlowe's cross-confessional representations of protagonists who appropriate religious rhetoric thus engage with the issues raised by post-Reformation polemic; in Marlowe's writings, however, it seems that the clash of competing voices has left an ideological vacuum. In a fictional world where the fraudulent manipulation of religion is a near-universal phenomenon, Marlowe's characters can no longer identify religious truth; instead, they substitute false performances of piety for true faith. Genuine belief is virtually absent from Marlowe's writings; and, where it does exist, it is emphatically incompatible with secular advancement. Thus Marlowe transfers the oppositional voices he encountered in post-Reformation polemic into a fictional context, demonstrating the universality of politic religion in a world where religious truth is called into question on all sides.

This book is a study of Marlowe's literary scepticism, and in it I suggest that Marlowe's writings invite his readers and spectators to recognise the near-universal prevalence of religious fraud. In particular, I emphasise the debt that his scepticism owes to the competing and mutually deconstructive claims of post-Reformation religious polemic, situating Marlowe's fictional depictions of politic religion within the specific historical context in which his plays and poems were written, read and performed. The introduction surveys this historical background, exploring the relationship between the contemporary discourse of politic religion and the confessional conflicts that raged in sixteenth-century Europe. The following chapters then illustrate the sustained connection between Marlowe's literary representation of religious fraud and the post-Reformation polemical tracts that attributed such fraud to their confessional rivals.

The first chapter explores instances of visual and verbal deceit in Marlowe's writings, from Mephistopheles' temptation of Faustus to Barabas's cunning use of equivocation to trick his enemies. In Marlowe's writings, eloquent characters regularly employ persuasive rhetoric to induce a form of 'conversion'; this theme of conversion is explored in more detail in Chapter Two, which relates episodes of feigned conversion in works such as *The Jew of Malta* to Elizabethan anxieties about false conformity and practical godlessness. Such fraudulent performances of 'conversion' often result from or lead to acts of political betrayal; the association between religious deceit and treachery is pursued in Chapter Three, which examines acts of oath-breaking by Marlovian protagonists from Aeneas to Ferneze. Intriguingly, these characters justify their perjury by alluding to religious duty at a time when oath-breaking in the name of religion had strong political connotations. The seditious implications of oath-breaking are explored in the fourth chapter, which considers more overt acts of religiously justified resistance, rebellion and regicide in Marlowe's writings. The last chapter focuses on Marlowe's *Doctor Faustus* and its unusually active Christian setting; I argue that by staging the tragedy of a man who is damned by his failure to manipulate religious rhetoric effectively, Marlowe's most famous play provocatively illustrates the indispensability of politic religion for success and even survival. Finally, the coda demonstrates the influence Marlowe's cross-confessional engagement with politic religion in his writings had on the work of his contemporaries and literary successors, paying particular attention to the plays of William Shakespeare, Ben Jonson and John Webster.

At this point it may also be helpful to clarify my use of religious terminology, since to capitalise 'Catholic' and 'Protestant' while leaving 'puritan' in lower case may appear inconsistent. I have chosen to use the term 'puritan' because it provides a useful shorthand for the various groups of early modern English Protestants who carried their discontent with the Elizabethan Church to the length of conscientious non-conformity. However, it is important to acknowledge that this usage is potentially misleading for a modern reader. In Elizabethan polemic the term 'puritan' was used collectively to denounce the diverse sects and churches who expressed dissatisfaction with the established Elizabethan Church, including radical non-conformist sects such as the Family of Love; indeed, far from being a precise confessional category, 'puritan' was originally a term of generalised abuse. In order to draw attention to these tensions, I have therefore left 'puritan' uncapitalised, to distinguish between modern usage and the sense in which the term was understood in early modern England.

INTRODUCTION

POLITIC RELIGION AND POST-REFORMATION POLEMIC

On 27 May 1593, shortly after Christopher Marlowe's twenty-ninth birthday, the Elizabethan councillor Sir John Puckering received a message from the government spy Richard Baines. The note contained a scathing indictment of Marlowe and his 'damnable Judgment of Religion', with Baines reporting that:

> Almost into every company he cometh he perswades men to Atheism, willing them not to be afeard of bugbears and hobgoblins and utterly scorning both god and his ministers.

This characterisation of Marlowe as a proselytising atheist forms the central thrust of the so-called 'Baines Note', which attributes various anti-Christian statements to the Elizabethan dramatist – including the provocative claim that Jesus Christ was a promiscuous bastard born to a dishonest mother.[5] Marlowe was called in for questioning, but apparently never had the chance to respond to Baines's accusations; three days later he died at the hand of the shady business entrepreneur Ingram Frazier, who stabbed him in the eye with his own dagger on 30 May 1593. Already, however, the charges of atheism against Marlowe had begun to snowball. In the days after Marlowe's death Puckering received two communications from Marlowe's fellow playwright Thomas Kyd, who had been arrested in mid-May on the charge of possessing a 'hereticall' treatise. Thrown into prison and probably tortured, Kyd sacrificed Marlowe to the gathering wolves by claiming that the papers in question belonged to his notoriously unorthodox former room-mate. When Puckering demanded further details

Kyd reiterated and elaborated upon Baines's accusations, detailing Marlowe's sacrilegious readiness to 'jest at the devine scriptures, gybe at praiers, and stryve in argument to frustrate and confute what hath byn spoke or wrytt by prophets and such holie men'.[6]

The reliability of these testimonies is uncertain to say the least. Baines presumably held a grudge against Marlowe, who had accused him of treason the previous year, while as a professional informer he had a clear financial motive to testify – especially against a man he disliked and distrusted.[7] Indeed, as Roy Kendall has pointed out, many of the blasphemous opinions attributed to Marlowe in the Baines Note bear a suspicious resemblance to those Baines had publicly confessed to a decade earlier.[8] It is also significant that Kyd's letters, perhaps given under duress, reached Puckering in the days immediately following Marlowe's death; by the time he wrote to the Lord Keeper, Kyd knew that Marlowe was beyond the reach of the Elizabethan judicial system. Scrambling desperately to get out of trouble, the imprisoned playwright found an ideal scapegoat in the form of his deceased colleague; like the Baines Note itself, Kyd's statements must be taken with a pinch of salt.

Despite the suspect veracity of the state's witnesses, however, the weight of the evidence was on their side. Though the Baines Note was the first official charge of atheism lodged against Marlowe, the reports delivered by Baines and Kyd were simply the last in a long line of contemporary accusations. References to the dramatist as an unbeliever or atheist had proliferated from 1588 onwards, often framed through allusive references to Marlowe's fictional characters. Notable examples include the author Robert Greene's attack on 'that Atheist Tamburlan' for daring God out of heaven; Greene's more overt condemnation of Marlowe's atheism in his deathbed tract *Greenes groats-worth of witte* (1592); and the Cambridge scholar Gabriel Harvey's 1593 description of atheism as 'tamberlaine contempt'.[9] Nor did the flood of accusations dry up with Marlowe's death. In subsequent decades the story of his violent end became a staple element of cautionary literature, as exemplified by the puritan writer Thomas Beard's moralising account. Writing in stridently providentialist terms, Beard vilifies 'Marlin' as a 'barking dogge' who,

> giving too large a swinge to his owne wit, and suffering his lust to have the full raines, fell (not without just desert) to that outrage and extremitie, that hee denied God and his sonne Christ.[10]

Comparable denunciations abounded in early modern England: while researching his 2004 biography David Riggs counted seven contemporaries of Marlowe who refer in writing to his blasphemy, and suggested that the number rises to eleven if pseudonymous allusions are included.[11] Even in the course of his own short lifetime, Christopher Marlowe speedily gained a reputation for provocative profanity and daringly unorthodox behaviour.

The figure of Marlowe the atheist has been eagerly embraced by modern critics. A cautionary tale to his contemporaries, Marlowe is now celebrated as the figurehead of an intellectually dynamic atheist movement – the brave Prometheus of his age, challenging the gods in heaven. While Michael Hattaway conservatively identifies Marlowe as a 'true but tentative atheist – the kind who is going to need to blaspheme', the historian G.E. Aylmer classes Marlowe as one of the very hardest cases of early modern atheism; and David Riggs goes so far as to assert that within the history of modern disbelief Marlowe 'bestrides the moment when English atheism comes out of the closet and acquires a public face'.[12] Though his soaring enthusiasm leads Riggs into hyperbole, there is certainly a good case for describing Marlowe as a religious sceptic. From the myriad contemporary sources identifying Marlowe as a blasphemer to the provocative statements he places in the mouths of his fictional literary speakers, it is easy enough to find supporting biographical and textual evidence for this hypothesis. One particularly striking instance is Marlowe's emphatic vernacular re-inscription of classical scepticism, as the speaker of his translation of *Ovid's Elegies* provocatively confesses that 'I am forbod / By secret thoughts to think there is a god' (3.8.35–6) – a statement that was consigned to the flames within a decade of its publication, when Marlowe's *Elegies* and the jointly bound *Epigrams* of Sir John Davies were condemned as part of the 1599 Bishops' Ban on subversive texts.[13]

Marlowe was accused of disbelief by his friends and enemies alike, and his literary output apparently did little to re-establish his reputation. Yet to classify him as an atheist is a tricky proposition, since accusations of atheism were thrown about with abandon in early modern England, while the modern terminology of atheism can be unhelpfully reductive when applied to an Elizabethan writer. Over the past few decades there has been considerable debate about the extent to which early modern disbelief can be termed 'atheism' in the modern sense, with a number of historians arguing that sixteenth-century thinkers did not possess the necessary philosophical and ideological framework to deny God's existence: indeed, the French historian Lucien Febvre has stated that it is 'absurd and puerile' to think that the early modern experience of unbelief was in any way comparable to our own.[14] While Febvre's sweeping conclusion is now generally considered too severe, it is true that the Elizabethan version of atheism rarely constituted an explicit denial of God's existence. Instead, an early modern atheist might express disbelief by challenging God's capacity to intervene in the world, by denying God's power as creator, by rejecting the immortality of the soul, or by questioning the authority of scripture. Marlowe's own fictional writings drew upon and responded to such contemporary discourses, being both conditioned by and inextricably bound up with the specific historical circumstances in which he lived, wrote and died.

In addition, Marlowe's developing modern fame as the poster-boy of Elizabethan atheism does not reflect a universally accepted critical consensus. On the contrary, scholars continue to identify Marlowe and his works with a veritable abundance of theological positions. Catholic rebel, Protestant radical, patriotic conformist, gnostic and atheist: Marlowe has been them all, and his literary writings have generated an equally varied range of interpretations. Indeed, the very fact that such diverse readings of Marlowe as orthodox Christian, militant Protestant or dissident Catholic can be constructed on the basis of the available biographical and textual evidence reflects the extent to which his writings were shaped by the urgent religious questions of his day. Fictionalising religious conflict and controversy at a time when literal and polemical warfare raged between conservative members of the Elizabethan Church, the radical Protestant fringe and the outlawed and exiled English Catholics, Marlowe stood at the centre of the debate: a man who trained to become an Elizabethan divine and may have worked as a government spy, but was accused by Baines of believing that 'if there be any god or any good Religion, then it is in the papistes' – and describing all Protestants as 'Hypocriticall asses'.[15]

MARLOWE'S ENGLAND: THE RELIGIOUS BACKGROUND

The charges of atheism that Baines and Kyd brought against Marlowe were potentially deadly, though in the event he died before he could be questioned. Sixteenth-century England was a Christian society, and attendance at weekly services and adherence to the English Church was rigidly enforced by law. Political considerations informed this emphasis on religious uniformity; the authorities were deeply anxious about religious divisions during a period when violent conflicts between Protestants and Catholics raged across Europe, and France and the Netherlands were ravaged by civil war. Marlowe's contemporaries were apprehensive that England might meet a similar fate, being only too aware that the established religion had changed course with dizzying rapidity during the course of the sixteenth century. Following Henry VIII's break away from the Roman Catholic Church and the introduction of royal supremacy over an independent English Church, England had experienced a series of dramatic confessional transitions: from the reformed Protestantism of Edward VI's reign, to Mary I's stringent enforcement of Catholicism, and back to a comparatively mild version of Calvinist Protestantism under Elizabeth I. Such transformations had momentous spiritual implications; indeed, for many members of Elizabeth I's government the enforcement of religious uniformity was perhaps as much about saving souls as it was about avoiding civil unrest. In a society where religion was central to everyday life, and many people worried that adherence to the wrong faith might damn them forever, the theology of the established church was a matter of vital significance.

In Marlowe's day the official English state religion was Protestant and predominantly Calvinist. Yet it seems that some Elizabethans, including perhaps the Queen herself, were not quite ready to jettison every religious tradition that had originated in England's Catholic past. Radical Protestants often complained that the Elizabethan Church remained too 'popish' and the most extreme, including the group known as presbyterians, sought to separate from the Church of England by refusing to attend services. These separatists, along with the other minor sects who also distanced themselves from the established church, were commonly known as puritans; of the minor sects, the Family of Love was particularly notorious. At the same time, Catholic belief remained strong in Elizabethan England; while some Catholics were content to conform outwardly to the English Church and practise their faith in private, others (known as recusants) firmly refused to attend 'heretical' Protestant services.

Despite the confessional diversity that existed in early modern England, however, the choice between faiths was not a free one. Conformity to the established religion was consistently equated with political loyalty, and the Elizabethan regime regarded any English subjects who deviated in their religious beliefs as potential traitors. Thus Catholics and puritans who refused to obey the law and conform to the Elizabethan brand of Protestantism were fined and imprisoned. Those whose behaviour was regarded as seditious might even be executed: the puritan separatist John Greenwood, an old college acquaintance of Marlowe's, was hanged in 1593, while the Catholic priests who secretly and illegally entered England were commonly tortured and executed as traitors if captured by the authorities. Atheism was regarded as an especially pernicious threat to both the church and the state, an extreme form of religious dissidence; thus the accusations of disbelief lodged against Marlowe in 1593, whether true or not, represented a serious threat to his well-being and perhaps even his life.

English fears about non-conforming religious dissidents became particularly acute from the 1580s, when Marlowe was writing. Elizabeth I had been excommunicated by Pope Pius V in 1570, which meant that England's Catholics theoretically had a religious duty to depose their queen, while 1581 saw the launch of a high-profile Jesuit mission to restore England to Catholicism. The Jesuits had a reputation among Protestants for promoting rebellion and regicide and, while the missionaries denied having a political agenda, the authorities accused them of promoting sedition: there were several Catholic conspiracies against Elizabeth I's throne and life during the 1580s, including the 1583 Throckmorten plot and the 1586 Babington plot. In response to these conspiracies and a succession of invasion attempts by Catholic Spain, including the famous Armada expedition of 1588, the 1580s and 1590s saw a more stringent enforcement of the laws against Catholicism in England. At the same time, the radical Protestants were also implicated in a series of arguably seditious episodes, from the 1588–9 publication of texts known as the Martin Marprelate tracts which outspokenly attacked the Elizabethan Church to a small-scale attempt to incite rebellion in 1591. Thus the later 1580s and early 1590s also witnessed an increasingly rigorous campaign against the puritan separatists, which culminated in the 1593 executions of John Greenwood, Henry Barrow and John Penry.

SCEPTICISM, MACHIAVELLIANISM AND RELIGIOUS FRAUD

Widespread paranoia about resistance to Elizabeth I's Protestant regime meant that the authorities were keen to gather as much information as possible about English dissidents. Although there was no formal spy service in early modern England, various members of Elizabeth's Privy Council recruited their own personal intelligence agents to spy on the Catholics and the puritans, many of them well-educated young men eager for advancement. It is generally believed that Christopher Marlowe, like his nemesis Richard Baines, worked as a government informer at some point in his life: perhaps as a student at Cambridge, when he was reportedly employed 'in matters touching the benefit of his country'; or during his 1592 visit to Flushing, haven of religious exiles, in the company of the same Richard Baines.[16] Possibly Marlowe was tasked with gathering information about dissidents for Sir Francis Walsingham or the powerful Privy Councillor Sir Robert Cecil, a commission that might have required him to pose as a religious radical: Elizabethan informers regularly feigned religious beliefs for the sake of their profession, a practice that perhaps heightened Marlowe's sensitivity to religious fraud. Indeed, many of Walsingham's operatives were brazen about shifting confessional allegiance for personal advantage, with spies such as Gilbert Gifford and Michael Moody masterminding the very plots they then disclosed for money.[17] By the 1590s, the religious frauds practised by English spies had become public knowledge: the Catholic priest Robert Southwell exposed the deceitful 'Hypocrisie' of informers such as Robert Poley in his *Humble Supplication* to Elizabeth I, while Marlowe's colleague Thomas Nashe reported in 1596 how the intelligencer 'frame[s] his religion and alleageance to his Prince according to everie companie he comes in'.[18] Marlowe, whose literary patron Thomas Walsingham was Sir Francis's cousin and who dined with the spy Robert Poley on the day of his own death, was very much part of this world of paranoia, deceit and religious fraud.

Not all informers were merely self-interested; Walsingham, the man at the centre of the web, was deeply and genuinely committed to the English Protestant cause. Nonetheless, Marlowe's personal acquaintance with men who manufactured religious poses for political and financial gain may have predisposed him to regard the intersection of religion and politics with a sceptical eye. This practical experience was complemented by his book-learning, which provided an intellectual basis for doubt and disbelief. As the young Kit Marlowe moved through the Tudor education system, from his early days at the King's School in Canterbury, to his years at Cambridge as a scholarship student of divinity, he would have encountered a wide range of classical 'atheist' writings. Among the most notorious were those by the Greek philosopher Epicurus, his Roman disciple Lucretius and the Roman poet Lucian, who suggested that organised religion had been invented by rulers eager to control their subjects and proffered natural explanations for supposedly miraculous phenomena. The provocative impact of these writers was augmented by that of staple figures in the Tudor education system such as Aristotle, Cicero and Plutarch: Aristotle for instance denied the immortality of the soul, while Plutarch drew attention to the secular origins of organised religion.[19] Finally, Cicero was connected with a classical tradition of scepticism that was also available to Renaissance readers through Diogenes Laertius's *Lives of Eminent Philosophers* and the writings of Sextus Empiricus, which gained influence within the context of Reformation debates over religious truth.[20]

Marlowe's own brand of religious doubt had much in common with this philosophical tradition of scepticism; his literary interest in fraudulent poses of faith perhaps responds to contemporary scepticism about whether belief has an inherent spiritual value or whether value is conferred through observation, remaining dependent on the interpretations of individuals. Although diverse in tone and content, these classical writings all discuss religion as a tool of policy – a distinctly controversial theme in early modern Europe, since the suggestion that religion might be manipulated in a political cause potentially invited the atheist corollary that faith is subordinate to secular politics. Marlowe, whose humanist education introduced him to classical authors, may have first learned to question the political implications of religious discourse by following the example of the great Cicero, or (as his fellow Cantabrigian Gabriel Harvey suggested) by becoming a disciple of Lucian.[21]

According to the writer Robert Greene, Marlowe was also strongly influenced by the sceptical Roman histories of Livy, or rather by the paraphrased version of these histories produced by Niccolò Machiavelli, the Florentine politician whose name became a byword for atheism in sixteenth-century Europe. Writing from his deathbed in 1592, Greene beat Baines to the post to accuse Marlowe (the 'famous gracer of Tragedians') of denying God's existence, maintaining that Marlowe learned such 'Atheisme' as a 'disciple' of Machiavelli. He demands:

> Why should thy excellent wit, his gift, bee so blinded, that thou shouldst give no glorie to the giver: Is it pestilent Machivilian pollicy that thou hast studied? O peevish follie! [22]

We cannot be positive that Greene's assumptions are accurate. But it is certainly likely that Marlowe, an educated young man with a flair for controversy and a demonstrable interest in questions of religion and policy, took an active interest in Machiavelli's writings and their popular reputation. A bookseller's account discovered by N.W. Bawcutt records the delivery of texts entitled *Antimachiavellus*, *Discourse de Machiavel* and *Machiavelli Princeps* to a Cambridge retailer in May 1584, as Marlowe was completing his BA, and there is evidence that Machiavelli's works were widely read in Cambridge throughout the period of Marlowe's residence. By 1579, the Cambridge scholar Gabriel Harvey reported that Machiavelli was more popular with the students than Aristotle; he added that he could 'name you an odd crewe or tooe that ar as cuninge' in Machiavelli's *Discourses* as in the Greek philosopher's works.[23] And where a diligent student such as Gabriel Harvey trod, we can assume that wilder spirits such as Marlowe might have dashed.

Available to the Elizabethan reader in Italian, French and Latin printed editions or manuscript English translations, Machiavelli's political theories were considered 'atheist' because the Florentine took a secular interest in religion and openly discussed its political utility. In the *Discourses*, for instance, Machiavelli argues that 'it was religion that facilitated whatever enterprise the senate and the great men of Rome designed to undertake'; he then describes the clever strategy of King Numa who, to ensure the obedience of his subjects, 'turned to religion as the instrument necessary above all others for the maintenance of a civilised state'. These Roman tactics are not completely at odds with the conventional Elizabethan vision of a mutually supportive church and state, but Machiavelli's analysis of Numa's actions is troubling: by describing religion as an 'instrument' or item (*cosa*) that 'facilitated' (*facilitò*) Rome's political agenda, the Florentine theorist demotes faith to a subordinate role. Moreover, Machiavelli explicitly prioritises the security of the state above religious truth, suggesting that the ruler ought to 'foster and encourage everything likely to be of help . . . even though they be convinced that it is quite fallacious'.[24] In this formulation the state and the church are no longer mutually dependent; instead, the church has become a servant of the state.

Machiavelli's emphasis on the political efficacy of even a false religion earned him an abiding reputation as an atheist in Elizabethan polemic. It also ensured that accusations of Machiavellianism featured regularly in Catholic, Protestant and puritan polemic, as each writer sought to brand his confessional opponents as self-interested atheists. Thus as early as 1572 the Catholic tract *A Treatise of Treasons* characterised the English Reformation as a Machiavellian enterprise, and described how

> to set up a lawlesse Faction of Machiavellian Libertines, that should not (by conscience or feare of synne) be restrayned from any maner mischiefe, a new Religion was pretended, that with helpe of Authority, shouldred out the olde.[25]

Sir John Davies, whose epigrams were published alongside Marlowe's Ovidian elegies, similarly denounced England's radical puritans as 'matchlesse Machivilian mates . . . Such Saints in shew, such devils in deed', while Protestant propagandists declared that 'righter Machevels than the Popes themselves Christendome hath not bred'.[26] The latter charge, by the Oxford divine Thomas Bilson, perhaps caught Marlowe's own attention: in *The Jew of Malta*, his stereotyped caricature of Machiavelli boasts loudly of having helped his disciples to become popes (Prologue, 11–12).

'POLITIC' RELIGION AND ELIZABETHAN POLEMIC

Accusations of Machiavellianism acquired great potency in Elizabethan polemic. Yet there was nothing inherently radical about Machiavelli's premise that religion and politics should operate in partnership, however controversial the weighting of his model. For many supporters of the Tudor regime, Elizabeth I's dual role as reigning monarch and supreme governor of the English Church symbolised a positive and mutually beneficial alliance between church and state. Marlowe might have encountered this attitude in any number of theological tracts. In 1580, for example, the Protestant polemicist William Charke celebrated the symbiotic interdependence of the Elizabethan church and state, whereby 'our blessed estate of policie standeth in defence of religion, and our most blessed religion laboureth in the mayntenance of the common wealth'.[27] The moderate Protestant theologian Richard Hooker, echoing Jean Bodin, similarly acknowledged that 'the saftie of all estates dependeth upon religion' in a monumental treatise published in the year of Marlowe's death. As Hooker revealed in 1593, however, the danger with this symbiotic model is that certain readers (and perhaps we should include Marlowe in their number) might thereby conclude 'that religion it selfe is a meere politique devise, forged purposelie to serve'. Hooker's term 'forged' is particularly telling: as Machiavelli's writings had illustrated, it was only too easy to conclude that religious deceit or even 'plaine forgeries' might be an acceptable means of ensuring political success.[28]

Popular awareness of religion's role as an instrument of state control was enhanced by the doctrinal uncertainties of the English Reformations. As the Jesuit leader William Allen pointed out in 1581, the established religion in England had changed four times within a mere thirty years;[29] and one consequence of such rapid theological transitions was an increased sensitivity to the ways in which religious ideology could be controlled by and dependent upon political circumstance. The establishment of an English state church further strengthened this perceived association between religion and politics – and, as Debora Kuller Shuger remarks, sixteenth-century thinkers had few illusions about the holiness of the state.[30] Indeed, religious dissidents even began publicly to condemn the Elizabethan Church as an institution that had subordinated religion to politics, as in Robert Southwell's 1587 *Epistle of Comfort*, which suggests that

> should the Prince but commaunde them, to adore Mahomett or renewe the memorye of the olde Godds, and Goddesses, as Jupiter, Juno, Venus, with the rest of that crew, there would be thousandes, as readye to embrace them.[31]

As Southwell's scathing comment suggests, the confessional conflicts raging in post-Reformation Europe played a central role in encouraging new attitudes towards faith; the role of the state in prescribing religious practice became at once more self-evident and more subject to criticism by rival confessions.

Tullio Gregory has similarly demonstrated how, in seventeenth-century France, the disorientating effect of the Wars of Religion between Catholics and Protestants combined with a new understanding of classical scepticism to inspire new theories about religion's role in imposing civil order. In an especially well-known passage, the brilliant essayist and French 'politique' Michel de Montaigne thus argued that people may adopt a religion simply because they fear the punishments meted out to non-believers or desire the rewards promised to the faithful. Considering the external pressures that might be brought to bear, he described how in sixteenth-century France rival confessions 'toss theological arguments to and fro' in order to bring people over to their side, taking religion into their own hands and twisting it 'like wax'.[32] This latter simile is particularly telling, suggesting that Montaigne's exposure to the cross-confessional polemic of the French civil wars has alerted him to the widespread manipulation of religious rhetoric in contemporary discourse – a realisation he shared with the English writer Christopher Marlowe. While the knowledge that religion might be exploited for political or even personal ends was not new, it seems that the 1580s and 1590s witnessed a newly energised alertness and a growing willingness to discuss the fraudulent or 'politic' dimensions of faith within the marketplace of print.

By the later sixteenth century, the conflicts raging between Catholics, Protestants and radicals reminded contemporaries to be constantly alert to questions of belief. Accusations of religious deceit were central to the polemical battles between English Protestants and English Catholics. Protestant spokesmen branded Catholicism a skin-deep counterfeit of Christianity and derided Catholic priests as dishonest hypocrites who 'color and counterfeit' treason 'with profession of devotion in religion'.[33] Catholic polemicists responded with reciprocal accusations against Protestantism and the English Church, condemning the Elizabethan campaign against Catholic priests as 'the manifold slanders and calumniations of certain heretics or politiques' and criticising the theologically suspect policy of enforcing outward religious conformity.[34] England's puritans were equally active in print, while such debates could also extend beyond the Christian arena. As modern critics such as Jonathan Burton, Matthew Dimmock, James Shapiro and Daniel Vitkus have ably demonstrated, early modern readers and writers remained fascinated by the belief systems of Islam and Judaism even as they denied their spiritual validity.[35] Polemical denunciations of non-Christian religion were comparatively common in this period: the founding father of Protestantism, Martin Luther, for instance denounced the destructive power of Jewish exegesis and, in 1518, characterised the 'turke' as the 'scourge of God'.[36] Although responses by Islamic and Jewish writers were comparatively rare in a European context, early modern readers were kept informed about the conflicting beliefs and religious practices of these Abrahamic faiths by a succession of published travel accounts and histories.

The regularity with which Marlowe depicts Jewish and Muslim characters in his writings suggests that he was aware of this wider contest for religious authority; as Catholics, Protestants and puritans competed within the Christian sphere, so Christianity sought to surpass Islam and Judaism on the world stage. In early modern England this latter conflict gained a particular resonance insofar as it could be related to the post-Reformation battles raging between rival Christian confessions. Elizabethan writers often drew parallels between Jews and Catholics or Jews and Protestants that implicitly criticised their confessional rivals: Henry Blount for instance likened Jews to England's radical puritans in his *Voyage to the Levant*, reporting that Jews have 'light, ayeriall, and fanaticall braines, spirited much like our hot Apocalyps men'.[37] Similarly, the Catholic writer William Rainolds composed a thousand-page Latin tract showing how similar Protestant beliefs were to those of Islam; Matthew Sutcliffe responded with *De Turco-Papismo*, in which he insisted that it was Catholics who resembled the Turks in their beliefs and ceremonies.[38] Marlowe exploited such analogies when he brought Jewish and Muslim characters on to the Elizabethan stage, with protagonists such as Barabas and Tamburlaine possessing a religious multivalency that potentially enables them to be associated with any religion – or none. Yet the episodes of religious fraud Marlowe depicts are most strongly indebted to contemporary Catholic, Protestant and puritan discourse; Marlowe's cross-confessional scepticism was sparked by the post-Reformation debates that were of most immediate and pressing concern to the Elizabethans.

The effect such oppositional and mutually contradicting polemic might have on a reader who was constantly urged to mistrust the religious truths of his or her society was recognised by a number of Marlowe's contemporaries. As Alexandra Walsham has demonstrated, Catholic–Protestant discourse displays acute anxiety about the perceived rise of practical godlessness in a generation which witnessed sustained inter-confessional conflict, while Sir Francis Bacon defined 'divisions in religion' as one of the primary causes of atheism.[39] Bacon's realisation that post-Reformation England's divisions in religion might lead to doubt and even disbelief was apparently shared by his contemporaries, who were convinced that English atheism was on the rise. George Whetstone, for example, reported in 1586 that 'a fourth part of christendome is inhabited by Atheists', and the pamphleteer Thomas Nashe warned the readers of *Christs teares* (1593) that 'there is no Sect now in England so scattered as Atheisme'. With sixteenth-century polemicists repeatedly accusing each other of politic fraud, religious truth became progressively harder to distinguish from its false counterpart. Ultimately, as Bacon and his contemporaries recognised, such uncertainty might lead by degrees to the type of doubt captured by Thomas Nashe in his literary portrait of the atheist, who

> makes conscience and the Spyrite of God a long side-cloake for all his oppressions and pollicies. A holie looke he will put on when he meaneth to do mischiefe, and have Scripture in his mouth even whiles hee is in cutting his neighbours throate.[40]

Nashe's definition signals the extent to which Elizabethan atheism was ideologically associated with the 'politic' appropriation of religion: that is, the hypocritical exploitation of religious language or imagery for self-interested secular ends. Indeed, 'politic religion' was a popular shorthand for the use of religious fraud in the political arena; accusations of 'Machiavellianism' and 'politic religion' were frequently used to tar polemical and confessional opponents. Blending the fifteenth-century sense of 'policy' as pragmatic, cunning statesmanship with the new term 'politique', a name given to religious moderates who valued secular peace above spiritual considerations, this Elizabethan terminology of 'policy' rapidly acquired negative connotations of religious hypocrisy, political expediency and self-interest.[41]

FRAMING FAITH: GUISE'S POLITIC RELIGION

Elizabethan polemicists frequently exploited the popular association of 'policy' with religious fraud to condemn those of an opposed confessional or political inclination. In 1592, for instance, the Jesuit Robert Parsons vilified Protestant England's Privy Councillors as 'politiques, and men of no conscience or religion', while the presbyterian John Fielde denounced Parsons and his fellow priests as 'politiques', 'enemies and traitorus to oure sovereigne prince the Queene'.[42] By suggesting that the Jesuit priests are manipulating the 'simpler sort' of English Catholics for their own suspect ends Fielde also connects religiously inflected deception with political transgression – a pattern that occurs frequently in Marlowe's literary works.

In Christopher Marlowe's plays and poems the term 'policy' appears sixteen times (including thirteen references in *The Jew of Malta*). In virtually all these instances, it is employed within a context of religious hypocrisy and self-interested secularism. In *The Jew of Malta*, for instance, 'policy' is identified as the 'profession' of the Knights who preach Barabas out of his possessions (1.2.161); the term 'profession' also carries connotations of religious fraud, punning on the genuine profession of confessional identity and the false professing of fraudulent faith. While modern editors and critics often emphasise the political implications of the term 'policy', its contemporary association with religious fraud crucially foreshadows the Maltese governor Ferneze's exploitation of scriptural precedent to confirm the 'wrongs' he inflicts upon the Jews (1.2.111).[43] 'Policy' is similarly associated with dishonesty in *Edward II*, in which Warwick's 'policy' to destroy his enemy Gaveston entails a treacherous attack on Warwick's ally Pembroke (9.96); the episode invites Marlowe's readers and spectators to equate 'policy' with fraud and political duplicity. And in *The Massacre at Paris*, policy's potential to jointly invoke religious hypocrisy and political ambition is realised to the full, with the protagonist Guise declaring that religion 'hath fram'd' his 'policy' (2.62).

Towards the start of *The Massacre at Paris*, the Duke of Guise reflects on the possibilities and limitations of faith in a characteristically outspoken and politically driven soliloquy:

> For this, hath heaven engender'd me of earth;
> For this, this earth sustains my body's weight,
> And with this weight I'll counterpoise a crown
> Or with seditions weary all the world;

For this, from Spain the stately Catholics
Sends Indian gold to coin me French ecues;
For this, have I a largess from the Pope,
A pension and a dispensation too;
And by that privilege to work upon,
My policy hath fram'd religion.
Religion: *O Diabole!*
Fie, I am asham'd, however that I seem,
To think a word of such a simple sound,
Of so great matter should be made the ground.
(*Massacre at Paris* 2.53–66)

The temptation when evaluating this speech is to head straight to Guise's condemnation of 'simple' faith and his 'atheist' conviction that religion is subordinate to politics. Guise's conclusion is undoubtedly significant: Marlowe's verse reinforces its dramatic impact by supplying the rhyming couplet of 'sound' and 'ground', while the shortened exclamation of 'Religion: *O Diabole!*' is metrically distinct in the 1594 editorial layout. However, the context of the quatrain is as important as these individual lines. In the course of his soliloquy Guise moves from a religiously inflected statement of purpose to a celebration of the material advantages of faith, culminating in a shockingly explicit repudiation of 'simple' religion as unworthy to further his ambitions. His anti-religious attitude develops over the course of fourteen lines, during which Guise's political agenda is presented in religious terms: an allusion to heavenly purpose supplies the initial justification for his monarchical ambitions, while the Catholic network represented by Spain and the Pope provides financial support and further ideological vindication. Guise consistently depicts religion as a tool of secular politics; in consequence, religion becomes aligned with rebellion, fraud and dissimulation. Yet the politic Guise continues to hide his scepticism in public – and will still 'seem' pious.

The same concept of religion as an instrument of policy appears time and time again in Marlowe's writings. His plays and poems regularly show characters utilising religious rhetoric for personal ends, and feature numerous episodes in which religion operates as a tool of secular power. It is this concept of religion as the 'simple' servant of politics, the 'ground' upon which the ambitious opportunist will tread, that shapes the disparagement of religion in Marlowe's work; the vulnerability of faith to appropriation inevitably inspiring contempt in the Marlovian protagonists who exploit the rhetoric of religion so hypocritically – and magnificently.

FROM PROVIDENCE TO THE POLITIC: MARLOWE'S INNOVATIONS

Marlowe was not the only Elizabethan writer to take a literary interest in the politic appropriation of religious rhetoric. As Paul Strohm has compellingly argued, the term 'policy' was used to identity selfish and potentially fraudulent political practice as early as the late fifteenth century, and this equation of 'policy' with self-interest and (on occasion) religious fraud had its impact on the drama which followed.[44] Elizabethan playwrights continued to utilise models of religious fraud inherited from the medieval moralities: thus Robert Wilson's *Three Ladies of London* (*c*. 1581), a possible influence on Marlowe's *Jew of Malta*, uses the morality convention whereby characters embody vices and virtues to stage an ongoing conflict between Conscience and Dissimulation (*Three Ladies of London*, 2.7–17, 142–96).[45] This medieval influence was complemented by the inspirational impact of classical drama. The Roman tragedies that became popular in sixteenth-century England regularly feature characters who exploit religious rhetoric and mythological precedents to challenge the gods: in Seneca's well-known tragedy *Hercules Furens*, for instance, Hercules defies his father Jove in terms that anticipate Marlowe's Tamburlaine, threatening to 'free Saturn from his chains' and set him 'against the wicked reign of my treacherous father' (*Hercules Furens* ll. 965–7).[46]

By the 1580s this literary interest in religious fraud and politic religion had acquired a new edge, honed by an awareness of and exposure to the confessional conflicts of post-Reformation Europe.

Playwrights and poets created fictional episodes of religious hypocrisy that closely reflected the specific historical context in which they were written, read and performed; episodes of false conversion, oath-breaking and rebellion in the name of religion are common in the literature of the 1580s and 1590s. George Peele's play *The Battle of Alcazar* for instance mocks the propensity of a Catholic bishop to convert 'to anie forme may fit the fashion best' (l. 437); stages Stukeley's historical attempt to invade Ireland 'by pope Gregories command' (l. 395); and dramatizes the career of an atheist usurper who attempts to legitimize his conquests by claiming divine sanction and support (ll. 214–21). Such episodes are however carefully qualified, being placed within an overarching moral framework. *The Battle of Alcazar* includes the providential prediction that heaven will punish the Spanish king Philip II for breaking his 'holy oaths' to Sebastian of Portugal, and that 'the time may come that thou and thine shall faile' (ll. 821–6); in a play of the late 1580s, it seems likely that Peele's 'prophecy' is a patriotic reference to England's recent victory over the Spanish Armada.[47] Similarly, in Peele's children's drama *The Araygnement of Paris* the audience is assured that the protagonist Paris will suffer for breaking his lovers' oath in Venus's name: the prologue affirms that as a result of Paris's actions, 'proude Troy must fall, so bidde the gods above, / And statelie Iliums loftie towers be racet / By conquering handes of the victorious foe' (*Araygnement* ll. 8–10).[48]

Peele's emphasis on the operation of divine justice is characteristic of the Elizabethan drama of the 1580s and 1590s. Plays from this period feature episode after episode in which characters manipulate religion for selfish secular reasons, but against a backdrop of sincerely portrayed and effective divine justice. In Robert Greene's *Alphonsus King of Aragon*, for example, the authoritative character Medea reassuringly identifies Alphonsus's military campaign to depose King Belinus as a just cause ratified by the 'fates' (ll. 1210–3).[49] Although this tragi-comedy was heavily influenced by Marlowe's *Tamburlaine*, Greene unlike Marlowe consistently stresses the role played by provid-ential justice in his hero's success: Alphonsus is a divinely appointed king, the rightful heir by birth and legal right as well as force of arms (ll. 139–79), and his victory and subsequent marriage are openly credited to Jove's divine intervention (ll. 2080–4). Tamburlaine's more dubious characteristics, including his willingness to attack the gods themselves, are cautiously displaced onto the villain Amurack (ll. 996–1001).

The emphasis Elizabethan dramatists such as Peele and Greene place on the operation of divine providence is significant, signifying the essentially orthodox nature of their work. Though the sixteenth-century version of atheism rarely constituted an explicit denial of God's existence, challenges to God's providential power to intervene in the world were treated as equivalent evidence of disbelief. Yet Marlowe's own writings, in contrast to most fictional works of the period, lack a clear providential structure. Prayers and curses are almost invariably ineffective, and the deaths of Marlowe's protagonists rarely conform to a straightforward moral pattern. Indeed, Marlowe sometimes seems to deliberately discredit the operation of divine justice: even if an audience accepts that Tamburlaine's death is a providential punishment rather than a natural illness, for instance, the most obvious architect is the Islamic prophet Mahomet; a difficult proposition for an early modern Christian audience to accept. Similarly, Barabas's death in *The Jew of Malta* is publicly credited to the just intervention of heaven, but is in reality attributable to the treachery of his purported ally Ferneze. Even in *Doctor Faustus*, the only one of Marlowe's works in which Christianity possesses an existential status, God is silent and Faustus seems deaf to the words of his angelic messenger.[50] At a time when the Protestant theologian Philippe de Mornay could state adamantly that divine providence 'is the peculiar effect of God' and that 'he which denyeth that, denyeth the Godhead it selfe', the virtual absence of a providential framework in Marlowe's plays and poems is almost equivalent to a literary declaration of disbelief.[51]

Greene's reluctance in *Alphonsus King of Aragon* to associate his hero with Tamburlaine's hypocritical religious rhetoric highlights another distinctive characteristic of Marlowe's work. During the

1580s and early 1590s, Marlowe's fellow writers associate the politic appropriation of religion almost exclusively with villains. One of the most infamous early examples is William Shakespeare's *Richard III*. Richard first uses linguistic equivocation to fatally deceive his brother Clarence (1.1.115), then covers his related campaign against the Queen's allies with a pose of pious innocence:

> But then I sigh, and, with a piece of scripture,
> Tell them that God bids us do good for evil;
> And thus I clothe my naked villainy
> With odd old ends stol'n forth of Holy Writ,
> And seem a saint when most I play the devil.
> (*Richard III* 1.3.333–7)

Later, in Act 3, Richard stage-manages his first public appearance as prospective ruler so that he is discovered praying 'with two right reverend fathers' (3.7.60); his ally Buckingham exploits Richard's pretence of piety to build a 'holy descant' of rhetoric that secures the latter's accession to the throne (3.7.48). But, though Shakespeare equates religious deceit with political advantage more overtly than George Peele and Robert Greene, even the amoral Richard eventually experiences the pangs of 'coward conscience' (5.3.179): on the night before the play's final battle the ghosts of his victims appear to him, their presence suggesting that Richard's subsequent defeat is ordained by providential justice.

Marlowe's more theologically conservative contemporaries carefully distinguished between the religious hypocrisy practised by their villains and the genuine piety of their heroes, a trend that continued into the seventeenth century. In Thomas Heywood's *Fair Maid of the West*, for instance, the honourable Muslim Joffer is persuaded to convert to Christianity after witnessing 'the virtue in these Christians' (*Part II* 5.4.185), while the English hero Spencer's determined integrity contrasts with the oath-breaking treachery of the lecherous Muslim ruler Mullisheg (*Part II* 1.1.233–8; 3.2.100–5).[52] Yet the orthodox distinction between heroic piety and hypocritical villainy maintained in this play contrasts with the vein of sceptical ambivalence that characterises much seventeenth-century drama, a development at least partly attributable to Marlowe's literary influence. Thus in Marlowe's writings the politic appropriation of religion became a cross-confessional and indeed almost universal phenomenon, as Marlowe's amoral, hypocritical yet brilliant protagonists blur the conventional boundaries of religious practice on the early modern stage. Placing his politic characters within fictional universes devoid of providential significance, Marlowe followed pragmatic politicians such as Machiavelli by removing spiritual constraints from his consideration of religion. Instead, Marlowe's plays and poems treat religious rhetoric as a secular tool of political or personal advantage, ready to be framed to the purposes of self-interested protagonists such as Guise, Barabas and Tamburlaine.

Was Christopher Marlowe an atheist? We may never know for certain, though in recent years his name has become so popularly eloquent of Elizabethan disbelief that literary critics and religious historians can almost automatically label his beliefs unorthodox. Yet the source of the poetic and theatrical vocabulary with which Marlowe articulates doubt in his plays and poems has been less rigorously investigated. Whatever his personal opinions, Marlowe's writings undoubtedly express scepticism about the relationship between religion and politics and the related capacity for religious fraud. His specific interest is in politic religion, and the fictional episodes in which he explores religious deceit present situations familiar to Elizabethan readers from the post-Reformation polemic exchanged by confessional rivals. Marlowe, reading such polemic with a sceptical eye, thus found within its mutually incompatible claims a source of doubt about the viability of any religious truth – a doubt that pervades his literary depictions of self-interested religious fraud.

While critics and biographers regularly relate the scepticism Marlowe's writings express to his knowledge of Greco-Roman philosophy, these classical treatises were not the most significant catalyst for Marlowe's literary scepticism.[53] Instead, Marlowe's most direct and personal experience of religious scepticism was his exposure to the spiritual anxieties suffered and the battles of belief fought by the men and women of sixteenth-century London, England and Europe. It was the theological and political polemic spawned by the Reformation and Counter-Reformation, a polemic inflected by urgent contemporary fears of rebellion, fraud and deception, which shaped Elizabethan England's acquaintance with religious doubt. And it was this understanding that animated Marlowe himself, the actors who performed his plays, the publishers who printed his work, and the readers and spectators who encountered his poems and plays; it is this understanding, rather than Marlowe's hidden conscience, that we need to try and recreate to appreciate fully the sceptical attitudes encoded in and expressed by Marlowe's plays and poems.

As with the French essayist Montaigne, Marlowe's experience of the disorientating effects of post-Reformation controversy combined with his knowledge of classical scepticism to shape his understanding of religion as an ideology of control. As he explores the conjunction of religion and politics in his literary works, engaging over and over again with instances in which religion is manipulated and exploited by self-interested protagonists, Marlowe develops a vocabulary of disbelief that is deeply rooted in the specific historical circumstances in which he wrote: his literary scepticism, as Sir Francis Bacon would have recognised, draws both its impetus and its inspiration from the inter-confessional controversies and divisions of post-Reformation England. The terminology of politic religion is thus a significant linguistic thread in Marlowe's work, as too are the broader early modern lexicons of Machiavellianism and religious fraud. These discourses frame Marlowe's fictional reproduction of a self-interested and hypocritical 'piety' which cloaks a broad spectrum of misbehaviour, with the specific Elizabethan terminology of politic fraud providing the scaffolding upon which Marlowe's literary exposé of religion is constructed.

The appropriation of religious rhetoric for personal advantage was a theme that preoccupied Marlowe throughout his writing career. The translations *Ovid's Elegies* and *Lucan's First Book*, most probably written in the early 1580s while Marlowe was a student at Cambridge, give an early indication of his interest in the subject.[54] These translations suggest that Marlowe inherited from his classical sources an awareness that religious discourse was a strategic fiction, a theory that operated powerfully on his mind at a time when accusations of hypocrisy dominated debate between Catholics and Protestants. Inter-confessional polemic became particularly virulent from the mid-1580s and Marlowe's next work, the children's company drama he wrote in collaboration with Thomas Nashe, more overtly responds to contemporary religious controversy. *Dido Queen of Carthage* cannot be dated with any accuracy, but it is usually tentatively allotted to 1585–6 due to its strong thematic and linguistic links with Marlowe's Ovidian translations and his *Tamburlaine* plays – a period during which the intensification of England's war with Catholic Spain resulted in heightened anxieties about the loyalties of Elizabeth I's Catholic subjects. This tension is perhaps reflected in Marlowe and Nashe's drama, in which the protagonist Aeneas breaks a political oath in the name of a conflicting religious duty – with disastrous consequences for the ruler and the kingdom he abandons.[55]

As Elizabethan concerns about religious dissidence intensified in the late 1580s, Marlowe's engagement with politic religion escalated. First came the two *Tamburlaine* plays (*c.* 1587), in which Marlowe explores the role played by religious rhetoric in rationalising acts of perjury, rebellion and even regicide – all political issues of immediate concern to Elizabethan subjects.[56] Although as with *Dido Queen of Carthage* the immediate contemporary implications are somewhat softened by the historically and geographically distanced nature of the narrative, and by the fact that hypocritical appeals to religion are often directed towards a broadly Greco-Roman pantheon, Marlowe's next play extends the Catholic themes that emerge in *Part Two* by staging an explicitly Christian narrative of religious deceit and treachery. *Doctor Faustus* is more openly concerned with religion than the rest of Marlowe's works; it is the only one of his plays or poems to give Christianity an existential status, as Faustus encounters angels and demons and launches a rebellion against a recognisably Protestant deity. Yet the play's strong thematic and linguistic affinity with *Tamburlaine* suggest that it was most probably written around 1588–9,[57] and like the two *Tamburlaine* plays it is by no means as conventional as the Christian narrative of damnation might suggest. The play survives in two separate editions, known as the A-text (published 1604) and the B-text (published 1616), and there are significant variations between the two versions; the 1616 B-text apparently also includes additions by Samuel Rowley and William Birde, commissioned by the theatrical manager Philip Henslowe in 1602. While these additions seem designed to establish *Doctor Faustus* as a more straightforwardly patriotic Protestant drama, extending for instance a scene in which Marlowe's protagonist attacks the Pope, both versions of Marlowe's tragedy continue to raise questions about the relationship between Faustus's Protestant rhetoric and his demonic conjuring, and to emphasise the role deceptive religious rhetoric plays in Faustus's damnation. A similar association between linguistic dissimulation and the repudiation of former religious loyalties also surfaces in the epyllion *Hero and Leander*, this time in a Greco-Roman mythological context: though the date Marlowe wrote this poem is unknown, it shares with *Tamburlaine* and *Doctor Faustus* an interest in portraying politic religious behaviour at a slight remove from the politicised controversies of post-Reformation Europe.

In his next trio of plays, however, Marlowe threw such caution to the wind. *The Jew of Malta* (*c.* 1590), *Edward II* (*c.* 1591–2) and *The Massacre at Paris* (*c.* 1592) are often termed Marlowe's 'plays of policy' by critics; and in these three dramas of the 1590s he again introduces themes of urgent importance to his original audiences, but now within a more explicitly contemporary context.[58] *The Jew of Malta* features representatives of all three Abrahamic religions within an up-to-date political setting; *Edward II* depicts a proto-Protestant English king deposed by rebels who cite Catholic theories of religious resistance; and *The Massacre at Paris* deals with historical events that took place just a few years earlier. The content of these three plays is equally controversial in

Elizabethan terms, with Marlowe representing false conversion for material gain, rebellion against anointed Christian rulers and, most provocatively, regicide in the name of religion. In the works that were probably his last Marlowe thus takes his engagement with politic religion one step further, attributing fraudulent religious practices to Catholic and even Protestant characters who thereby achieve secular advantage within recognisably European settings.

Marlowe's engagement with politic religion is not limited to a denunciation of Catholic, Turkish or puritan dissidence, but exposes characters of various denominations as practitioners of religious fraud. It is this cross-confessional, universalising approach to politic religion that sets Marlowe apart from his contemporaries. While an awareness of the politic (mis)appropriation of religious rhetoric was common in the 1580s and 1590s, Marlowe is almost unique in his willingness to show characters of all faiths (or none) exploiting religion to their own ends. Moreover, Marlowe portrays such politic behaviour within fictional universes where divine providence is either absent or ineffectual, suggesting that in a secular world only the fraudulent appropriation of religion can offer any hope of success or safety. It is the comprehensive need to exploit religion in Marlowe's writings that, more than anything else, illustrates his sceptical assumption that all faith is negotiable; and that the true value of religion is defined by the protagonist's ability to cloak his or her secular, self-interested ambitions successfully in the rhetoric of belief.

CHAPTER ONE

EQUIVOCATION, DISSIMULATION AND DECEIT

In Marlowe's *Massacre at Paris*, the notorious rebel Guise declares in his first soliloquy that his policy has 'fram'd' religion (2.62). The verb 'fram'd' implies an intentional shaping of his religious thoughts and actions, hinting at the possibility of deception; although these connotations of deceit were less overt in sixteenth-century English than they are in modern usage, the verb 'frame' could refer even then to the framing of a false account or fraud.[59] As the linguistic and performative connotations of 'to frame' suggest, the power Guise gains through his pretence of religious conviction is grounded in his ability to construct this pose rhetorically: to verbally fashion a counterfeit conscience. Guise himself also prioritises linguistic skill in his eulogistic account of how his policy frames religion, reporting that he daily wins King Charles IX with his words (*Massacre at Paris* 2.62, 70). Marlowe's protagonist Tamburlaine similarly uses 'working words' to tempt the Persian general Theridamis into a treacherous alliance against his king (*1 Tamburlaine* 1.2.226–31), while the devil Mephistopheles is renowned for the seductive rhetoric that convinces Faustus to sign away his soul.

The power words possess in these plays is not a coincidence: as a poet and a playwright Christopher Marlowe was fascinated by the possibilities of language, by rhetoric's capacity to move audiences. Linguistic dexterity is a characteristic feature of the Marlovian protagonist, and Marlowe's works regularly incorporate great oratorical set pieces. Moreover, the impact of these spectacles goes beyond words alone. Rhetoric in the sixteenth century was an art of public speaking, and the manner in which the orator addressed his audience was as important as the composition of his speech; with manuals such as Thomas Wilson's *Arte of Rhetorique* instructing their readers to deliver orations with an appropriate 'framyng of the voyce, countenaunce, and gesture', early modern rhetoric was very much a performance art.[60] Marlowe's eloquent protagonists similarly pair the aural and the visual, combining persuasive argument with striking effects; the convergence of words and spectacle aptly mirrors their creator's fascination with the power of theatrical display.

The poetic and theatrical powers of rhetoric can be a source of profit and delight in Marlowe's writings. But rhetoric's threatening capacity to deceive spectators and listeners is also emphasised, through a series of episodes that explore the deadly consequences of surrendering to verbal and visual temptation. The dangers are especially evident in *Doctor Faustus*, a tragedy in which language and spectacle combine to seal the title character's damnation. By the final act, a newly cautious Faustus warns his fellow scholars to 'be silent then, for danger is in words' as they watch the spirit of Helen of Troy cross the stage (5.1.25); voiced by a magician who has been led towards damnation by Mephistopheles' sweet speech, the warning resonates strongly. But Faustus ignores his own advice: a few lines later he requests 'heavenly Helen' as his paramour, and greets her with a famous paean to the beauty 'that launched a thousand ships / And burnt the topless towers of Ilium' (5.1.85, 91–2). The act of speech apparently seals the damnation that Faustus's written and verbal contract with Mephistopheles promises: as Marlowe's magician orates in Helen's honour, the spirit's lips meet his in a kiss that 'sucks forth' his soul (5.1.94). Physical utterance proves dangerous, allowing Faustus's soul to escape the confines of his body: with prayers believed to ascend to heaven from the lips, the dual significance of the mouth as physical source of speech and as metaphorical egress for the conscience was well established in early modern thought. The sucking forth of Faustus's soul by a beautiful spirit who apparently serves the devil is the direct consequence of his earlier decision to bargain with Lucifer; his soul's departure reiterates the role played by dangerous words and seductive spectacle in Faustus's damnation.

Faustus is an extreme example, but early modern writers, readers and spectators were deeply conscious that the wrong words could invite damnation. The verbal crime of blasphemy against God and the Holy Spirit was regarded as an unforgiveable sin, and critics sometimes suggest that it is Faustus's blasphemous utterances that seal his fate. Faustus's creator Christopher Marlowe was himself accused of that same crime in 1593, when Richard Baines detailed his 'damnable' pronouncements in a letter to the Elizabethan government and concluded that 'the mouth of so dangerous a member' should 'be stopped'.[61] Yet while words are consistently acknowledged to be dangerous in Marlowe's writings his characters rarely take refuge in silence, as Faustus's encounter with Helen illustrates. On the contrary, Marlowe's protagonists employ a range of linguistic strategies to filter their words past hostile auditors, adopting in thc proccss tactics of dissimulation that Marlowe's contemporaries might have associated as much with religious and political dissidence as with spiritual blasphemy.

Using the stage's multiplicity of fictional voices or the ambiguities of figurative language to evade government censorship were strategies familiar to Marlowe and his fellow writers. Yet while his personal experience might have influenced Marlowe's representations of linguistic dissimulation, the most infamous early modern strategies against repressive censorship were those discussed in and employed by post-Reformation polemic. In Elizabethan England the voices the Protestant regime strove most to silence were those of their puritan and Catholic opponents, who were accused of using verbal and visual trickery to evade the law and deceive English subjects. In his 1582 tract *A Discoverie of Edmund Campion*, for instance, the playwright and government agent Anthony Munday characterised the Jesuit priest as a deceptive rhetorician,

> eloquent in phrase, and so fine in his quirkes and fanasticall conjectures: that the ignorant he wun by his smoothe devises, some other affecting his pleasaunt imaginations, he charmed with subtiltie, and choaked with Sophistrie.

Munday stresses the fraudulent quality of Campion's teachings, reporting that 'what was sounde he would make Sophisticall' in order to delude the people and 'purchase him credit and affection'.[62]

Denouncing the 'Sophisticall' eloquence of the Catholic missionaries, Protestant polemicists also condemned Catholicism in general as empty and fraudulent. Catholic priests were accused of enticing the gullible with false miracles and conjuring tricks, with the Catholic ceremony of mass termed a sham. The Protestant John Foxe claimed that the Catholics 'altogether delight in untruths' and built their religion on 'fained fables, lying miracles, [and] false visions',[63] while the notorious public exorcisms performed by the Jesuit priest William Weston and his companions during the 1580s were a target of Protestant antagonism. Moreover, Catholics were accused of using specific linguistic strategies to trick and deceive. The most notorious of these were mental reservation and equivocation: the former method involved qualifying an external statement with a silent internal stipulation intended only for God, while the latter exploited the inherent ambiguities of discourse to deceive a reader or listener into interpreting a statement in the wrong sense, secretly reserving an alternative meaning. While this precise definition of equivocation as a deception that exploits the double meanings of words did not become widely prevalent until after the Jesuit priest Robert Southwell's 1595 trial, the term 'equivocation' could denote linguistic trickery in a confessional context as early as 1533: in that year, Sir Thomas More accused his Protestant adversary William Tyndale of 'juglynge' or equivocating with two different definitions of the word 'church'.[64]

By the 1580s and 1590s, Elizabethan Catholics, presbyterians and members of the Family of Love were all actively exploiting ambiguous double meanings to evade hostile questioning. Jesuit priests trained at the English College in Douai were advised to 'reply sophistically' when questioned by the Elizabethan authorities, and were taught to mislead hostile listeners through mental reservation;[65] similar tactics were adopted by radical Protestant groups such as the presbyterians in response to persecution by the Elizabethan authorities. The linguistic deceit practised by the comparatively obscure separatist sect the Family of Love was also notorious: while Catholics were forbidden to lie directly to their interrogators, whatever their Protestant enemies might claim, the former Familist Leonard Romsey informed the authorities that 'the disciples of H.N. make no conscience of lyinge and dissemblinge to all them that be not of their religion'.[66] Finally, the verbal trickery employed in mainstream Protestant propaganda came under reciprocal attack from Catholic and puritan authors: England's Protestant polemicists were for instance accused of misquoting and manipulating scripture to support false arguments, a charge that relates intriguingly to Marlowe's *Doctor Faustus*. An association between dangerously persuasive eloquence, linguistic dissimulation and confessional conflict thus permeated English polemic of the 1580s and 1590s, as accusations of fraud and deceit raged between rival confessions.

It seems likely that Marlowe's plays and poems, in which articulate characters regularly tempt their fictional listeners into treason, bear the imprint of these post-Reformation debates. Marlowe's writings demonstrate a sustained interest in the fraudulent practices denounced by contemporary authors; his exposure to cross-confessional accusations of visual and verbal deceit combined with his literary interest in the power of language and theatrical show to shape his fictional representation of characters who manipulate religious rhetoric. This chapter explores Marlowe's enduring fascination with those who use language to deceive others, arguing that these episodes resonate closely with early modern concerns about fraudulent religious rhetoric. Thus the devil-friar Mephistopheles and Hero's lover Leander cite religious precedents to seduce their listeners with pseudo-spiritual syntax, while in Marlowe's later plays protagonists such as Barabas and Mortimer embrace the specific tactics of linguistic dissimulation associated with Elizabethan religious conflict: Barabas and Abigail use mental reservation in *The Jew of Malta*, and the regicide Mortimer scripts an equivocal order for the king's death in *Edward*

II. The self-interested appropriation of religious rhetoric is a pervasive trope in Marlowe's writing; beginning with Mephistopheles' temptation of Faustus, this chapter will explore his imaginative preoccupation with linguistic dissimulation and fraudulent show.

DANGER IS IN WORDS: VISUAL AND VERBAL DECEIT IN 'DOCTOR FAUSTUS'

In *Doctor Faustus*, Marlowe's audiences encounter a demonic character whose deceitful rhetoric convinces Faustus to damn himself with a 'conversion' to the worship of Lucifer. Contemporary accounts suggest that sixteenth-century spectators recognised and feared Mephistopheles as the devil's representative; the image of a devil threatening Faustus decorates the title page of the

Woodcut from the title page of the 1616 B-text edition of *Doctor Faustus*. Christopher Marlowe, *The tragicall history of the life and death of Doctor Faustus* (London, 1618; STC 10713).

1616 edition, indicating that Mephistopheles' demonic qualities were very evident to an early modern audience. Yet it is also significant that Lucifer's messenger is explicitly instructed to don Catholic garb, and appears onstage dressed as a friar. At a time when Catholic priests were believed to be seducing English subjects away from their natural allegiances through a combination of misleading rhetoric and false show, Mephistopheles' adoption of near-identical tactics is arresting. In fact, during the course of Marlowe's tragedy Faustus's decision to sell his soul to Lucifer is consistently associated with forms of rhetorical deceit that parallel those denounced in contemporary religious polemic. While the connection between the devil and Catholicism is visually striking, Mephistopheles' verbal duplicity and Faustus's efforts to justify his behaviour also invite comparison with puritan and Protestant strategies; this blurring of denominational boundaries is characteristic of Marlowe's writings, which consistently universalise the various types of politic religious fraud denounced in post-Reformation polemic.

At the start of *Doctor Faustus*, Faustus's demonic conjuring is perhaps most closely associated with Catholicism. His mentor Valdes rejoices at the power magic has to 'canonise' its practitioners (1.1.121–2), and the rites Faustus uses to summon Mephistopheles include several elements conventionally associated with the Catholic sacrament of baptism – most notably, the sprinkling of holy water and appeals to the 'holy saints' (1.3.10). The Catholicised nature of these rites has often been noted by modern critics and audiences. In a recent production at the Manchester Royal Exchange, for instance, the ritual's Catholic nature was underscored by the use of a censer to dispense incense during the summoning sequence, while the 2011 Shakespeare's Globe production similarly stressed the Catholic element by having a chorus of robed scholars chant Faustus's Latin incantations in plainsong while Paul Hilton's Faustus spoke the main invocation.[67] Both productions were based on the 1616 B-text of *Doctor Faustus*, which features additional anti-Catholic elements not present in the 1604 A-text, including an extended Pope-baiting episode and a more overt emphasis on papal corruption. Despite these variations, however, the 1604 A-text equally associates Faustus's magic with Catholic ritual: Faustus's command that Mephistopheles should dress as a holy friar is common to both versions, while the conjuring scene is virtually identical in the two editions.

Mephistopheles' costume was not Marlowe's invention. In the *English Faust Book* (*EFB*), which seems to have been the main source for *Doctor Faustus*, the spirit summoned by John Faustus appears 'in the manner of a grey friar, asking Faustus what was his request'; Marlowe's Mephistopheles takes on the shape of 'an old Franciscan friar' in accordance with Faustus's directive (1.3.26).[68] Nonetheless, Marlowe's decision to retain the friar's costume tellingly enhances the Catholic aura that surrounds Faustus's demonic conjuring. On the Elizabethan stage, in fact, Mephistopheles conforms to a Protestant and anti-papal theatrical tradition which expects demonic characters to shroud themselves in Catholic garb: in the biblical drama *Abrahams Sacrifice*, for instance, Théodore de Bèze's Satan exults that his 'Cowle' will conceal much mischief.[69] Marlowe's devil-friar would also have invoked England's Reformation history in a more concrete and material form: since Catholic clerical garments were sold to the playing companies during Elizabeth I's reign, the robes worn by the actor playing Mephistopheles might have previously belonged to a Marian priest: the literal remnants of the Catholic past brought onstage to decorate a devil.[70]

Since Marlowe's devil is presumably still wearing friar's robes when he tempts Faustus into signing his soul away to Lucifer, his costume may imply an affinity with the Catholic priests proselytising secretly in Elizabethan England. The mendicant order of the Franciscans or Grey Friars could be readily associated with the missionary zeal of the latter, especially since the great Protestant hagiographer John Foxe had accused Marian friars of tricking Protestants into converting to Catholicism. In his famous account of Thomas Cranmer's temptation, for example, Foxe describes how 'the wily papistes flocked about hym, wyth threatning, flattering, entreating, and promising', emphasising in particular the role played by 'frier John'.[71] It is plausible that Foxe's narrative influenced spectator responses to Mephistopheles, given that Cranmer was a well-known English Protestant martyr; in *Doctor Faustus*, Marlowe's audiences likewise witness a demonic friar convincing a Protestant scholar to reject his faith in favour of satanic rites infused with papist tradition. Faustus's 'conversion' seems to echo contemporary fears about the English Catholic mission; such fears may take on a particular resonance in Act 2, as Mephistopheles exclaims 'O, what will not I do to obtain his soul?' (2.1.73).

Mephistopheles' mastery of visual spectacle and the way he seduces Faustus with splendid shows offers another parallel between his temptation of Faustus and Elizabethan anxiety about the proselytising missionary priests. His technique is strongly reminiscent of the radical Protestant exile Henry Ainsworth's complaint that 'by the abundance of her pleasures' the Church of Rome 'bewitcheth and deceiveth many soules, betraying them unto Satan'.[72] Indeed, Protestant polemic sometimes condemned Catholic services as fraudulent magical shows or illusions and denounced them in theatrical terms, as in Samuel Harsnett's 1603 accusation that the Pope and the Catholic missionaries 'do make a pageant of the Church, the blessed Sacraments, the rites and ceremonies of religion'. According to Harsnett, the purpose of such spectacle was

> to gull, terrifie, and amaze the simple ignorant people, and by bringing them into an admiration of the power of their priest-hood . . . to enchaunt, and bewitch their innocent simple soules.[73]

These contemporary associations between Catholic ritual and demonic magic even had a linguistic impact: while the verb 'conjuration' usually meant 'to call a spirit to appear', for the Protestant reformers it could also mean 'to consecrate in the Roman Mass'.[74]

Puritans were also occasionally accused of practising dangerous and rebellious magic, but the association between Roman Catholicism, the devil and fraudulent magic was particularly pervasive in the sixteenth century. These popular associations are significant for Marlowe's *Doctor Faustus*, in which a demonic spirit conjures up various fantastic and eroticised spectacles – from the masque of the Seven Sins to the appearance of Alexander the Great and his paramour. Mephistopheles' tactics perhaps also echo early modern Protestant accusations that Catholic rituals seduced the senses rather than appealing to the rational mind: though Faustus is initially tempted by the devil's offer of knowledge, he quickly allows himself to be distracted by show. As he signs the fatal contract with the devil, Mephistopheles diverts him (in both senses of the word) with a demonic dance and gifts of royal regalia. Sara Munson Deats notes the parodic significance of these 'hollow crowns without kingdoms', which mockingly anticipate Faustus's abandonment of his heavenly crown for an earthly authority he never attains.[75] Afterwards Faustus spends much of the play seeking distraction in Catholic locations, from papal Rome to the court of Charles V of Spain. While such diversions are especially elaborate in the 1616 B-text, both the A- and B-texts seem to invite comparisons between Mephistopheles' tactics and the deceptive, distracting practices attributed to missionary priests by Protestant commentators. Thus, in *Doctor Faustus*, Marlowe indirectly reveals the power of the demonic and quasi-Catholic show that frames Faustus's descent into damnation; a few years later the informer Richard Baines would accuse Marlowe himself of falling for these visual enticements, attributing to him the statement that if there be any good religion 'it is the papistes because the service of god is performed with more ceremonies'.[76]

This emphasis on visual spectacle in *Doctor Faustus* is a deliberate theatrical innovation by Marlowe. In the *The English Faust Book* the main focus is not on sight but sound, with John Faustus 'ravished' by 'the sweetest music that ever he heard'.[77] But, while this auditory component is not completely absent from Marlowe's play, it is words rather than music that fill Faustus's ears, from those Valdes and Cornelius use in Act 1 to praise magic to the seductive sayings of 'sweet' Mephistopheles. Mephistopheles' honeyed words are especially important, with Marlowe's devil using a range of rhetorical tricks to dazzle and mislead his victim.

The impact these tricks have on protagonist and spectator alike is evident in performance, and modern productions often emphasise Mephistopheles' eloquence: in the 1993 Greenwich Theatre production, for instance, Hugh Ross played Mephistopheles as a 'smooth spy master' who spoke his lines with cool plausibility.[78] This skill is equally apparent at the textual level: Marlowe crafted his devil's lines with care, and his Mephistopheles is a skilful orator who employs a range of subtle techniques. For example, as Douglas Hayes has demonstrated that Mephistopheles uses the rhetorical flourish *epistophe* (turning to the same sound in the line end) to build upon Faustus's use of the word 'Lucifer' (1.3.71–4), adding an amplifying corollary to Faustus's questions that serves to pull Faustus the interrogator into the position of Faustus the damned.[79] Mephistopheles also relies heavily on the rhetorical figure of *protrope* or *adhortatio*, whereby the auditor is exhorted to action by means of promises and threats; although examples of this figure are plentiful in the Bible, Marlowe's contemporary Henry Peacham warned that it could also be used to move 'sedition, tumults, or rebellion' and seduce 'unstable mindes into false religion' – events that 'Sathan doth alwaies further to the uttermost of his power'.[80] In the context of Faustus's decision to rebel against God by pledging allegiance to Lucifer, Mephistopheles' use of this figure is especially suggestive.

For the play's original spectators, then, the theatrical narrative of a Protestant scholar lured to damnation by an eloquent devil dressed in friar's robes surely recalled contemporary warnings against deceptive Catholic rhetoric. However, the correlation between Mephistopheles and Catholic eloquence is not as simple as it might at first appear. Although he relies on sensuous spectacles to distract Faustus, Mephistopheles is surprisingly restrained in his speech. In fact, as Hayes suggests, there are times when this representative of Lucifer, the father of lies, seems to damn Faustus by telling him the truth. There are several moments in *Doctor Faustus* when Mephistopheles adopts honesty as his best policy, most notably his ostensibly truthful but almost suspiciously detailed description of the horrors of hell (1.3.78–82; 2.1.122–6). The rhetorical excesses of this speech trick Faustus into dismissing the devil's hyperbole as a weakness to be countered with 'manly fortitude' (1.3.87), as emphasised in the 2011 Globe production: Paul Hilton's Faustus spoke the lines mockingly, inviting the audience to share his disdain for Mephistopheles' cowardice.[81] Such descriptive flamboyance contrasts strikingly with Mephistopheles' usually restrained style – it is Faustus who commonly indulges in elaborate rhetorical display – and his ostensible truthfulness may be deliberately misleading. Such an interpretation was perhaps hinted at in the Young Vic production of 2002, in which Richard McCabe's Mephistopheles gave a 'sly knowing smile' as Jude Law's Faustus blustered that damnation did not scare him.[82]

Mephistopheles' reliance on plain speech and misleading truthfulness disrupts a straightforward alignment between Marlowe's devil and the seductive, eloquent priests denounced by English Protestant polemicists. Emphasis upon a plain-speaking style was, on the contrary, characteristic of puritan and Protestant preaching during this period: texts written in the service of the Elizabethan state church claimed that 'plain words of Scripture have their aucthoritie' and that 'Christe taught us plainly'.[83] At the same time Protestantism could also be associated with linguistic dissimulation. Even the founding father of Protestantism, the Wittenberg scholar Martin Luther, was prepared to acknowledge the value of equivocation: in his commentary on Romans 13, Luther argues that 'as the apostle has become all things to all men, so he also speaks to everyone in his own terms . . . [and] must necessarily become equivocal when he uses the words "liberty" and "servitude"'.[84] Marlowe's devil may be dressed as a Catholic friar, but the linguistic strategies he uses to deceive that other Wittenberg scholar Faustus owe as much to early modern ideals of godly Protestant style as to denunciations of Catholic sophistry.

It may be that scholars of Protestant Wittenberg were commonly associated with equivocation in late Elizabethan England:[85] Hamlet, who has also studied at Wittenberg (1.2.113), is the first character to use the term 'equivocation' in Shakespeare's drama. Hamlet even practises his own form of dissimulation by adopting an 'antic disposition' (1.5.170), while his warning to Horatio against doubtful phrases and 'ambiguous giving out' perhaps hints at the problematic early modern association between linguistic ambiguity and disloyalty (1.5.183–6). Hamlet is a comparatively positive character, however, whereas Marlowe's prior representation of linguistic equivocation in Protestant Wittenberg more problematically links such deceit to Faustus's demonically inspired rebellion against God. Indeed, it seems possible that Marlowe's characterisation of Mephistopheles was influenced by the contemporary tendency to conflate Catholicism and puritanism as joint threats to English security; as his fellow writer Thomas Nashe suggested, the devil, once a Catholic and still robed as one, 'of late is growen a puritane'.[86]

Although Faustus's decision to sign his soul away is usually credited to Mephistopheles' winning words and seductive spectacles, his arguments fall on fertile ground: Faustus is already predisposed to accept Mephistopheles' logic on the basis of his own manipulation of the Bible. Thus Marlowe's tragic protagonist is at least in part condemned by his own words, contributing to his damnation through an equivocal interpretation of scripture that preempts Mephistopheles' words of temptation, and which he uses to justify summoning the devil in the first place. In the 1616 B-text it is just about possible to blame Faustus's initial error on the wiles of the devil, who gloats towards the end of the play that

> 'Twas I that, when thou wert i'the way to heaven,
> Damned up thy passage. When thou took'st the book
> To view the Scriptures, then I turned the leaves
> And led thine eye.
>
> (B-text 5.2.98–101)

This passage does not, however, appear in the 1604 A-text, where Faustus's own responsibility for crafting the suspect syllogism that inspires his damnable progress is more evident. And even in the B-text, the extent to which Mephistopheles has had to distort Faustus's reading remains ambiguous: earlier in this edition the devil reminds Faustus that damnation was 'thine own seeking, Faustus. Thank thyself' (B-text 2.3.4).

To use the Bible as an instrument of damnation sounds like something a good Elizabethan Protestant would never even consider, yet the role played by the scriptures in Faustus's damnation is striking. Listening to the Good Angel's consistent entreaties that Faustus 'lay that damnèd book aside' and 'read the Scriptures' (1.1.72–5), Marlowe's audiences are liable to recall that Faustus's interest in magic was sparked by the conclusions he drew from reading the Bible in the first place. Indeed, the ambiguous application of the Angel's phrase 'that is blasphemy' (1.1.75), hovering syntactically between the 'damnèd book' and the 'Scriptures', may even direct our attention back towards this problematic progression; modern productions tend to iron out the ambiguity by having the Good Angel gesture in the appropriate direction at this point, but we cannot know if the Elizabethan actor did the same. Certainly, while the Angel prioritises the act of scriptural interpretation in accordance with standard Protestant dogma, such advice is problematic following Faustus's earlier misreading of 1 John 1.8:

> *Si peccasse negamus, fallimur*
> *Et nulla est in nobis veritas.*
> If we say that we have no sin,
> We deceive ourselves, and there's no truth in us.
> Why then belike we must sin,
> And so consequently die.
>
> (*Doctor Faustus* 1.1.42–7)

For the Elizabethan Church, the implications of Faustus's misreading were especially challenging. While in the Bible itself the crucial latter verse from 1 John is followed by a statement assuring the reader that 'if we acknowledge our sinnes, he is faithful and just, to forgive us' (1 John 1.9), this progression was not mirrored in the articles of the Elizabethan Church.[87] In the 1559 Book of Common Prayer, for instance, the quotation from 1 John is used to preface the exhortation to repentance and the Order for General Confession, and is thus separated from the consolatory message of verse 9. In the Thirty-Nine Articles, the fifteenth article likewise ends with the conclusion that 'if we say we have no sin, we deceive ourselves and the truth is not in us'; there is no mention of the subsequent verse.[88]

In the event, the dangerous implications of this comparison are softened by the fact that the biblical passages through which Faustus reaches such a damnable conclusion are purportedly drawn from Jerome's Bible (1.1.38), a fourth-century Latin translation that was associated with Roman Catholic teaching; in fact, it seems that Marlowe translated passages from the Geneva Bible into Latin to sustain this illusion.[89] Yet even if his choice of Bible perhaps hints that Faustus is not following accepted Protestant practices, Marlowe's protagonist still co-opts Calvinist logic to construct a devilish syllogism supported by the articles of the Elizabethan Church. In combination with Mephistopheles' fondness for plain, puritanical language, Faustus's misreading of the Bible threatens to undercut a simple assumption that the demonic magic which damns him is exclusively Catholic in nature.

In some respects, the challenging implications of Faustus's scriptural misreading are not especially unusual. Early modern writers were fully alert to the dangers of misinterpreting the Bible: Thomas Nashe, more theologically conservative than his colleague Marlowe, warned in *Christs teares* that 'Scripture as it may be literally expounded and sophisticallie scande, may play the Harbinger as well for Hell as Heaven.'[90] Comparable accusations of scriptural misquotation were also exchanged by Catholic and Protestant polemicists. In 1581, for instance, William Charke said of Edmund Campion that

> If he alledge the scriptures for his cause, as satan did, and as heretikes doe, using some of the words, and leaving the fulnes of the sentence, or perverting the words to another sense then the holy Ghost delivereth, then shall he prevaile as Satan did.[91]

Charke's reference to Satan's equivocal rhetoric recalls Mephistopheles' boast in the 1616 B-text that, by turning the pages of the Bible, he tricked Faustus into an act of misinterpretation. Ben Jonson similarly mocks the foolish gull who deceives himself with religious references in *The Alchemist*, in which Sir Epicure Mammon ironically defends the trickster Subtle's fraudulent alchemical practices by citing 'a treatise penned by Adam' (2.1.79–83). Yet it is with the anti-Protestant accusations voiced by the Catholic mission's propagandists that we come closest to the type of linguistic deception Marlowe depicts in *Doctor Faustus* – especially if we consider the possibility that Faustus may be deliberately obscuring those passages that contradict the conclusion he desires. Robert Parsons, for instance, accused Charke himself of 'fraudulently' turning a scriptural passage from the same Book of John backwards to change 'all the meaning of the sentence' and of cutting from a quotation 'the woordes that folowed immediatlie', an action characterised as a 'moste willfull falsehoode'.[92]

Such techniques of cutting and re-ordering a scriptural sentence to construct a false syllogism are identical to the tactics of biblical quotation Faustus uses to justify summoning the devil, whether we assume that he is being deliberately manipulative or whether (as in the 1616 edition) Mephistopheles is the deceiver who leads him astray. Here, denominational divisions blur once more. With misguided and even deliberately deceptive practices of biblical interpretation attributed to both Catholics and Protestants during this period, the Protestant scholar Faustus's misinterpretation of scripture is not easily categorised as the equivocating device of a Catholic devil. Rather, Faustus's scriptural citation operates in concert with Mephistopheles' deceptive truths and seductive spectacles, hinting that visual and verbal religious fraud might be practised by any individual seeking to bolster his or her secular ambitions.

SAINT-SEDUCING SOPHISTRY: RELIGIOUS PRECEDENTS IN 'HERO AND LEANDER'

In *Doctor Faustus* there are moments when Faustus's temptation verges on literal seduction: Faustus is 'ravished' by magic and 'sweet Mephistopheles' (1.1.112; 5.1.70), claiming to sign his soul away 'for love of' the latter (2.1.53). Throughout Marlowe's tragedy Faustus consistently credits Mephistopheles with the same qualities as 'sweet Helen', the beautiful spirit whose lips suck forth his soul (5.1.93); these linguistic parallels imply that Mephistopheles too has seduced Faustus. In modern performances, the possible homoerotic tension between Faustus and Mephistopheles is often hinted at: in the RSC's 1989 production, for instance, Gerard Murphy's Faustus embraced David Bradley's Mephistopheles on the line 'for love of thee', while in 2011 Arthur Darvill's Mephistopheles gratified Faustus's longing for Helen – 'this, or what else my Faustus shall desire' (B-text 5.1.92) – with his hands clasped lovingly around Faustus's neck, kissing Faustus's forehead at the end of the exchange.[93]

In early modern England, Mephistopheles' seductive sweetness also had implications that went beyond the erotic. The same terminology of sweetness was sometimes used in religious polemic to characterise the smoothly deceptive rhetoric of England's religious dissidents: William Charke, for instance, described in 1581 how Edmund Campion's letters were sent out to 'comfort the Papists, and sweetely to feed them with hope of a great conquest'.[94] Mephistopheles' temptation of Faustus may also recall the accusations directed by Elizabethan Protestants against Catholic priests and separatist sects such as the Family of Love, who were reputed to entice converts with the prospect of sexual pleasure. The Familists were accused of promiscuity and even of holding orgies, while in the Elizabethan morality play *The Conflict of Conscience* the character Sensual Suggestion embodies the fleshly temptations associated in contemporary polemic with Catholic proselytising.[95] This terminology of seduction was often employed to discredit Catholic missionaries: one suggestive parallel to Mephistopheles' temptation of the Protestant scholar Faustus is the Earl of Leicester's 1582 warning against the 'secret and lurking Papists' who have infiltrated the University of Oxford to 'seduce your youth and carry them over by flocks to the Seminaries beyond Seas'.[96]

A similar association between religious rhetoric and seduction can be identified in Marlowe's erotic epyllion *Hero and Leander*. In this poem, Marlowe's protagonist Leander adapts Faustus's strategy of scriptural citation, invoking religious allusions to seduce

Hero away from her existing allegiances. But whereas in *Doctor Faustus* Mephistopheles' misleadingly plain language and seductive showmanship are equally to blame for Faustus's fall, and his misreading or misrepresentation of scripture is merely one aspect of the deceit that permeates the play, Leander's references to religious precedent play a more significant and central part in his own strategy of seduction.

Although critics sometimes dismiss Marlowe's poetry as 'a deliberate escape from thought into the world of simple, sensuous things', the dividing line between erotic and political disorder was rarely so clear cut in Elizabethan England.[97] This was particularly true during a period in which religious dissidence was equated with civil disobedience and polemicists regularly denounced conversions to rival confessions in sexualised language, arguing that using sensual enticements to win converts exposed the internal corruption and spiritual impurity of that faith. Such accusations are especially common in Protestant polemic: in 1582 the playwright and government agent Anthony Munday denounced the English Catholic missionaries as 'secrete seducing Priestes', while at the start of James I's reign the dedicatory epistle to *An Answer to a Catholike English-Man* termed them 'seducing spirits' who veil treason 'under the title of Religion'.[98]

It seems likely that an awareness of these early modern debates about eloquence, seduction and religious belief influenced Marlowe's depiction of the two lovers in *Hero and Leander*. His epyllion is apparently based upon the classical Greek poem by Musaeus, but in Marlowe's version the tension between Hero's religious duty and the worldly desires represented by Leander is conspicuously emphasised. First, Marlowe makes it clear that Hero's position in Venus's temple and her vow to the goddess of love are explicitly religious in nature. She is described by the narrator as 'Venus' nun' and Leander refers to her occupation as 'sacred priesthood' (ll. 45, 293), while her formal ecclesiastical commitment to Venus is physically confirmed by the 'sacred ring' with which 'she was endowed / When first religious chastity she vowed' (ll. 593–4). Secondly, whereas Musaeus originally represented Hero's sacred vows and her parents' concern for her social position as equal constraints on her love life, Marlowe omits all domestic references to focus on the religious issue.[99] Finally, while in Musaeus's poem Hero's vow of chastity was sworn to Urania, the aspect of Venus associated with platonic affection, in Marlowe's version Venus is an explicitly sexual figure and Hero's oath of chastity is overtly incongruous.[100] Indeed, Hero's oxymoronic title 'Venus' nun' seems to draw attention to the logical flaw in her oath, while perhaps also ironically recalling the Elizabethan slang that termed prostitutes 'nuns'.

As well as enhancing his poem's comic appeal, Marlowe's emphasis on the incongruity of Hero's oath enables Leander to frame his rhetorical assault on her chastity in elaborately theological terms. Thus Marlowe's protagonist argues that Hero's vow is 'heedless' because it is contrary to the tenets of Venus (l. 294), and threatens her status by denying the power of sexual love:

> 'Thee as a holy idiot doth she scorn,
> For thou in vowing chastity hast sworn
> To rob her name and honour, and thereby
> Commit'st a sin far worse than perjury,
> Even sacrilege against her deity,
> Through regular and formal purity.'
>
> (*Hero and Leander* ll. 303–8)

In this speech Leander characterizes Hero's vow as an act of 'sacrilege', since it violates her goddess's precepts. In fact, he concludes, the only way for Hero to truly serve her divine mistress is to share her physical favours freely: 'Such sacrifice as this, Venus demands' (l. 309). He goes on to argue that

> 'Though neither gods nor men may thee deserve,
> Yet for her sake whom you have vowed to serve,
> Abandon fruitless cold virginity,
> The gentle queen of love's sole enemy.
> Then shall you most resemble Venus' nun,
> When Venus' sweet rites are performed and done.'
>
> (*Hero and Leander* ll. 315–20)

Though the rough outline of this argument was present in Musaeus's narrative, in which Hero is urged to 'attend to the works of Cypris' 'since you are Cypris' priestess', Marlowe significantly expands the theological angle.[101] Appeals to mythological precedent become central to his protagonist's seduction strategy while the overall significance of the religious context is greatly enhanced.

Despite Leander's appeals to the precedent of Venus, the reader is aware that his argument is self-interested, manufactured to serve his own desires. Whereas in John Lyly's 1584 children's drama *Campaspe* Venus is described by the lover Apelles as a pure deity who must be prayed to with 'vows irrevocable' and honoured with 'hearts ever sighing, never dissembling' (3.3.36, 38), Marlowe's Leander uses all manner of linguistic arts to assimilate Venus's mythology to his own project of seduction.[102] Indeed, Leander's speeches are riddled with linguistic deception. His description of Venus's rites as 'sweet' and 'gentle' contrasts sharply with the narrator's earlier description of the 'heady riots, incest, rapes' enjoyed by the gods (l. 144), while his own conquest of Hero is a 'cruel' rough wooing metaphorically likened to an act of war or hunting (ll. 754–80). Leander's duplicity is further emphasised by a parallel episode featuring the quick-talking god Mercury. In a lengthy digression added by Marlowe, Mercury, Leander-like, is shown using 'speeches full of pleasure and delight' to seduce a country maid (l. 420); yet he too proves 'deceitful' and 'reckless of his promise' (l. 446, l. 461), his behaviour mirroring Leander's sophistry.

Perhaps inspired by *Hero and Leander*, Marlowe's contemporaries and literary successors introduced similar associations between elaborate appeals to religious precedent and self-interested sexual desire in their own work. In Robert Greene and Thomas Lodge's scriptural drama *A Looking-Glass for London*, for instance, the villainous Rasni cites the classical precedent of Juno and Jove to seduce his sister into an incestuous relationship (ll. 77–92);[103] Giovanni similarly uses religious rhetoric to justify incest in John Ford's Jacobean tragedy *'Tis Pity She's a Whore*, casting his sister Annabella as a divine intercessor (1.2.186–90, 231–8). By 1613, the connection between sexual desire and religious argument could even be explicitly related to the doctrinal upheavals of Reformation England: in Shakespeare and Fletcher's *Henry VIII* the king's plans to divorce Katherine are framed by a religious discourse in which his appeals to his conscience are motivated by lust for Anne Boleyn; the lascivious Old Lady employs this sexualised terminology of conscience most explicitly, describing suggestively how Anne's 'soft cheveral conscience' 'would receive, / If you might please to stretch it' (2.3.31–3).

Leander's eloquence is equally suspect in Marlowe's poem. Nonetheless, he eventually persuades Hero to abandon her chaste commitment to Venus (the religion of Urania) and instead worship Venus in her sexual aspect. The narrator's description of Leander as a 'bold sharp sophister' (l. 197) highlights the role played by persuasive rhetoric in Hero's 'conversion': the term 'sophister', commonly designating a person who used reason speciously,[104] was also an epithet used in early modern England against the Jesuit missionaries and other religious dissidents. The Protestant William Fulke denounced the Jesuit Cardinal William Allen as a 'prophane heathenish sophister' in 1577, while Allen's successor Robert Parsons was likewise described by William Barlow as a hypocrite and 'sophister'.[105] While the term 'sophister' could have more neutral associations, being used for example to identify a student in his second or third year at Cambridge University, the sexual dimension to Hero's conversion is suggestive: religion, unlike the university syllabus, was often discussed in eroticised metaphors during this period. Moreover Leander's sophistry, like that of the Elizabethan dissidents, has treasonous implications: he encourages oath-breaking and seizes Hero's 'diadem' of chastity (l. 561), an action that Harry Levin and Patrick Cheney believe may evoke the contemporary political challenges to Elizabeth I's crown.[106] Thus Hero, yielding to Leander because 'treason was in her thought' (l. 777), potentially realises English fears about the deceptive religious rhetoric of Catholic and puritan dissidents; Leander, the 'sophister' who seduces Hero, might remind Marlowe's readers of how those same eloquent dissidents had reportedly 'seduced' English subjects into open rebellion.[107]

MENTAL RESERVATION IN 'THE JEW OF MALTA'

Marlowe returns to these themes of sophistry, seduction and sedition in *The Jew of Malta*. The play's main character Barabas practises another type of rhetorical manipulation often identified with Elizabethan England's religious dissidents: mental reservation. Mental reservation was particularly associated with the Catholic missionaries and the puritans, and Barabas's adoption of such tactics marks a transition in Marlowe's writings; in *The Jew of Malta* and *Edward II* Marlowe depicts rhetorical strategies that conform more formally and overtly to the linguistic evasions advocated by early modern theorists. The first hints of this shift emerged in *Doctor Faustus*, in which Mephistopheles equivocates by answering the words of Faustus's inquiries rather than their intended meaning: in the notorious seventeenth-century Jesuit *Treatise of Equivocation*, the reader is advised that 'whan unto one question may be geven many aunsweres, we may yeelde one and conceale the other'.[108] In *Doctor Faustus*, however, the scarcity of asides and in Mephistopheles' case the absence of soliloquies leave the interiors of the characters opaque, inaccessible; it is impossible to evaluate accurately how frequently Faustus and Mephistopheles use deceptive and misleading language, because we can never be certain when they are telling the truth. In *The Jew of Malta*, on the other hand, Marlowe's unusually frequent use of asides provides spectators and readers with insight into the processes whereby Barabas and on occasion Abigail manipulate language, exposing the mechanics of their dissimulation to his early modern audiences.

Marlowe's Malta is a dangerous place, an island where no one can be trusted and the only choice is to either 'dissemble that thou never mean'st' or 'mean truth and then dissemble it': between 'a counterfeit profession' and 'unseen hypocrisy' (*Jew of Malta* 1.2.290–3). England's Jesuit missionaries, who were forbidden to tell a direct lie, would presumably opt to 'mean truth and then dissemble it'; but a radical sect such as the Family of Love, who were reputed to 'make no conscience of lyinge and dissemblinge', might have embraced the alternative.[109] Marlowe's Barabas also decides that he will 'dissemble that thou never mean'st', falsifying a courtship between Ferneze's son Lodowick and his daughter Abigail in order to trick her suitor Mathias into killing Lodowick. In his instructions to his daughter Barabas uses religious precedents to justify this deception: after urging Abigail in Lodowick's hearing to treat him 'with all the courtesy you can afford', he adds in an aside (as marked by parentheses): 'as if he were a (Philistine. / Dissemble, swear, protest, vow to love him, / He is not of the seed of Abraham.)' (2.3.230–2). Barabas later elaborates on his argument, contending in another aside that

> (This offspring of Cain, this Jebusite
> That never tasted of the Passover,
> Nor e'er shall see the land of Canaan,
> Nor our Messias that is yet to come,
> This gentle maggot Lodowick I mean,
> Must be deluded)
>
> (*Jew of Malta* 2.3.303–8)

In these lines, it seems that it is not merely permissible to deceive those of a rival faith; rather, such deception becomes a duty that 'must' be practised. Marlowe's terminology here hints at the sixteenth-century English context of inter-confessional antagonism. Although ultimately drawn from Judges 19.11–13, Barabas's charge that Lodowick is a 'Jebusite' also reflects the use of the term in Protestant polemic to vilify the Jesuits: as William Charke argues in his *Answere to a Seditious Pamphlet* (1580), 'these that corruptly have called themselves Jesuites, may be called Jebusites, without offence to the Lord Jesus, and most aptly in respect of their dealings'.[110] Barabas's speech can be difficult for modern spectators who may not recognise the significance of his allusions, and it is sometimes cut in performance, but for Marlowe's original audiences Barabas's terminology implicitly aligned his appropriation of religious rhetoric with the dissimulation practised by England's Catholic and puritan dissidents.

Within this sixteenth-century context, Barabas's scriptural allusions are also intriguing. Early modern writers sometimes cited biblical precedents to defend dissimulation and equivocation: common examples included Christ's pretence in Luke 24.13–31 that he would travel farther along the road; Abraham and Isaac's claim that their wives were their sisters (Genesis 20.1–12; 26.6–7); and Jehu pretending to worship Baal in order to destroy the false god's worshippers (2 Kings 10.18–28).[111] But, while Jehu's actions have a thematic affinity with Barabas's mission of destroying Malta's Christians, the actual examples cited by Marlowe's Jew are less harmonious. For instance, Barabas's exclamation that 'as sure as heaven rained manna for the Jews, / So sure shall he and Don Mathias die' frames his action with a scriptural precedent (2.3.250–1) – but the tenuous applicability of the allusion, which forcibly pairs divine mercy and generosity with a cruel and vengeful intent, implicitly mocks his sophistical manipulation of biblical quotations. Certainly, the discrepancy between such posturing and the true meaning of Barabas's references is a source of comedy in modern performance, with the audience's ability to discern such disparities contributing greatly to their enjoyment of the play. In Barry Kyle's 1987 RSC production, for instance, the audience laughed loudly at Barabas's announcement that he holds Abigail 'as dear / As Agamemnon did his Iphigen' (1.1.136–7).[112]

As well as claiming scriptural precedents for his actions, Barabas invokes the notorious Catholic argument that

> It's no sin to deceive a Christian;
> For they themselves hold it a principle,
> Faith is not to be held with heretics;
> But all are heretics that are not Jews
>
> (*Jew of Malta* 2.3.311–14)

Despite his wide-ranging appropriation of religious models, however, the effectiveness of Barabas's arguments remains in doubt: Abigail's ambiguous response generates uncertainty about whether or not she has been convinced by his reasoning (2.3.318). Whatever inner reservations she may possess, however, Abigail outwardly conspires with her father to entrap the Christian 'maggot' Lodowick. From Barabas we learn that the pair have exchanged mutual vows of love offstage, and they then openly plight their faith to each other within the audience's sight (2.3.248–9, 319–20). Although this audience is aware that Abigail loves Mathias and does not really intend to marry Lodowick, the Jew's daughter convinces her unwanted suitor that she genuinely cares for him. In addition, Barabas carefully emphasises the validity of the engagement by framing it in legal and contractual terms: he designates the engagement an 'account' (2.3.244), describes Abigail's consent as an act of granting (316) and pledges financial consideration to her suitor by offering a dowry of 'many a golden cross / With Christian posies round about the ring' (298–9).

However, the marriage vows between Lodowick and Abigail are simultaneously undercut by numerous interpolations that remind Marlowe's readers and spectators of their false nature. Barabas is shown promising Mathias that 'thou know'st, and heaven can witness it is true, / That I intend my daughter shall be thine' at the very moment that Lodowick and Abigail exchange their offstage vows (2.3.255–6), while Abigail's pledges to Lodowick are disrupted by the qualifications she adds for the audience's benefit. Barabas and Abigail's frequent use of asides in this scene is intriguing; while these comments do not necessarily provide Marlowe's spectators with the whole truth, they do enable an audience to evaluate the public performances delivered by Barabas and Abigail from an informed perspective that recognizes their deceitful nature. In his exchanges with Lodowick, for instance, there is a pointed contrast between the declarations Barabas makes to his Christian victim and the running commentary he provides for an audience in the form of asides:

> O my lord
> We will not jar about the price; come to my house
> And I will give't your honour (with a vengeance).
> (*Jew of Malta* 2.3.66–8)

These asides, as indicated in the original 1633 quarto, equate to a form of mental reservation whereby Barabas qualifies his external statements to Lodowick with private comments audible only to the audience and (presumably) his god. Thomas Heywood, who oversaw the 1633 revival of Marlowe's *Jew of Malta*, certainly seems to have recognised that theatrical asides could be used to stage expressions of mental reservation: in his own play *The Golden Age*, the character Jupiter similarly uses asides to register 'internal' caveats when, disguised as a woman, he supposedly swears fealty to Diana (2.1).[113]

During the Elizabethan period the doctrine of mental reservation was most fully theorised by the Jesuits. By the mid-1580s a number of Jesuit treatises on the subject were available in print on the Continent, including Martín de Azpilcueta's *Enchiridion* and his *Commentary on the Chapter Humanae Aures* (1584). In this latter treatise examples are given of mental reservation being used in the context of marital vows, offering an interesting insight into the strategies employed by Abigail and Barabas in *The Jew of Malta*.[114] Indeed, one of the scenarios discussed by Azpilcueta features a man who privately tells a woman that he takes her as his wife with the mental reservation that he has no intention of doing so;[115] this conceptual conflation of counterfeit marriage with mental reservation aptly mirrors Abigail's use of qualifying asides when pledging love to Lodowick:

> LODOWICK: Why, loves she Don Mathias?
> BARABAS: Doth she not with her smiling answer you?
> ABIGAIL: (He has my heart, I smile against my will.)
> (*Jew of Malta* 2.3.287–9)

The final qualification crucially hints at Abigail's reluctance to follow her father's instructions and her attempt to register her resistance through linguistic dissimulation: when this aside was cut from Barry Kyle's 1987 RSC production, Abigail seemed far more complicit in the deception. As noted by David Bevington and Eric Rasmussen, Abigail also exploits tactics of equivocation to avoid outright perjury. While her statement to Lodowick that 'nothing but death shall part my love and me' is presumably understood by him to mean that 'I will love you till death do us part' (2.3.319), the phrase is ambiguous and carries a double meaning; an alternative interpretation is that she will die before she gives up her true love, Mathias.[116] Abigail's equivocating technique and the parallels between her situation and Azpilcueta's marriage scenario perhaps hint that Marlowe was thinking of the Jesuit model of mental reservation when he penned this scene, especially since Barabas's habit of appealing to the precedent of the Old Testament patriarch Abraham is one he shares with the sixteenth-century theorists of dissimulation.

Marlowe's *Jew of Malta* may elicit a degree of sympathy for the intelligent trickster Barabas and his loyal daughter Abigail, who use mental reservation to counter religious persecution and seek to hold their own against an oppressive regime. Yet as the play progresses it also speaks to urgent Elizabethan concerns about the possible connection between linguistic trickery and treason in God's name. Barabas's mastery of mental reservation is always somewhat troubling, potentially recalling the Catholic priests who entered England secretly and used dissimulation and disguise to evade capture and prosecution. These associations between dissimulation and sedition converge when Marlowe's Barabas uses mental reservation to bring about the deaths of two Christian subjects, initiating a sequence of violence that culminates in his betrayal of Malta to the Turks. By using linguistic trickery to bring about the death of his Christian enemies, Barabas perhaps hints at the real-life threat that England's secret dissidents posed to the Protestant Elizabethan regime. Indeed, Abigail's supporting role in Barabas's original plan may even foreshadow (however coincidentally) the scheme's seditious conclusion: she shares her name with the biblical Abigail, who is mentioned in several sixteenth-century resistance tracts advocating rebellion against heretical rulers.[117] More explicitly than in *Hero and Leander* or *Doctor Faustus*, where characters defy social mores or spiritual decrees, in *The Jew of Malta* Marlowe stages the dangerous secular consequences of a linguistic dissimulation grounded in and justified through reference to religion.

THE 'UNPOINTED' LETTER: EQUIVOCATION IN 'EDWARD II'

The association between linguistic dissimulation and sedition is even more explicit in Marlowe's *Edward II*. Gaveston provides the first intimation of the play's interest in persuasive rhetoric, invoking the classical precedent of the 'sophister' Leander to celebrate the power of King Edward's words:

> these thy amorous lines
> Might have enforced me to have swum from France,
> And, like Leander, gasped upon the sand,
> So thou wouldst smile and take me in thy arms.
> (*Edward II* 1.6–9)

Yet by casting Edward as Hero Gaveston implicitly identifies himself with Leander, the 'sophister' who seduced Hero. He too uses elaborate speeches, coupled with seductive spectacles reminiscent of *Doctor Faustus*, to manipulate the king; in fact, in this opening scene he explicitly celebrates the conquering power of verbal and visual rhetoric (*Edward II* 1.54–70). Like his creator Marlowe, Gaveston's arena of profit is the theatre: he uses show to tempt Edward into generosity, exulting that with 'music and poetry' he can 'draw the pliant King which way I please' (1.52) – indeed, Gaveston's words even win him his own royal crown.

As Edward's impulsive gift of the crown of Man indicates, Gaveston's power over the king subverts traditional social hierarchies. His transgressive ambitions are brought into focus when he imagines himself as a military conqueror, appropriating the imperial role of Caesar:

> It shall suffice me to enjoy your love,
> Which whiles I have, I think myself as great
> As Caesar riding in the Roman street,
> With captive kings at his triumphant car.
> (*Edward II* 1.170–3)

Gaveston's reference to captive kings in this speech is particularly provocative. Since the preposition 'at' implies that the kings draw

Gaveston's chariot after the precedent set by Marlowe's Tamburlaine, and since Gaveston's imagined status as 'Caesar' stems from his rhetorical conquest of Edward II, the passage hints that the English king himself may draw his low-born favourite's 'triumphant car'. Gaveston's profitable performances thus connect theatrical show and seductive rhetoric with the seditious acquisition of political power. His rhetorical prowess may also gesture towards the fears about verbal and visual manipulation publicised in contemporary propaganda: Gaveston is like Mephistopheles a master of the sense-seducing, erotically charged spectacles associated by Protestant polemicists with Catholic deceit – spectacles which might ultimately threaten the safety of Elizabeth I's own royal crown. Even Gaveston's choice of metaphor is interesting: the same conventional motif of a rhetorical 'brydle' that holds the listeners in 'slavishe servytude' appeared in a polemical tract of 1589, which denounced Elizabethan government propaganda as lies invented 'to blynde and bleare, the eyes of the people'.[118]

In spite of his theatrical skills, however, Marlowe's Gaveston is soon supplanted by a character whose command of rhetoric is more subtle and more threatening. Rejecting visual excess for verbal subtlety, Mortimer Junior uses the form of linguistic trickery known as equivocation as he brings about the death of two royal favourites (including Gaveston) and finally murders the English king himself. By employing the equivocating tactics ascribed to Elizabethan Catholic and puritan dissidents to commit regicide, Marlowe's rebel raises problematic questions about the relationship between linguistic deceit and sedition – questions that were worryingly relevant for Marlowe's original audiences.

Mortimer's equivocating tactics accord with the guidance supplied in the seventeenth-century *Treatise of Equivocation*, sometimes attributed to the Jesuit Henry Garnett. This tract defines equivocation as using words or expressions 'which hath many significations . . . We understand it in one sense, which is trewe, although the hearer conceave the other, which is false'.[119] Mortimer's exploitation of such double meanings is evident in his plan to kill the king:

This letter, written by a friend of ours,
Contains his death, yet bids them save his life:
'*Edwardum occidere nolite timere, bonum est*;
Fear not to kill the King, 'tis good he die.'
But read it thus, and that's another sense:
'*Edwardum occidere nolite, timere bonum est*;
Kill not the King, 'tis good to fear the worst.'
Unpointed as it is, thus shall it go,
. . .
Maltravers and the rest may bear the blame
And we be quit that caused it to be done.
(*Edward II* 23.6–16)

As the last two lines of the speech suggest, Mortimer's primary concern is to evade punishment and avoid being executed as a traitor and regicide; the context recalls that in which England's Jesuit priests employed their own version of equivocal deceit, as a defence against a Protestant regime that accused them of treason.

Mortimer's specific exploitation of syntactic ambiguity is a technique that the author of the *Treatise of Equivocation* terms *amphibole* or *amphibology*, in which ambiguity is achieved through 'the manner of poynting or deviding the sentence'.[120] While the *Treatise* was not written until several years after Marlowe's death, the presumed author Henry Garnett and his fellow theorist of equivocation Robert Southwell had been present in England since July 1586; it is at least plausible that Marlowe, who had links with the English Catholic community via his friend Thomas Watson, was aware of their advice by the 1590s. It is even possible that Mortimer's reference to the 'secret token' worn by his Italianate assassin Lightborne, by which 'shall he be murdered when the deed is done' (23.19–20), was intended to signal the Catholic connection to his original audiences: the 'secret token' perhaps suggests the *agnus Dei* worn by the first missionary priests to England, an unambiguous symbol of Roman Catholicism that could seal a priest's death warrant if discovered by the Protestant authorities. Such associations were certainly available in the play's subsequent performances: the Jacobean spectators who viewed the play at the Red Bull in 1622, after the 1605 Gunpowder Plot had rendered Jesuit equivocation notorious, would surely have recognised the implied connection between dissimulation and sedition. Shakespeare's 1606 tragedy *Macbeth* certainly implies that early seventeenth-century audiences were alert to instances of linguistic deception, associating equivocation with sedition and even regicide. Thus Shakespeare's Macbeth, tempted into killing King Duncan by the equivocal predictions of the play's witches, uses pious pretence to facilitate this murder; concluding that 'false face must hide what the false heart doth know', he deceitfully attributes the murder to his chosen scapegoats, employing various mental reservations in the process (*Macbeth* 1.7.83; 2.3.98–116).

Mortimer's own equivocating tactics are equally intriguing as a preparation for regicide. However, it is important to remember that Marlowe did not invent this use of syntactical ambiguity; instead, he adopted and elaborated upon the hints he found in the historical record. Raphael Holinshed's *Chronicles*, for instance, describe how the Bishop of Hereford wrote to the king's murderers 'under a sophisticall forme of words', wrapping his instruction that they should kill Edward in a riddle that might 'be taken in two contrarie senses, onlie by placing the point in orthographie called Comma'.[121] Holinshed's reference to 'orthographie' mirrors the advice about syntactical ambiguity given in *A Treatise of Equivocation*, while John Stow's version of the letter episode is even more suggestive. He describes the riddling command '*Edwardum occidere nolite timere bonum est*' as 'the great deceyte of Sophisters'; as discussed in the section on *Hero and Leander*, the term 'sophister' could be associated in early modern England with Jesuit equivocation. Stow's account also explains that this 'Sophistical' saying could be resolved into two propositions, suggesting that its ambiguity signalled deliberate manipulation by the guilty parties.[122] But, while these histories remind us that the equivocating letter is not Marlowe's own invention, and that statements with a double meaning were a fairly common dramatic device, details such as Stow's reference to 'the great deceit of sophisters' suggest that the early modern chroniclers may themselves have had the contemporary phenomenon of equivocating dissidents in mind as they wrote. Such conclusions were certainly available to an imaginative Elizabethan who knew about equivocation, and it is at least possible that Marlowe introduced an Italianate assassin and the contextualising detail of the 'secret token' because he too was thinking in such terms.

Equivocation was most notoriously associated during this period with English Catholics and particularly with the Jesuit missionary priests. However, similar methods of verbal and mental evasion were also practised by England's puritan dissidents. It was an open secret that the more radical Protestant clergy had used tactics of equivocation when subscribing to Whitgift's Three Articles in 1583, and that presbyterians as well as Catholics used dissimulation to avoid taking the prescribed oath in support of the Elizabethan Church. This popular awareness that puritans used linguistic tricks to deceive their government is suggested by a passage in the anti-Marprelate tract *An Almond for a Parrat*, tentatively attributed to Marlowe's colleague Thomas Nashe:

> Is perjury such a matter amongst puritans? Tush, they account it no sin as long as it is in the way of protestation, being in the mind of a good old fellow in Cambridge . . . Why, quoth hee, I neither respect oath, statute, nor conscience, but only the glory of God.[123]

Thus, while the type of equivocation practised by Mortimer is more reminiscent of Jesuit practices than of puritan, an audience might have linked Mortimer's regicidal dissimulation to a broader climate of religious dissidence. Indeed, Marlowe adapted his historical sources in a way that seems to invite this more universal reading: whereas in Holinshed's and Stow's chronicles the device of the 'unpointed' letter is explicitly attributed to the Catholic Bishop of Hereford, Marlowe's version emphasises Mortimer's involvement and dismissively ascribes the actual act of writing to an unidentified 'friend of ours' (23.6). Moreover, Mortimer has by this point in the play performed a confessional *volte-face* and is busy securing his political position with a pose of 'bashful Puritan' piety (23.57), thus further blurring the denominational significance of his equivocating tactics.

The possible parallel between Mortimer and Puritan dissimulation is complemented by another connection that might have struck a chord with Marlowe's original audiences. As David Riggs suggests, it is possible that Mortimer's letter-trick reminded Elizabethan spectators of their own Protestant government's actions in the aftermath of the 1586 Babington plot. Marlowe's literary patron Thomas Walsingham and the spy Robert Poley, one of the three men present at Marlowe's death in 1593, were both personally involved in exposing this conspiracy, suggesting Marlowe's potential familiarity with a historical episode involving linguistic dissimulation and misunderstandings over letters that culminated in the execution of the former Scottish queen Mary Stuart.[124] Elizabeth I's behaviour – she signed the warrant for Mary's execution but later claimed that she had done so unwittingly – is perhaps especially indicative of the English regime's capacity for linguistic and textual deceit, and in a form that seems highly relevant to Marlowe's play. Indeed, potential parallels between Mortimer's regicidal plot and Mary Stuart's execution may even have been strengthened in Marlowe's day by rumours that Elizabeth had secretly ordered the captive queen's murder: the historian John Warren reports that Elizabeth asked Mary's puritan gaoler Sir Amyas Paulet to dispose of his prisoner quietly, but Paulet refused to 'shed blood without law or warrant'.[125]

Such contemporary associations are implicit at best, their challenging insinuations softened by the intervening presence of Marlowe's historical sources. Yet it is worth noting that Mortimer's behaviour (however treacherous and deceitful) need not have reminded Marlowe's original audiences exclusively of Catholic treason and Catholic equivocation. Instead, Mortimer's dissimulation can be situated within a broader spectrum of confessional behaviour that encompasses Catholics, puritans, Familists and English Protestants. The same blurring of denominational lines can be found in Marlowe's other scenes of visual and verbal deceit:

the eloquent 'sophister' Leander seduces a 'nun'; Mephistopheles, dressed as a Catholic friar, adopts the plain linguistic style beloved of puritan divines; and Barabas, drawing on stereotypically Catholic methods of mental reservation, uses these methods to bring about the deaths of his Catholic enemies. If confessional identities are frequently unfocused, however, what is clear is that in Marlowe's writings dissimulation is a universal trait. The religiously inflected episodes of visual and verbal deceit that Marlowe portrays in his plays and poems are not characteristic of one creed in particular. Instead, rhetorical dissimulation is a politic tool employed by almost every character seeking advantage in the secularised universe of Marlowe's literary imagination.

CHAPTER TWO

FALSE CONVERSION AND CONFORMITY

In 1993 the historian Christopher Haigh described the strength of religious conviction during the English Reformations, writing that 'Protestants marched steadfastly towards the horror of the heretics' fire, Catholics towards the ordeal of the traitors' gallows.'[126] But what about those who were less committed to their faith? What about those who got cold feet? The martyrs may have grabbed the historical limelight, but for most people in sixteenth-century England religious change was experienced as a series of accommodations and compromises, with individuals striving to reconcile their inner consciences with the political and theological attitudes dictated by the state. During Mary I's reign, many of the leading Protestant figures of Elizabeth I's government had avoided confrontation by quietly dissembling their faith: those who had outwardly conformed to Mary's Catholic Church included Sir Nicholas Bacon, Sir William Cecil and, most notoriously, the Princess Elizabeth herself. When Elizabeth ascended the English throne in 1558 such practices were not eliminated, merely reversed. The newly reformed national church was now Protestant and predominantly Calvinist in its theology, but with regular attendance at services prescribed by government statute most English subjects adhered to the minimum standards of church attendance regardless of their personal religious beliefs.

As Alexandra Walsham argues in her ground-breaking study *Church Papists*, sixteenth-century men and women were concerned by the implications of outward conformity: the term 'church papist' was applied pejoratively to those who, while rejecting the theological tenets of the state church, still attended services as required by law.[127] For the English government such outward conformity was an indication of political loyalty, as well as an opportunity to convert Catholics and dissident puritans to the Elizabethan brand of Protestantism.[128] Committed Catholics and puritans, on the other hand, believed that attendance at the 'heretical' services of the Elizabethan Church would endanger their very souls. Such religious dissidents, known as recusants, refused to attend the state church's services; indeed, the term 'puritan' was originally a derisive synonym for 'schismatic', used to condemn those who distanced themselves from the Church of England. Recusancy or separatism was illegal and carried heavy financial penalties, but it enabled those whose faith was incompatible with the state-prescribed Protestantism of the Elizabethan Church openly to declare their inner convictions. For this reason, recusancy was advocated by most Catholic theologians as well as the radical Protestant separatists known as puritans. Despite occasional claims that feigned conformity was a permissible solution for the laity, endorsed by the scriptural precedents of Naaman and Gamaliel, the majority of authors agreed that to hide one's faith through fear was a damnable offence that cut the schismatic off from God.

Recusancy was a key characteristic of post-Reformation English Catholicism from the 1570s onwards, and was strongly advocated by the missionary priests. The Jesuit Cardinal William Allen argued that for English Catholics to attend the wicked and profane services of the 'hæretical' Elizabethan Church would be 'no lesse damnable, then it was in olde time . . . to commit Idolatrie, by Sacrificing to Idoles'; his second-in-command Robert Parsons, writing under the pseudonym John Howlett, summarised the many reasons that wavering Catholics should refuse to attend Protestant services in his *Brief Discours* of 1580.[129] Puritan separatists such as John Greenwood and William Perkins also enjoined the faithful to cut themselves off from the 'time-serving' Church of England. Perkins cited Revelation 18.4, warning his listeners that 'all those who will be saved, must depart and seperate themselves from the faith and religion of this present Church of Rome [the Elizabethan Church]', while Greenwood argued that Jesus 'would not himself, nor his Disciples, obey and observe the traditions of the Elders'.[130] Propaganda advocating recusancy escalated rapidly as church attendance became central to Elizabethan ideas of religious observance: indeed, Robert Parsons noted that 'goynge or not goeyng to the Church' is 'made a signe now in England distinctive, betwixt religion, and religion'.[131]

The Elizabethan government, fearful of potentially disloyal subjects and eager to save both souls and the state, responded swiftly to the threat of recusancy. The initial legislation enforcing church attendance, as set out in the Act of Uniformity (1559), was reinforced by two Acts of 1581 and 1587 which cumulatively increased the financial penalties for non-attendance at weekly services. These measures were largely successful. Despite the frantic denunciations of polemicists, most English subjects adhered to the standards of church attendance dictated by the state. However, using social, political and financial pressures to exact conformity created a new difficulty for the Elizabethan authorities: how to distinguish between outward conduct and inner belief. Whereas English recusants advertised their refusal to attend church services as a matter of conscience, the conforming 'church papists' quietly kept their true convictions to themselves.

For many contemporaries, the implications were alarming. Catholic propagandists mocked the Elizabethan authorities for thinking they could benefit from forcing Catholics to 'professe that outwardly, which is knowen they hate in their hartes inwardly', and warned that 'Catholiques in hartes by goinge to Protestantes Churches, must needes bee brought ether to flat athisme' or 'lyve in contynuall torment of mynde'.[132] Mere conformity was equally distasteful to godly Protestants. Advocates of the puritan Robert Browne's separatist policies denounced the mixed congregations of the English Church as 'false and adulterate', and even loyal Protestants occasionally questioned the value of extorting a feigned outward conformity through financial pressure: in a 1572 letter to Lord Burghley, Archbishop Matthew Parker (who sponsored Marlowe's Cambridge scholarship) described the policy as a 'Machiavel government' that 'bringeth forth strange fruits'.[133] The 'Machiavel' reference suggests Archbishop Parker's anxiety about hypocritical religious fraud; as Alexandra Walsham's illuminating study has demonstrated, such 'strange fruits' were a real threat for the many Elizabethans who equated false outward conformity with practical godlessness. The fearful realisation that it was impossible to determine true belief was exemplified by the church papist, a person who could 'keepe their conscience to themselves, and yet goe to Church'.[134] While outward conformity and inner indifference may not have been anything new, early modern commentators treated it as if it was – and condemned it on these terms.

In Christopher Marlowe, a man predisposed towards religious scepticism, such comments found an attentive audience. Absorbing his society's concerns about mere conformity and forced conversion, Marlowe translated these anxieties into rich and evocative dramatic spectacles. Indeed, he went further. In his later plays Marlowe explores the relationship between religious persecution and outward conformity, but also provocatively aligns false conversion with a sceptical secular agenda, depicting characters who adapt their faith in response to political circumstances. Thus Ithamore in *The Jew of Malta* feigns a bewildering variety of beliefs in his search for material profit, while in *The Massacre at Paris* Henry III, abandoned by his former Catholic allies, adopts a proto-Protestant Gallican pose and renounces papal authority in favour of an independent French Church. Even *The Massacre*'s nominal hero Navarre is arguably implicated in this process of politically motivated conversion, shorn of spiritual significance.

THE COST OF CONVERSION: RECUSANCY FINES IN 'THE JEW OF MALTA'

Christopher Marlowe's interest in questions of outward conformity and conversion was no doubt stimulated by his personal experience of these issues. As one of Elizabeth I's subjects Marlowe was unavoidably implicated in the debate over church attendance; like his spectators, his actors and his literary patrons, he was legally required to attend the state church's services on a weekly basis.

While contemporary accounts suggest that many Londoners were rather careless about church attendance, instead prioritising entertainments such as the theatre, citizens would have been fully aware of the penalties for repeated absence. Including those incarcerated in London's prisons, the Pipe Rolls of the Exchequer record more than 250 convictions for recusancy within the main city boundaries between 1581 and 1592, while Londoners also witnessed the regular executions of priests, Catholic laymen and puritan separatists condemned by the authorities as traitors. Southwark, where audiences gathered to see Marlowe's plays performed at the Rose theatre, seems to have been a particularly dissident area: 124 references to local recusants are recorded in the Pipe Rolls for 1581–92.

Marlowe may have been personally acquainted with some of the London recusants prosecuted by the authorities. During the approximate period he was living in Norton Folgate two of his near neighbours in the Bishopgate Ward, Richard Webster and Dorothy Hankin, were convicted of recusancy, while his friend and fellow poet Thomas Watson appears to have been a known recusant: in June 1581 Watson's name was entered on a list of 'strangers that go not to church'.[135] If Marlowe was a government informer his acquaintance with the recusant community was presumably far more extensive, but even this brief survey suggests the extent to which he and his contemporaries would have been surrounded by the reality as well as the discourse of enforced religious conformity.

When Marlowe wrote about religious tensions and persecution in his drama, these experiences provided him with material and inspiration. For instance, the contemporary Elizabethan awareness that religious difference carried monetary penalties provides a suggestive background to Marlowe's *Jew of Malta* and in particular to the Maltese governor Ferneze's plans to tax the island's Jewish population. The financial demands imposed by Ferneze are a response to a political threat; if Malta cannot raise the tribute money demanded by their Turkish allies, the island will be attacked by 'a fleet of warlike galleys' (1.1.145). Ferneze's solution is to transfer responsibility for this tribute on to Malta's Jews:

OFFICER [*reading*]: First, the tribute money of the Turks shall all be levied amongst the Jews, and each of them to pay one half of his estate.

. . .

OFFICER [*reading*]: Secondly, he that denies to pay, shall straight become a Christian.

. . .

OFFICER [*reading*]: Lastly, he that denies this, shall absolutely lose all he has.

(*Jew of Malta* 1.2.68–77)

When Marlowe's protagonist Barabas demands whether all will pay 'equally' (1.2.62), the governor defends the disproportionate demands made of Malta's Jewish population in terms of religious difference. The Jews are to be taxed 'like infidels', since 'through our sufferance of your hateful lives, / Who stand accursèd in the sight of heaven, / These taxes and afflictions are befallen' (1.2.62–5). As Emily Bartels points out, however, Ferneze's rhetoric is tellingly undercut by his reduction of the religious signifier 'Jew' to a purely secular definition; Ferneze locates Jewish identity in monetary value, rather as the Elizabethan authorities categorised English recusants according to their financial 'valew' or 'worth'.[136]

Critics typically relate Ferneze's demands to medieval legislation against the Jews, suggesting that Marlowe is basing the scene upon the expulsion of the Jews from England in 1260. Even when they look beyond the thirteenth century, modern scholars and editors still focus on instances of specifically anti-Semitic persecution: Roma Gill for instance suggests that Ferneze's demands are based on the 1492 expulsion of Malta's Jews, when exemption was granted to those who agreed to 'buy baptism' at a cost of forty-five per cent of their total wealth.[137] But, while Marlowe may have come across an account of this episode, it is doubtful that many of the play's spectators would have recognised the connection. Marlowe is perhaps more likely to have been interested in contemporary controversy than in events one or even three centuries earlier, and in fact Ferneze explicitly states that the unconverted Jews will *not* be exiled (1.2.101). Such a statement is at odds with the historical banishment of the Jews from either thirteenth-century England or fifteenth-century Malta. However, it is intriguingly reminiscent of the situation in Elizabethan England. During Marlowe's lifetime the Protestant government sought with increasing urgency to enforce outward religious conformity through financial pressure. While Catholic and puritan dissidents sometimes chose voluntary exile, however, the authorities often took steps to prevent lay religious non-conformists leaving the country, spying on those who intended to travel abroad and placing strict controls on foreign passports. Ferneze's financially motivated persecution of the Jews, which does not threaten them with exile, perhaps has more in common with the religious tensions of the sixteenth century than it does with the banishment of the Jews from England in 1260.

On closer investigation there are a number of suggestive parallels between Marlowe's fictional tax, justified by religious difference, and the contemporary context of English separatism and recusancy fines. The designation of Ferneze's demands as 'articles' potentially recalls the Elizabethan church settlement detailed in the Thirty-Nine Articles – and principled Catholic and puritan recusancy was inspired by a refusal to conform to these terms. Ferneze's terminology might also invoke the notorious Three Articles of 1583–4, which threatened to deprive nearly four hundred non-conforming ministers of their benefices; thanks to the scandal surrounding the publication of the Martin Marprelate tracts in 1589–90 and the arrest of the presbyterian leader Thomas Cartwright in 1591, general awareness of puritan dissidence was at its height when Marlowe wrote *The Jew of Malta*. As Elizabethan England exacted fines from those separatists who refused to conform to the established state church, so Ferneze's demands similarly put a tax on religious difference. In both cases, financial penalties are imposed in response to the threat of invasion: Ferneze fears the Turkish fleet, while the Elizabethan authorities were anxious that English Catholics might support England's

Catholic enemies in the event of a French or Spanish invasion. Ferneze's subsequent decision to fight the Turks, presumably funding the campaign with appropriated Jewish wealth, perhaps also echoes the way in which Elizabeth's government tried to force recusants to pay for the war against Catholic Spain.[138]

The immediate price of Barabas's refusal to conform is the loss of his goods and property, with his house being seized and converted into a convent (1.2.130–1). The fractional sequestration of a recusant's possessions was relatively common in Marlowe's England, especially after the 1587 parliamentary ruling that one conviction for non-attendance at church would result in a cumulative monthly fine of £20 until the offender submitted; since few could afford to pay such a penalty, an alternative often pursued by the Crown was the sequestration of two-thirds of the offender's property.[139] Though this fractional division is not directly analogous to that proposed by Ferneze, the seizure of wealth and the wholesale confiscation of property were penalties familiar to many Elizabethan separatists. Moreover, Marlowe's Maltese governor explicitly links his financial penalties to questions of conversion and religious conformity, stating that 'he that denies to pay, shall straight become a Christian' (1.2.73–4). This condition is again relevant to the sixteenth-century context of enforced church attendance, since for convicted English recusants submission to a rigorous conversion process was the only sure way to avoid being fined for skipping church.[140] Marlowe's London spectators might not have been emotionally invested in the thirteenth-century expulsion of England's Jewish population or the anti-Semitic antics of Malta's fifteenth-century inhabitants, but Elizabethan recusancy was a very different matter.

Barabas's Jewish identity may still be relevant to this play's interest in religious separatism and recusancy fines. London's population of 'Marranos' (Jewish converts to Christianity) were notorious for supposedly dissimulating their faith for financial reasons: in 1611, for instance, John Florio described the Marrano as 'one descended of Jewes or Infidels and whose Parents were never christned, but for to save their goods will say they are

Christians'.[141] Yet to limit consideration of religious politics in *The Jew of Malta* to the Jewish experience alone seems unduly restrictive – rather, Barabas's experiences could strike a chord with religious dissidents of all denominations, at a time when Elizabethan attitudes towards separatism were hardening and many English Christians found themselves in a precarious situation. The financial penalties threatened by Ferneze suggest an affinity between Barabas and England's Catholics, who faced increasing pressure to conform as fears of Spanish invasion grew: Jewish stereotypes were often applied to English Catholic missionaries during the 1580s. At the same time, Barabas's allusions to the Old Testament and his Jewish heritage potentially align him with the puritan separatists who sought to establish their own 'synagogues' outside the Elizabethan Church: the Catholic writer William Rainolds suggested sarcastically that the English clergy 'prefer this synagoge before the Church, and Jewes before the Christians'. In fact, Zachary Lesser considers that during the play's 1633 theatrical revival Barabas would have been most likely to remind London audiences of the city's Dutch Protestant community, and notes that Ferneze's articles are oddly if coincidentally reminiscent of Archbishop Laud's contemporary attacks on these puritan 'Stranger churches'.[142]

Marlowe's Jew thus preserves an unfixed and shifting denominational identity that allows his own sufferings to reflect those of religious non-conformists in general rather than Catholics or presbyterians in particular; the experience of religious alienation and financial threat was common to all recusants, regardless of their precise beliefs. Ultimately, Barabas takes his separatist values to an extreme that borders on atheism, refusing in practice to conform even to the Jewish faith with which he rhetorically aligns himself: facing persecution, he characterises the other Jews as 'a multitude' and himself as 'but one' (1.2.179). Barabas's resistance to any straightforward notion of confessional identity perhaps raises again the threatening spectre of practical godlessness, a worry that lurks behind Marlowe's fictional representations of outward conformity and false conversion.

Initially, Barabas seems to be a committed and even principled recusant. He adopts a hard militant stance in the second scene; when Ferneze, taking his wealth, mockingly asks, 'Why Barabas wilt thou be christened?', Marlowe's Jew instantly replies, 'No, Governor, I will be no convertite' (1.2.82–3). Although in Act 4 Barabas confesses to the friars that he 'would for lucre's sake have sold my soul' (4.1.53), his behaviour in Act 1 tells a different story: conversion to Christianity might in theory allow him to evade Ferneze's demands, but he does not seem to entertain the thought for a moment. However, Barabas's principles do not extend to a rejection of *false* conversion, particularly when it is his daughter rather than himself who performs the deception. To return to his statement in Act 4, it would perhaps be more accurate to say that 'for lucre's sake', he would willingly sell Abigail's soul.

Discovering that the house in which his wealth is hidden has been turned into a convent, Barabas decrees that his daughter must pretend to convert to Christianity in order to enter as a religious novice. To regain her father's wealth, the Jew's daughter must learn to play the role of a 'precise' 'convertite' – an intriguing instruction, given that Marlowe and his fellow Elizabethans often applied the term 'precise' to England's puritans:

> be thou so precise
> As they may think it done of holiness.
> Entreat 'em fair, and give them friendly speech,
> And seeme to them as if thy sins were great,
> Till thou hast gotten to be entertained.
> (*Jew of Malta* 1.2.284–8)

Abigail, following her father's instructions to the letter, then gives a moving performance of penitence and the desire to convert as she pleads for admittance to the newly established convent:

> Fearing the afflictions which my father feels
> Proceed from sin, or want of faith in us,
> I'd pass away my life in penitence,

And be a novice in your nunnery,
To make atonement for my labouring soul.
(*Jew of Malta* 1.2.320–4)

Her show of remorse duly deceives Marlowe's Catholic friars; concluding that Abigail's spiritual epiphany 'proceedeth of the spirit', the pair entreat the abbess to admit her to the convent (1.2.325).

A possible source for this episode can be found in Robert Wilson's earlier play *Three Ladies of London*, in which the act of conversion again has financial implications: the villainous Christian trader Mercadorus threatens to convert to Islam in order to write off his debt to the Jew Gerontus (14.13–47).[143] Although Wilson's character Mercadorus secretly advises the audience that he does not intend to convert and that his purpose is to 'cozen da Jew' (13.21–4), he goes so far as to begin formally pledging his religious allegiance:

JUDGE: Signiore Mercadorus, draw near:
Lay your hand upon this book, and say after me.
. . .
Say: I, Mercadorus, do utterly renounce before all the world my duty to my Prince, my honour to my parents, and my goodwill to my country.
MERCADORUS: Furthermore, I protest and swear to be true to this country during life, and thereupon I forsake my Christian faith –
(*Three Ladies of London* 14.21–8)

Only Gerontus's intervention stops Mercadorus from proceeding further; perhaps unexpectedly, the Jewish merchant chooses to forgive Mercadorus's debt rather than watch him forsake his faith (14.38–40). Yet the threat of 'conversion' is emphatically false, as Mercadorus's closing words affirm: 'Me be a Turk? No. It will make my Lady Lucre to smile / When she knows how me did da scald Jew beguile' (14.58–9). Wilson's turning-Turk episode may reflect contemporary concerns about the high conversion rate to Islam among Christians trading in the Ottoman Empire; but his depiction of a hypocritical merchant who feigns conversion for financial advantage also provides a possible model for Marlowe's Barabas, who persuades his daughter to practise a similar deception.

Abigail's false conversion, which stems from Barabas's desire to reclaim his appropriated wealth, is equally motivated by financial considerations. Their scheme may also allude to the contemporary situation in Elizabethan England, locating the threat of feigned conversion in a context closer to home. In 1581 the English government had introduced a series of new regulations against recusants; however, this act specified that all financial sanctions for non-attendance could be avoided if the offender 'submit and conforme himselfe before the Bisshop of the Diocesse where he shalbe resident, or before the Justices' (23 Elizabeth I, c. 1). Limited attendance at official church services was thus common among practising Catholics who wished to evade recusancy fines. Some English Catholics were even prepared to undergo formal conversion to the Elizabethan Church to escape financial retribution, and Michael Questier suggests that these men and women regarded limited church papistry simply as a means of recovering property from the Crown: as, indeed, a 'form of estate management'.[144] If so, the possible connection with Abigail's own feigned conversion to Christianity is intriguing – especially given the potential parallels between Ferneze's exactions and Elizabethan recusancy fines.

A number of early modern commentators attacked those who outwardly conformed to the English church for financial reasons. In his play *The Captives*, for instance, Thomas Heywood characterises the 'convertite' Mildew as a villain eager for material 'gayne' (ll. 3047–9), while in 1628 John Earle pungently described the church-papist as 'one that parts his Religion betwixt his conscience and his purse'; 'he loves Popery well, but is loath to lose by it'.[145] Earle's scepticism was nothing new. As early as the 1580s, the perceived prevalence of financially motivated false conversion is suggested by a clause in the 1581 recusancy statute that forbids recusants from taking financial advantage of a second submission to the church; potentially relevant to Abigail's second conversion in *The Jew of Malta*, which brings no material profit, this clause suggests Elizabethan trepidation about false conversion for financial gain.

Catholic polemicists also advertised the prevalence of false outward conformity: Robert Parsons's uncompromising *Brief Discours* for instance denounces those who, 'albeit they doe judge al other religions besides theire owne, false and erroneous, and damnable', consider that 'for some worldly respecte, as for savinge their offices, dignities, liberties, credytes or the like' they may 'shewe themselves conformable'. Significantly for Marlowe's *Jew of Malta*, some of these polemicists drew direct parallels between Jewish conversion and outward conformity. The Catholic moderate Alban Langdale uses the example of Christ's apostles joining the Jews in the temple to argue that church papistry is a justifiable response to persecution; while, even more intriguingly, Robert Parsons's counter-argument for recusancy utilised the very comparison between Catholic and Jewish conformity that Marlowe's staging of Abigail's false conversion may exploit. According to Parsons, the iniquity of English Catholics who attend Protestant services is comparable to the wickedness of a Jew who swears against his conscience 'that theire weare a blessed Trinity' – as Marlowe's Abigail does in entering the convent.[146]

In *The Jew of Malta* Barabas's daughter enters the convent not once, but twice. On the first occasion she deceives the abbess with a pretence of conversion in order to retrieve her father's wealth, now that their house has been seized and transformed. The second time, however, Abigail is motivated not by financial or political considerations but by grief, and the only reward she wants is to survive (3.3.63–7). As Emily Bartels suggests, Abigail converts not to be saved by Christ but to be rescued from the Jew; seeing no 'pity in Jews, nor piety in Turks', Abigail becomes Christian by a process of elimination (3.3.49–50).[147] But though she affirms the reality of this conversion in death, receiving Catholic rites and asking Friar Bernardine (and the audience) to 'witness that I die a Christian' (3.6.40), Marlowe's spectators cannot be sure it is genuine until this final moment. Prior to her death, the rhetorical echoes between Abigail's two performances of conversion in fact license a degree of scepticism about the second as about the first: thus in Barry Kyle's 1987 RSC production, Alun Armstrong's Barabas invited audience laughter by comically emphasising the statement that 'Abigail [is] become a nun *again*' (3.4.1, my italics).[148] And, even if Abigail remains true to her second conversion, her final words still trigger yet another false conversion: when her deathbed confession tempts the friars who hear it to blackmail her father Barabas, Marlowe's murderous Jew takes refuge in religious pretence.

Barabas is well aware that religion 'hides many mischiefs from suspicion' (1.2.282). Faced with the financial and physical threat represented by the friars, he immediately turns to feigned conversion in an attempt to escape the law:

> (I must dissemble.)
> Oh holy friars, the burden of my sins
> Lie heavy on my soul; then pray you tell me,
> Is't not too late now to turn Christian?
> (*Jew of Malta* 4.1.47–50)

Crucially, Barabas builds his ostensible intention to convert upon a financial basis. Although he initially distances material from spiritual wealth, exclaiming 'what is wealth? / I am a Jew, and therefore am I lost' (4.1.56–7), his next lines indicate that the relationship between earthly and heavenly treasure is more complicated: 'I could afford . . . to pray, and wear a shirt of hair, / And on my knees creep to Jerusalem' (4.1.59–62). The term 'afford' is ambiguous, but its commercial associations suggest that literal wealth may play a role in achieving salvation. This hint of bribery is made explicit a few lines later, when Barabas directly offers his wealth in exchange for conversion: 'All this I'll give to some religious house / So I may be baptised and live therein' (4.1.75–6). Barabas buys a form of feigned conversion to secure the friars' silence; financial considerations lie at the heart of this conversion narrative. Similarly, the squabbling friars desire material wealth as well as spiritual credit, with Friar Jacomo celebrating the 'happy hour, wherein I shall convert / An infidel, and bring his gold into our treasury' (4.1.161–2). Though his speech ostensibly prioritises religious considerations, the opportunity for financial profit is of equal (or greater) importance.

In *The Jew of Malta* Barabas, like his daughter before him, seeks protection through an act of conversion. Marlowe later returned to this concept in *The Massacre at Paris*, in an episode where Catholic murderers threaten the Protestant scholar Ramus. The play is based on the events of 23 August 1572, when a surge of Catholic violence against Protestants broke out in Paris; thousands of French Protestants (known as Huguenots) died in the notorious St Bartholomew's Day massacre. When dramatising Ramus's death, however, Marlowe draws attention to the financial dimensions of religious persecution; drawing on historical reports that the Protestant scholar had tried to bribe his killers, he creates a scene in which self-preservation, monetary penalties and a form of conversion overlap and intertwine. Thus, in scene 9, Ramus's Catholic murderer Gonzago enters to demand 'more gold, or thou shalt have the stab' (9.16): his eagerness to profit from religious difference mirrors Ferneze's tactics in *The Jew of Malta*. Financial submission will enable Ramus to evade death by confirming that he is a 'Christian' rather than a Protestant, and Gonzago's request for '*more* gold' implies that Ramus has used this tactic before. Even his hesitation on Gonzago's reappearance seems less a question of faith than practical viability; Ramus, a poor scholar, quite literally lacks the resources to buy his way out of trouble (9.17–19). While the monetary exactions that underwrite Ramus's defensive 'conversion' predominantly mock Catholic greed, his belief that gold can buy a form of pseudo-conversion echoes Barabas's equation of conversion with bribery in *The Jew of Malta*; both episodes perhaps also allude to the role played by financial pressure in some Elizabethan 'conversions' to state Protestantism.

Staged at a time when conversion and outward conformity could become survival tactics, Barabas's obviously false and self-seeking behaviour may raise concerns about the reliability of any conversion made under duress. As Marlowe's Jew mockingly remarks, 'are not both these wise men to suppose / That I will leave my house, my goods, and all, / To fast and be well whipped'; he concludes emphatically that 'I'll none of that' (4.1.122–4). The tone of the episode is comically satiric, but the consequences are more threatening: Barabas follows up his false conversion with a striking act of treachery, betraying his Christians persecutors to their Turkish foes. Marlowe's portrait of a religious dissident who surrenders his city to an invading army he identifies as his confessional allies must have resonated powerfully in the 1580s and 1590s, as Elizabethan England agonised about the prospect of foreign invasion and domestic treason.

THE SERIAL CONVERTITE: ITHAMORE'S PROFESSIONS OF FAITH

Barabas's actions realise so many of the English state's greatest fears that it comes as no surprise when he is eventually compared to Judas, the arch-traitor of the Christian tradition. The only shock is that this comparison is expressed so flippantly: Ithamore jokes that the hat Barabas wears is one 'Judas left under the elder when he hanged himself' (4.4.64–5). While the image of the hat's physical removal from Judas to Barabas might be held to symbolise the transference of the former's tainted thoughts, in practice Ithamore's throwaway comment is simply one more anti-Semitic jibe in the long list he invents to amuse his mistress. If the comparison between Barabas and Judas proves clichéd and arbitrary, however, its presence is still worth noting. Since references to Judas were used in sixteenth-century polemic to condemn time-serving apostasy, Ithamore's taunts perhaps imply a rejection of his former master's religious hypocrisy at the very moment when his own performances of conviction come full circle: from Christian to Muslim, to Jew, and now back to Christian.

Compared to Barabas with his one feigned act of conformity and Abigail, who performs one false and one genuine act of conversion, Ithamore can be regarded as the play's most committed apostate – a serial 'convertite' who spins from one religion to another as fast as the political and financial winds of Malta carry him (1.2.83). Although Ithamore is ultimately no match for Barabas's ruthless cunning, in terms of religiously inflected opportunism he outdoes both the Jew and his daughter. His very name advertises his unfixed religious identity, recalling both the saintly Christian bishop Ithamar and Ithamar the son of the Jewish patriarch Aaron (Exodus 6.23), while simultaneously punning on the 'Islamic' designator 'Moor': Ithamore amply fulfils these semantic expectations. During the course of Marlowe's play we learn that he has followed or will follow every one of the major Abrahamic religions, turning from faith to faith in a search for security and secular advantage.

Barabas is perhaps the first to recognise Ithamore's confessional adaptability. When the two characters meet at a slave market, where the captive Ithamore is auctioned off, Barabas's interest is piqued by this slave's origins. Informed that Ithamore was born in Thrace and 'brought up in Arabia', Barabas instantly concludes that he is 'for my turn' and 'by my help shall do much villainy' (2.3.131–2, 136). While to a modern reader the connections Barabas is silently drawing may be unclear, his use of the verb 'turn' is suggestive: in early modern England the act of conversion was often referred to as 'turning', particularly when discussing multiple conversions. Thus Barabas's choice of words suggests that, as Mark Hutchings has convincingly demonstrated, Marlowe's Jew recognises and is pleased by the demonstrable elasticity of Ithamore's religious identity.[149]

Ithamore's birthplace Thrace, a region in the southern Balkans, was a Christian country that belonged to the Ottoman Empire in the sixteenth century. It was therefore subject to *devshirme*, a practice whereby young children were claimed as tribute by the region's Turkish rulers. These children were then raised to serve the empire as administrators, soldiers (known as Janissaries), or sailors, being converted to Islam in the process.[150] The practice of *devshirme* was relatively well known in Elizabethan England: for instance, George Gascoigne's 1572 'Devise of a Masque' features a twelve-year-old Anglo-Italian boy who is 'tane by Turkes' and lives 'a turkish life' until rescued through divine providence. The popular *Travellers Breviat* (1601), which was based upon earlier travel accounts, similarly describes the 'Janizars' as 'renegados' whom the Turkish ruler 'taketh as tithe from their parents in their childhood' and makes 'Mahumetans before they perceive it'.[151] As Mark Hutchings suggests, it seems likely that Ithamore's account of his history – born in Thrace but raised in Arabia – is meant to identify him as another product of *devshirme*. If so, as Barabas may realise, Ithamore has presumably undergone one conversion before Marlowe's play even starts: from Christian child of tribute to Muslim sailor.

For Ithamore, however, this forced childhood conversion is only the beginning. At the slave market he assures his new master that his 'profession' shall be 'what you please' (2.3.168); although Barabas here interprets profession to mean 'trade', the earlier punning by Ferneze and Barabas on pious profession might encourage Marlowe's audiences to read his offer in a more problematic religious light (1.1.115–17; 1.2.145–52). Ithamore soon follows through on his implied promise. While Barabas initially builds an alliance on the grounds that Jews and Muslims hate Christians equally (2.3.217), the situation alters after Abigail's defection to Catholicism. Though willing to employ a generic anti-Christian villain against Lodowick and Mathias, Barabas requires additional reassurance about Ithamore's commitment to killing Abigail; presumably because her status as both Jew and Christian complicates their earlier Judaeo-Muslim alliance against Malta's Christians.

Marlowe's Jew resolves this difficulty by promoting Ithamore to the rank of adopted son. In terms that echo those he once used to praise his daughter (2.1.48–50), he transforms his 'trusty servant' into a substitute child: 'For I have now no hope but even in thee; / And on that hope my happiness is built' (3.4.15–17). Having decided that 'she that varies from me in belief / Gives great presumption that she loves me not' (3.4.10–11), Barabas binds Ithamore to him in spiritual as well as material terms: the wealth promised to Ithamore is literal, but Barabas's offer of the keys to his strongroom may simultaneously invoke the allegorical 'keys to the kingdom of heaven' promised to religious converts (Matthew 16.19). Barabas's pronounced tendency to conflate spiritual and material concepts of wealth supports this interpretation, as does his adoption of Ithamore as his 'second self' and 'only heir' (3.4.15, 43) – an adoption that symbolically enfolds Ithamore into the Jewish family and, by inference, the Jewish 'nation' described in Act 1 (1.1.120). Barabas's offer proves false, but Ithamore was more than happy to change his 'profession' in exchange for his master's treasure; during this scene we witness the former Christian and former Muslim undergoing a form of presumptive 'conversion' to Judaism.

Ithamore's religious peregrinations are not yet over. While bribing the blackmailing friars with a false offer of conversion, Barabas dismissively refers to his 'adopted son' as 'the Turk' (4.1.111), and Ithamore's own notion of his identity also fluctuates. He reports that 'a Turk could ha' done no more' of a task which he has performed alongside Barabas (4.1.196), constructing an 'us and them' model which implicitly aligns him with the Jew, but then privately describes himself as 'a poor Turk of ten pence' during an encounter with Pilia-Borza (4.2.41–2). The instability is particularly intriguing since, in Marlowe's day, Ithamore's erratic status could not be easily explained as a distinction between religious and national identity: the terms 'Turk' and 'Moor' were often used interchangeably though inaccurately to describe any member of the Muslim faith.[152] Neither full Jew nor true Muslim in this section of the play, Ithamore occupies a limbo between faiths; his confessional identity is unfixed, shifting and uncertain.

Such discrepancies are subsequently exploited by the villainous Catholic Christians Pilia-Borza and Bellamira. Seduced by the courtesan Bellamira's protestations of love, Ithamore is quick to abandon any ties he has to the Jewish nation. In Act 4 Ithamore emphasises his former master's alien religious identity as he plots with Bellamira to blackmail Barabas: he addresses the latter as 'Sirrah Jew' (4.2.120); insults his eating habits and clothing in stereotypically anti-Semitic terms (4.4.59–67); and concludes aphoristically that 'to undo a Jew is charity, and not sin' (4.4.77). Like Ferneze before him, Ithamore justifies his financial depredations by reference to religious difference; his specious accusations align him with the Catholic community of Malta against the Jews, albeit at the lowest social level.

There is no explicitly spiritual dimension to Ithamore's alliance with Pilia-Borza and Bellamira, but it is perhaps telling that Bellamira seduces him. Seduction was an extremely common trope in early modern conversion narratives, and accounts of Christian conversions to Islam often alluded to the apostate's love or desire for a Muslim woman. Marlowe may have been influenced by Thomas Kyd's *Soliman and Perseda* (*c.* 1588), in which the clownish Basilico converts to Islam and then back to Christianity; his ostensible motive is to follow 'Perseda, whom I love so well' (3.5.17–18), though a sceptical Kyd later reveals that this cowardly convert's main concern is his own physical well-being (3.5.11).[153] While in Act 5 Ithamore is still identified as a 'Turk' by the Maltese governor Ferneze (5.1.27), his outward conformity to Christian Malta's anti-Semitic values and his alliance with the Catholic characters Bellamira and Pilia-Borza imply that he has undergone a type of quasi-conversion to Christianity. Ithamore remains a Turk in Ferneze's eyes, but in terms of his own rhetorical self-fashioning he has run the gamut from Christian child to Muslim sailor and from adopted Jewish heir to arguably Catholic lover; in the latter guise Ithamore also compares himself to the pagan Greco-Roman gods, parodying the tactics used by Marlowe's politic heroes.

Ithamore's religious transformations are not just about love or sexual desire: the alliance with Bellamira is also an opportunity to turn a profit. Ithamore's willingness to change loyalties at the drop of a coin recalls contemporary denunciations of self-seeking apostasy, and perhaps in particular the sixteenth-century European Christians charged with 'turning turk' for financial profit: English merchants who converted to Islam for trading purposes were often accused of greed. Thomas Heywood's seventeenth-century play *The Fair Maid of the West Part I* similarly associates conversion and financial profit, staging a comic episode in which the clownish tapster Clem is 'gelded' after he mistakenly equates conversion to Islam with material benefits and offers to be 'gilded' (5.2.90–104, 126–31); Heywood's play also refers to the heavy tax duties imposed on Christian traders by Muslim rulers (4.3.15–26).[154]

Marlowe's Ithamore, who 'turneth' for 'gaine' and betrays his former master Barabas, also has much in common with the former Catholics who turned to Protestantism as paid agents, informing on their old allies for financial reward.[155] Ithamore's status as a serial 'convertite' is particularly telling with regard to these Elizabethan Catholic–Protestant converts, many of whom switched religious allegiance on multiple occasions. Thus Anthony Tyrell famously changed confessions eight times during his lifetime, as publicised in a series of polemical tracts and sermons, while Marlowe was personally acquainted with at least one self-confessed apostate: Richard Baines, whose oscillations between Protestantism and Catholicism are recorded in his written recantation of 1583.[156] While contemporary converts claimed to be motivated by the dictates of conscience, Marlowe's serial convertite Ithamore openly trades in his faith for its financial value: his focus is resolutely secular, as he switches between Islam, Judaism and Christianity in the hope of acquiring Barabas's wealth. At the same time, the vacillating nature of his associated secular loyalties may also reflect contemporary Elizabethan concerns about the connection between religious belief and political allegiance.

PIOUS POSTURING IN 'THE MASSACRE AT PARIS'

The poses of piety adopted by Abigail and Barabas exploit a problematic distinction between outward faith and inner truth. Yet we are at least granted a glimpse beneath the mask; through dramatic soliloquies and an unusually high number of asides, Marlowe enables the readers and spectators of *The Jew of Malta* to experience the fantasy of absolute disclosure. This desire to access the hidden inner self was a common one in Elizabethan England. Elizabeth I may have disclaimed interest in the secret consciences of her subjects but her government emphasised the symbolic discovery of internal truth when prosecuting England's religious dissidents, often through the deconstruction of their physical bodies on the scaffold. Similar fantasies of revelation and disclosure occur regularly in early modern drama: in Ben Jonson's *Sejanus*, for instance, the Roman senator Arruntius fantasises about cleaving the tyrannical protagonist to the heart to find out his secrets (11.253–8).

In Marlowe's case, there may have been a personal dimension to this emphasis on exposure and revelation. His involvement in Elizabethan intelligence-gathering would have introduced him to men who practised dissimulation to expose the inner convictions of others; paradoxically, it was through the false pretence of religious dissidence that the state's operatives sought to expose the hidden consciences of England's Catholic and puritan 'traitors'. During the late 1580s many government agents moved between faiths at a startling pace, and even their employers struggled to identify their true convictions. Thus the government spy William Parry was executed in March 1585 for treason despite his claims that he had simply been gathering intelligence, while Sir Francis Walsingham's treatment of Gilbert Gifford in the aftermath of the Babington plot suggests that he may have temporarily lost faith in his agent's loyalties.[157] Similarly, Marlowe's characters are often surprisingly resistant to the fantasy of absolute disclosure: thus Ithamore's unfixed and shifting religious convictions cannot be easily reduced to one firm interpretation.

By the time he wrote *The Massacre at Paris*, Marlowe was apparently questioning the possibility of revealing anyone's inner conscience. It is possible that a revealing soliloquy has been lost in transmission; and the unusually short length and somewhat episodic structure of the play text as we have it has encouraged critics to speculate that the 1594 edition is a heavily truncated version of the original, although there is no evidence that any additional soliloquies ever existed. Certainly, in the version of the play text that survives the hidden thoughts of Marlowe's characters remain inscrutable – accessible only through guesswork and inference despite their familiar involvement in a series of suspect conversions.

The most sustained 'conversion' narrative in *The Massacre at Paris* belongs to the French prince Anjoy (later Henry III), who moves from rabid Catholicism to proto-Protestant Gallicanism during the course of the play. In the opening scenes, Marlowe introduces Anjoy as an aggressively proselytising Catholic. While contemporary sources disagreed about how deeply the real Duke of Anjou had been implicated in the St Bartholomew's Day Massacre, Marlowe's character is shown slaughtering French Protestants (Huguenots) as enthusiastically as his mentor Guise. He echoes the latter's febrile instructions to 'kill them, kill them!' (6.3); swears to 'not be partial, / But slay as many as we can come near' (5.51–2); and personally orders the degradation of the Huguenot leader Admiral Coligny's corpse in terms that potentially devalue the seminal event of Christianity, Christ's crucifixion: he announces that 'unto Mount Faucon will we drag his corse, / And he that living hated so the Cross / Shall, being dead, be hang'd thereon in chains' (5.45–7).

These early scenes also give the first hints of Anjoy's duplicitous nature. The arguments he uses to convince his brother King Charles IX to approve the planned massacre suggest that self-interest rather than religious conviction dominates his thinking (4.13–16). His indifference to the massacre's supposedly religious purpose is confirmed by his behaviour during the ensuing bloodbath: as he murders Huguenots in the name of Catholic faith, Anjoy begins to parrot the rituals of Protestant prayer. Standing over the body of the Huguenot Loreine, he mockingly asks Guise to 'let me begin the psalm' (7.6); his words mimic the Anglican service, which began with the preacher's greeting to his 'dearly beloved brethren' (a phrase parodied by Guise in line 5) and ended with the singing of a psalm.[158] Anjoy's eagerness to mouth Protestant formulae even as he slaughters Huguenot 'heretics' is shared by an equally irreligious Guise, but contrasts sharply with the behaviour of the other Catholic murderers, who instead actively impose the language and rituals of the Catholic Church on their dying victims.

Anjoy's irreverent attitude reveals his underlying lack of religious conviction. The Protestant terminology he adopts in these early scenes also prophetically and problematically anticipates his later switch from ostensible Catholicism to a public pose of anti-papal Gallicanism; the real-life French Gallicans sought to reject papal control and establish an independent state church comparable to the Protestant Church of England. During the massacre itself, however, Anjoy shows no qualms about murdering his future allies: his eagerness to kill Huguenots is qualified only by his desire to preserve the appearance of innocence. Having adopted a disguise to conceal his involvement (5.5–6), he then pretends a spurious sympathy for the Huguenot survivors:

> ANJOY: I have done what I could to stay this broil.
> NAVARRE: But yet, my Lord, the report doth run
> That you were one that made this massacre.
> ANJOY: Who, I? You are deceived; I rose but now.
> (*Massacre at Paris* 9.72–5)

As Navarre's awareness of damaging rumours indicates, Anjoy's ability to dissimulate is not yet fully developed. In these early scenes, however, Marlowe's readers and spectators catch the first glimpses of Anjoy's self-interest, his readiness to distinguish between public appearance and true reality, and his indifference to true faith.

Anjoy's religiously inflected trickery becomes more skilful in the course of the play. The ahistorical provisos he introduces when accepting the Polish crown for instance suggest a developing skill in manipulating public perception that contrasts with his brother Charles's political vulnerability (2.67–72). The real Anjou was said to have returned to France surreptitiously after Charles's death, acting 'against the oath he made to the Polish lords', but it seems that Marlowe deliberately altered the facts to characterise the young Anjoy as a cunning politician.[159] Following his accession to the French throne as Henry III, the new king follows the advice of sixteenth-century political theorists such as Machiavelli by surrounding himself with loyal advisors.[160] Although his mother

Queen Catherine and the Duke of Guise are contemptuously dismissive of Henry's 'minions', seeing his favouritism as a sign of political naivety (14.45–6), their attitude is a mistake – in the end, it is Henry's favourite Epernoun who advises the French king that 'it would be good the Guise were made away' and who helps him to outmanoeuvre the rebellious duke (19.82).

Henry's attitude towards the doomed Guise reveals his extensive political guile. As Julia Briggs has convincingly demonstrated, Marlowe's version of Guise's murder emphasises Henry's treachery through an ahistorical chronology that shows the French king reassuring Guise immediately before the murder is carried out.[161] Henry himself characterises his behaviour towards Guise as 'traitorous guile' (21.33), and his equivocating speech is carefully designed to mislead his 'sweet coz':

> 'Twere hard with me if I should doubt my kin
> Or be suspicious of my dearest friends.
> Cousin, assure you I am resolute –
> Whatsoever any whisper in mine ears –
> Not to suspect disloyalty in thee:
> And so, sweet coz, farewell.
>
> (*Massacre at Paris* 21.42–7)

Since the French king delivers this reassurance immediately before Guise is stabbed by his hired assassins, however, his dishonesty is evident to an audience.

Marlowe's version of Guise's death emphasises Henry's cunning, and this focus on the king's duplicity may also invite suspicion about his related 'conversion' to a proto-Protestant agenda. Henry is able to dispose of his former ally Guise thanks to the security provided by his new alliance with the Huguenot prince Navarre; yet, in such circumstances, the French king's suspect willingness to characterise the political murder of Guise as a quasi-religious epiphany casts a cloud over his subsequent anti-papal rhetoric (21.90–1). Indeed, as Sara Munson Deats comments, it remains questionable whether Henry's shift from Catholic to Protestant sympathies is an act of genuine conversion or merely the opportunistic choice of yet another Machiavellian politician.[162]

Having disposed of Guise Henry proceeds to consolidate his alliance with the Huguenots, exclaiming that:

> Brother of Navarre, I sorrow much
> That ever I was prov'd your enemy,
> And that the sweet and princely mind you bear
> Was ever troubled with injurious wars.
>
> (*Massacre at Paris* 24.1–4)

But, given his pressing need for Protestant support in his 'injurious wars' against the Catholic League, the politically convenient timing of Henry's repentance invites reservations about the truth of his 'conversion'. It is especially hard to accept this apparent change of heart after his previous enthusiastic participation in the 1572 massacre. Whereas some early modern writers blamed the real Henri III's *volte-face* on political incompetence, with Francis Bacon describing him as a foolish ruler who 'entered league for the extirpation of the Protestants' and then found the same league 'turned upon himself', Marlowe gives greater credence to his character's political abilities.[163] The Huguenots may suggest that the French king has backed himself into a corner and urgently needs their help (20.7), but Marlowe's version of Guise's death affirms Henry's cunning in an episode that bears no overt Huguenot imprint; on the contrary, Guise is tricked by the king and his Catholic favourite. Henry then negotiates for the practical support he requires to secure his political standing and defeat the Catholic League forces that oppose him, sealing this agreement with a new pose of anti-papal Gallicanism: for Marlowe's original audiences, his rhetorical attacks on papal authority and his proto-Protestant agenda evoke the English model of a state church free from papal control.[164]

Henry's suspect 'conversion' may be a political gambit, but the king commits thoroughly to the deception. Though antagonistic contemporary accounts derided Henri III as a hypocrite, at the very moment of his death Marlowe's character presents an unfaltering image of fervent religious conviction:

Navarre, give me thy hand: I here do swear
To ruinate that wicked Church of Rome
That hatcheth up such bloody practices,
And here protest eternal love to thee,
And to the Queen of England specially,
Whom God hath bless'd for hating papistry.
(*Massacre at Paris* 24.64–9)

Henry's speech celebrates the English Protestant Church in patriotic terms. At the same time, his performance is complicated by the past responsibility he bears for the 'bloody practices' of the St Bartholomew's Day Massacre. Memories of the earlier massacre are indeed doubly problematic for an audience: while the dying Henry acts as the mouthpiece of international Protestantism (24.97–105), Marlowe's spectators have already seen him engage in a comparable performance of Protestant prayer when he murdered the Huguenot martyr Loreine. These earlier events proved Anjoy's willingness to use religious rhetoric as part of a personal agenda, and hinted that the language of religious ritual means little to him. It seems likely that his 'conversion' to proto-Protestant Gallicanism might appear equally suspect to an Elizabethan audience: a self-interested pretence, grounded in religion but pursued for political advantage.

When Henry's final speeches are studied closely their surface platitudes begin to disintegrate, exposing the hypocritical reality. In particular, the speech he directs to Elizabeth I is likely to have resonated hollowly for an informed contemporary spectator:

Henry thy King wipes off these childish tears
And bids thee whet thy sword on Sixtus' bones
That it may keenly slice the Catholics.
. . .
I die, Navarre; come bear me to my sepulchre.
Salute the Queen of England in my name,
And tell her, Henry dies her faithful friend.
(*Massacre at Paris* 24.97–105)

Henry's vision of a loving mutual alliance between England and France is suspect: the contemporary agreement between Henri III and Elizabeth I was marked by distrust and deception, while the subsequent pact with Henri's heir Navarre, crowned Henri IV, was equally problematic from the English perspective. Moreover, the confessional politics of this scene contrast sharply and significantly with the historical reality: far from encouraging his heir to pursue an anti-papal policy, the dying Henri III had in fact urged Navarre to convert to Catholicism. Julia Briggs believes that Marlowe was trying to evade the 'unpalatable truth' of Henri III's final moments, but the close parallels between the historical reality and Marlowe's dramatic narrative actually seem to underscore the discrepancies between fact and fiction.[165] By drawing attention to the flaws in Henry's claims, Marlowe undercuts his character's ostensible 'conversion' to proto-Protestant Gallicanism. With the informed spectator aware that even Henry's staged conversion is false and that the real Henri III died a Catholic, the dramatic ironies of this scene invite scepticism about the dying king's motives; Henry may propose an international Protestant alliance against papal Rome, but it seems that his main concern is to secure his personal revenge against the Catholics who ordered his murder.

Henry's suspect deathbed 'conversion' nonetheless has an important dramatic, historical and propagandistic function; the French king then names the Huguenot prince Navarre as his rightful heir, bringing the action of the play almost up to Marlowe's present. Navarre quickly responds with a reciprocal pledge of Protestant loyalty. In a scene that recalls Elizabeth I's own use of providential rhetoric as well as Tamburlaine's suspect claims to act as the 'scourge of God' in Marlowe's earlier drama, Navarre uses the language of divine providence to buttress his claim to the throne. Having previously characterised his military triumphs against the Catholics as a sign of heavenly favour (18.12–17), he now vows to uphold the Protestant faith as the new French king. Navarre's formal oath to his dying predecessor ostentatiously aligns him with the anti-papal values of Protestant England, his political ally in the early 1590s:

> I vow for to revenge his death
> As Rome and all those popish prelates there
> Shall curse the time that e'er Navarre was king
> And rul'd in France by Henry's fatal death!
> (*Massacre at Paris* 24.108–11)

Critics usually take Navarre's promise to maintain Protestantism as 'the perfect truth . . . so long as life doth last' (18.13–14) at face value, describing Marlowe's character as an 'idealised Christian' and 'godly' hero; the real Henri IV's conversion in summer 1593 is regarded as a historical irony.[166] Despite Marlowe's death in spring 1593, however, this is not necessarily the case. Instead, the close proximity of Navarre's promise to Henry's suspect conversion may invite doubts about its validity, and even hint provocatively at Navarre's future confessional *volte-face*.

The reciprocal pledges depicted in the closing scene of *The Massacre at Paris* were ironic for informed spectators even during Marlowe's own lifetime. Not only did the dying Henri III urge Navarre to convert to Catholicism rather than upholding the Protestant cause; the new Henri IV's first public commitment was an undertaking to defend the French Catholic Church.[167] John Welles reported these facts to Sir Francis Walsingham as early as 1589, writing that 'the King did pray the King of Navarre to live and die a Catholic, and so he hath promised all the nobility and doth go to Mass'. Moreover, some French commentators suspected Navarre of duplicity and denounced his 'protestation to live Catholic' as 'but to dissemble': Marlowe's characterisation of Navarre as a self-interested politician of suspect religious loyalties might well have struck a chord with his contemporaries.[168]

If Marlowe was an agent for the Elizabethan government, he may have had privileged access to information about Navarre's confessional manoeuvrings. There is even a slight but tantalising possibility that Marlowe was personally involved in disseminating the relevant reports: John Michael Archer notes that a 'Mr. Marlin' delivered messages for the English envoy to Henri of Navarre during 1591–2.[169] But Marlowe and his audiences could also have acquired advance knowledge of Navarre's intentions in a more straightforward fashion. Henri III's favourite the Duke of Épernon (himself a cunning and duplicitous figure in *The Massacre*) was sent on a mission to convert Navarre to Catholicism in the summer of 1584, while in 1591 the London publisher John Wolfe printed two pamphlets discussing the possibility of Navarre's conversion: one of these pamphlets informed its English readers that debates about why the king does not become a Catholic are 'the daily speeche of divers'.[170] In addition, rumours that the French king was about to convert circulated early in 1593: his actual conversion to Catholicism in the summer came as no surprise.[171]

While there is no firm evidence that Marlowe was aware of these rumours, he displays a thorough familiarity with recent French politics in *The Massacre at Paris*; it is at least plausible that the play's final scenes knowingly anticipate Navarre's future conversion. Navarre's readiness to dissimulate his faith for political advantage is hinted at earlier in the play, and it seems likely that Marlowe introduces a deliberate gap between his inner thoughts and outwardly pious utterances. The precise connection between Henry III's politic transformation, Navarre's response and the real Henri IV's subsequent conversion remains ambiguous. Yet it seems perfectly possible that a sceptical spectator, viewing this play in 1593, might have interpreted Navarre's vow to the dying Henry III as an ironic commentary on the new French king's conversion – especially in a dramatic context where political ambition and false conversion have come to seem virtually synonymous.

CHAPTER THREE

OATH-TAKING AND OATH-BREAKING

The enforcement of outward religious conformity and the struggle to discern an individual's private beliefs were urgent concerns for an English Protestant regime that equated confessional allegiance with political loyalty. Elizabeth I's government and many of her subjects regarded Catholicism and treason in God's name as virtually synonymous, especially after the papal proclamation of 1570 which excommunicated the English queen and declared her subjects to be forever absolved from their political oaths of obedience. Explicitly linking oath-breaking with the religious duty to rebel, this papal bull consolidated English fears about the dual and conflicting allegiances owed by English Catholics. Concerns that English Catholics might prioritise their perceived religious duty over secular loyalty and rebel against the Protestant state were especially acute in the later 1580s, when England lived in fear of an imminent Spanish invasion, and were exacerbated by tracts such as William Allen's *Admonition to the Nobility* (1588). Writing in support of the Spanish Armada invasion attempt, the Jesuit Cardinal reminded Elizabeth's Catholic subjects that they had a religious obligation to break the secular oaths binding them to their 'heretic' queen, since 'this woman was by good Pius Quintus excommunicated and deprived, and all her subjects discharged of othe and obedience towardes her'.[172]

In the 1580s Elizabethan fears of invasion centred on Catholic Spain, but the struggle to reconcile conflicting loyalties was not an exclusively Catholic issue. The radical Protestant faction of presbyterians led by Thomas Cartwright similarly strove to resolve their divided allegiances, as did some of the more extreme separatist sects. While not tarred by association with an international

Catholic conspiracy, these groups were still regarded as an active political threat. In the case of the extreme Protestants or puritans the political implications were acute, since the 1559–60 revolt by the Scottish Lords of the Congregation had demonstrated that radical Protestants were as likely as Catholics to rebel in the name of their religion. Although Elizabeth I's newly established government had given military assistance to the Scottish dissidents in 1560, the English authorities were aware of the potentially subversive implications of such campaigns; the ideological justification for the Scottish rebellion was provided by the preacher John Knox, who argued in 1558 that 'neither can oath nor promise bind any such people to obey and maintain tyrants against God and against His truth known'.[173]

Elizabethan England's sensitivity to the dangers of puritan dissidence reached new heights in 1588–9, with the publication of the Martin Marprelate pamphlets. These radical Protestant tracts attacked the hierarchy of the Elizabethan Church in scathing terms, claiming that 'every archbishop is a petty pope'; the fictional Martin's violent assault on the established church was strongly condemned by the Elizabethan authorities, who characterised his rejection of ecclesiastical hierarchy as a threat to all social order.[174] When the English bishops hired propagandists to respond, the latter branded 'Martin' an outright rebel. The pamphleteer Thomas Nashe even linked the Marprelate scandal to the threat of Catholic invasion: in *An Almond for a Parrat* (1589) he imagines a scene in which Italian Catholics rejoice at Martin's success, discussing how this 'famous Schismatike' has

> brought that to passe which neither the Pope by his Seminaries, Philip by his power, nor all the holy League by their underhand practises and policies could at any time effect: for wheras they lived at unitie before . . . hee hath invented such quiddities to set them together by the eares that now the temporaltie is readie to plucke out the throtes of the Cleargie, and subjects to withdraw their allegeance from their Soverayne.[175]

The puritans soon gained a popular reputation for treason, particularly after a few radicals proclaimed their leader William Hackett the new Messiah and sought to depose Queen Elizabeth in his favour. While in practice most puritans were loyal to Elizabeth I, many members of her government shared Nashe's doubts. Thus in 1593 the Bishop of London, Richard Bancroft, publicly denounced the 'pretended refourmers', arguing that they were as 'traiterous' and 'seditious' as the 'divelish' Catholics, and adding that any oath taken by a puritan was worthless since 'they dally so exceedingly with it'.[176]

As Bancroft's critique of puritan loyalty indicates, the act of oath-taking was increasingly central to Elizabethan ideals of civil obedience. The English authorities relied heavily on oaths that tested the confessional and political loyalties of the queen's subjects: by 1563 England's lawyers, schoolmasters, university graduates and divines were all required to take the Oath of Supremacy, a promise of loyalty to Elizabeth and the established church, while from 1571 onwards members of the clergy had also to swear an oath accepting the authority of the 1559 Prayer Book and the Thirty-Nine Articles. Such oaths were often imposed in direct response to immediate state fears, casting political loyalty in contractual terms. For example, rumours in the early 1580s that Elizabeth I's life was in danger resulted in the Bond of Association, which created a sworn brotherhood of voluntary defenders of the realm. Elizabethan government propaganda similarly presented the act of oath-taking as a confirmation of the promiser's political allegiance: for instance, one anti-Catholic tract compiled on Lord Burghley's orders makes much of the public oath of loyalty given to the queen by Viscount Montague, a Catholic loyalist who 'did professe and protest solemnely' to defend England 'against all Invaders, whether it were Pope, King or Potentate whatsoever'.[177] Comparable oaths of political allegiance were exacted from Elizabeth's subjects as a preventive measure against rebellion, especially rebellion in the name of religion.

With England's security balanced upon a scaffold of promises, the government was naturally fearful of and antagonistic to claims that religious duty might take precedence over loyalty to the state. Yet, in an actively religious society, incidents in which spiritual considerations clashed with the demands of the state were comparatively common. In 1583, for example, there was a major scandal when at least three hundred clerics refused to subscribe to the Three Articles imposed by Archbishop Whitgift. In this instance the Earl of Leicester and Sir Francis Walsingham intervened on the ministers' behalf, and Whitgift eventually accepted an edited version of the oath; by the early 1590s, however, Leicester and Walsingham were dead and a new campaign against the puritans had begun. England's Catholics faced a more severe dilemma when it came to the nationally prescribed Oath of Allegiance: while a Catholic could not agree that Elizabeth was the Supreme Governor of the Church without breaking faith with the Pope, a refusal to swear this oath was considered treason. Indeed, any promissory undertaking that might supersede English bonds of loyalty was roundly condemned by Elizabethan propagandists: the government informer Anthony Munday for instance wrote that when English Catholic priests 'receive their Preestehood, they enter into theyr oath, which oath contayneth the sum of the Treason'.[178] English Protestant anxieties were further exacerbated by secular attacks on the inherent sanctity of political oaths; Niccolò Machiavelli's suggestion that considerations of self-interest might supersede abstract notions of contractual duty was particularly notorious.[179] Amplifying the Protestant government's existing fears about oath-breaking in the name of religion, such comments generated significant concern about the security of the Elizabethan regime and its complex, perhaps precarious network of promissory allegiance.

The Elizabethan preoccupation with oath-taking and oath-breaking is reflected in Christopher Marlowe's plays and poems. But, while literary critics have long been aware of the importance of contracts in Shakespeare's drama, Marlowe's writings have only recently attracted similar attention. The new studies remain fairly specialised: Richard Wilson's discussion of contract in *Tamburlaine* looks exclusively at commercial undertakings; Luke Wilson's perceptive analysis of Faustus's pact with Mephistopheles considers only the stage tradition of the demonic contract; while other critics have focused on discerning Machiavelli's influence.[180] Such research has made a valuable contribution, demonstrating Marlowe's familiarity with legal terminology and interest in contractual questions. However, the extensive spiritual and political significance of his contractual episodes has not been fully recognised. Crucially, these reflect Marlowe's extensive interest in the relationship between oaths, religion and political loyalty; indeed, he consistently creates scenarios in which characters are encouraged to break a legal contract or political treaty in the name of religion.

Marlowe's interest in oaths is wide-reaching: every one of his major poetic and dramatic works includes one or more episodes in which contractual undertakings are represented or reported. Writing in Elizabethan England, Marlowe responded to contemporary anxieties about oath-breaking as he portrays acts of perjury which his characters cast as religious duty; in Marlowe's sceptical imagination, however, such pious claims almost invariably ring hollow. This chapter explores how Marlovian protagonists from Aeneas to Ferneze call on their gods to vindicate acts of oath-breaking and perjury, while Marlowe simultaneously reveals their underlying financial and political motives. I begin with the broken lovers' vows of *Ovid's Elegies* and *Dido Queen of Carthage*, which relate indirectly to contemporary debates about promissory loyalty, before turning to *Tamburlaine Part Two* and *The Jew of Malta* – the two plays that most overtly show characters breaking political oaths in the name of religion.

VENUS AND FALSE VOWS IN 'OVID'S ELEGIES'

Marlowe's fascination with characters who appropriate religious precedents to excuse a self-interested repudiation of contractual loyalties is apparent throughout his literary career, complementing his broader exposé of the role religion plays in justifying selfish and often immoral actions. The first hints of his interest in oath-breaking are found in his vernacular translation of Ovid's *Amores*, usually considered to be one of his earliest works. In *Ovid's Elegies* Marlowe presents several episodes in which the narrator appeals to the goddess Venus, citing her as a precedent for and defender of his erotically inspired perjury. In Book Two, for instance, the paired elegies on the maid Cypassis create a vignette that exposes the false faith of the lover who narrates them. First, in Elegy 7, the reader encounters his denial of guilt and pledge of honesty. The speaker denies any sexual involvement with his mistress Corinna's maid Cypassis and appeals to the gods to free him from suspicion, vowing 'by Venus, and the winged boy's bow' that 'myself unguilty of this crime I know' (*Ovid's Elegies* 2.7.19, 27–8). Our trust in the unnamed speaker's word is short-lived, however, since the next elegy shows him berating Cypassis for her indiscretion:

> Who that our bodies were compressed bewrayed?
> Whence knows Corinna that with thee I played?
> Yet blushed I not, nor used I any saying,
> That might be urged to witness our false playing.
>
> (*Ovid's Elegies* 2.8.5–8)

The reader can recognise the dubious accuracy of these charges; the true 'bewrayer' is not the hapless slave but the speaker himself. Indeed, even he implicitly acknowledges that by making love to Cypassis he has been 'false' to Corinna. Yet, particularly in Marlowe's translation, there is no mood of contrition: rendering Ovid's phrase '*num tamen . . . num*' as '*non tamen . . . nec*', Marlowe transforms the guilty exclamations of Ovid's lover – 'Can I have blushed?' – into the speaker's self-satisfied statement that, under pressure, 'yet blushed I not'.[181] As the elegy continues, the speaker boasts about his success in deceiving Corinna. He openly admits his 'false playing' and marvels how 'by Venus' deity . . . did I protest!' (18), secure in the knowledge that 'thou, goddess, dost command a warm south blast / My false oaths in Carpathian seas to cast' (19–20).

The most significant element in these paired elegies is not the deception itself, though this obviously compromises the reader's trust in the narrator, but rather the means by which the speaker justifies his perjury – and his related assumption that Venus will excuse his behaviour. This point is made particularly forcefully in Marlowe's translation. Whereas Ovid's speaker ambiguously describes the vows he has made as '*periuria puri*' (pure or moral perjuries) in asking Venus to send them away, Marlowe's narrator openly acknowledges the falsity of his words.[182] In addition, the goddess becomes a more complicit conspirator in *Ovid's Elegies* than she was in the Latin original: when the speaker announces that Venus 'dost command a warm south blast / My false oaths in Carpathian seas to cast' (19–20), Marlowe's forceful use of the future verb 'dost' removes any sense of uncertainty or pleading from the speaker's statement. Nor is this concept of Venus as a champion of oath-breaking uncommon in Elizabethan writings. In the sixteenth-century emblem book *Amorum emblemata*, for instance, the emblem 'Love excuses from perjurie' is accompanied by a verse stating that 'venus doth dispence in lovers othes abused'; intriguingly, Donna Hamilton notes that this book's English translator Richard Verstegan was better known as a Catholic polemicist, and posits a connection between 'Love excuses' and the Catholic practices of equivocation I explored in Chapter One.[183] Any connection is implicit at best, but it is possible that appeals to a religious figurehead such as Venus might resonate with contemporary Elizabethan fears of oath-breaking: according to sixteenth-century Protestant propaganda, the Catholic missionary priests were equally guilty of committing perjury in the pope's name, and according to his mandate.

'AGAINST ALL LAWS OF LOVE': AENEAS'S BETRAYAL OF DIDO

While the idea that the goddess Venus can sanction an act of oath-breaking may arguably echo English concerns about the loyalties of Catholic and puritan subjects, in *All Ovid's Elegies* these possible allusions are glancing and indirect. In *Dido Queen of Carthage*, on the other hand, it seems that Marlowe and his co-writer Thomas Nashe exploited a coincidental connection between the mythological

Dido and Queen Elizabeth I to hint that their fictional narrative might speak to early modern English issues. Dido, a childless female ruler, was historically known by the name Elissa; various Elizabethan texts drew flattering comparisons between England's sixteenth-century 'Eliza' and the widowed Dido praised by Justin and Boccaccio for her chastity, including James Aske's *Elizabetha Triumphans* and Edmund Spenser's *Shepheardes Calender.*[184] Since the Tudor dynasty claimed Aeneas as their mythical ancestor, allusions to the Trojan prince in early modern literature might also have contemporary resonance. Indeed, in the so-called 'Siena Portrait' by Quentin Metsys the Younger England's monarch is compared to both the historical Dido and Virgil's *pius* Aeneas; as this portrait suggests, Elizabeth's iconography might simultaneously credit the queen with the chastity of the historical Dido and the martial, empire-building attributes of Aeneas.

But the Virgilian tale of Dido's love for Aeneas could also serve less flattering political ends. As Donald Stump notes, Elizabeth's detractors employed the same analogy to dispute her proposed marriage to the French Catholic Duke of Alençon and Anjou, Henri III's younger brother. In the case of the Siena portrait, for instance, it is possible that this ostensibly flattering painting is actually a warning against the French match, suggesting that Elizabeth risks becoming a second Dido.[185] William Gager's university play *Dido Tragoedia* (1583) similarly celebrates the English queen – 'Dido, our Virgin Queen is for all that far superior to you' (ll. 1260–1) – but stresses the dangers of marrying a foreigner; the Latin drama was, revealingly, commissioned by Elizabeth's English Protestant suitor the Earl of Leicester.[186] Through the story of Dido's doomed love, *Dido Tragoedia* implicitly censures Elizabeth's marriage plans, even demanding whether the queen's subjects will 'with impunity permit a stranger to be taken into the kingdom while the natives are despised' (ll. 447–8). The final chorus explicitly attributes Elizabeth I's political success to her moral decorum in affairs of the heart, and pointedly contrasts this success to the disasters caused by Dido's reckless passion. Subtly denouncing Elizabeth's unpopular marriage negotiations, Gager's play explores the fate of a queen whose marriage is incompatible with her political duty.

Marlowe's dramatic version of Dido and Aeneas's story may have been partly inspired by Gager's play. Indeed, some critics consider that Marlowe and Nashe's children's drama also engages with the controversy over Elizabeth's marriage negotiations and mocks her French suitor in the figure of Aeneas.[187] A sustained analogy between Aeneas and the Duke of Alençon and Anjou is doubtful, since *Dido Queen of Carthage* was most probably written after the latter's death in 1584, and the tone of the play is very different to that of Gager's didactic and moralising drama. However, Marlowe and Nashe do seem to follow Gager's lead in one major respect; in both plays, Dido's relationship with Aeneas might figuratively suggest an English encounter with Catholicism, when Queen 'Elissa' is betrayed by the legendary founder of imperial, Catholic Rome. But whereas Gager emphasises Dido's uncontrolled passion for a foreign prince, in Marlowe and Nashe's drama it is her contractual relationship with Aeneas that takes centre stage.

When readers of Virgil's *Aeneid* consider the morality of Aeneas's decision to leave Dido, little is left to chance. Although the epic shows sympathy for the abandoned queen, Aeneas's decision is presented as unequivocally correct. His parting words to Dido epitomise this approach, drawing upon both law and religion to justify his departure: 'I never held out the bridegroom's torch nor entered such a contract,' Aeneas explains, before adding his clinching argument: 'The messenger of the gods sent from Jove himself . . . has borne his command down through the swift breezes'.[188] Virgil's *pius* hero is justified, both legally and theologically, in leaving Carthage for Italy. The sixteenth-century English translators of the *Aeneid* endorsed Aeneas's defence, stressing that despite Ovid's claims in his *Heroides* there was nothing between Aeneas and Dido that could legally be termed a marriage. Henry Howard's Dido is 'led against honour with unhonest lust', and her claims to be married are merely a pretence whose 'fayre name' 'cloketh' her fault, while in Richard Stanyhurst's *Aeneis* the relationship between Dido and Aeneas is reductively termed 'thee bedmatch' and Dido is said to use 'thee name of wedlock' to cloak her 'carnal leacherye'. Thomas Phaer's *Eneidos* more sympathetically describes a Dido who is 'joyned in love' with Aeneas, but their relationship is still nothing more than a sexual 'cowpling'; again, Phaer's Dido uses 'wedlocks name' to hide 'her faut'.[189] Even Gager's *Dido Tragoedia* follows this tradition, as any doubts about Aeneas's abandonment of Dido are soothed by the epilogue's pronouncement that 'it is proper to be obedient to the predictions of the gods' (l. 1249).

In these sixteenth-century versions of the *Aeneid*, as in the Virgilian original, Aeneas can use religious and legal arguments to justify his departure from Carthage because his relationship with Dido does not constitute a binding marriage. Marlowe and Nashe were undoubtedly familiar with this tradition; both men would have studied the *Aeneid* extensively at grammar school, while Nashe's allusion to the Phaer and Stanyhurst translations in his 1589 preface to Robert Greene's play *Menaphon* may suggest that it was these particular editions he consulted for *Dido Queen of Carthage*.[190] Yet Marlowe and Nashe break with tradition in their play, staging a ceremonial agreement between Dido and Aeneas that seems to conform to accepted sixteenth-century nuptial practice. Thus, in a significant departure from Virgil, Marlowe and Nashe introduce the telling possibility that Aeneas owes a contractual duty to Dido as her husband. The shift ensures that their Aeneas, unlike Virgil's hero, faces a conflict between his religious and secular loyalties. When the gods command him to leave Carthage he must choose between his contractual obligation to his lawfully wedded wife and his religious duty to the gods – his fictional dilemma perhaps echoing the difficulties faced by England's religious dissidents.

The most important indication that Marlowe and Nashe's Aeneas is legally bound to Dido is the ceremony that takes place between the two characters as they shelter from a storm. The basic episode is taken from Virgil's *Aeneid*, but it has been extensively revised and expanded in *Dido Queen of Carthage*. Initially, the omens are poor: Aeneas's first words invoke the precedent of Mars and Venus, recalling a notorious adulterous coupling, while the rapid vacillation of Dido's emotions in this scene introduces a note of deflationary comedy (3.4.25–9). Yet Marlowe often uses comic parody to emphasise a more serious message: in *Doctor Faustus*, for instance, the parallels between the main narrative and the comic subplot call attention to the transitory nature of the gifts for which Marlowe's protagonist sells his soul. Aeneas's ominous reference to divine infidelity and Dido's comic indecisiveness perhaps similarly foreshadow Aeneas's ultimate abandonment of her; his thoughts later fluctuate wildly as he decides first to go, then to stay, then to go, while his betrayal of his lovers' vows accords with the precedent set by his adulterous mother Venus.

After this inauspicious start, however, the note of irreverent comedy seems to fade in the final exchange between the two characters. Aeneas, prompted by Dido but certainly not coerced, delivers a long and elaborate vow of love:

> With this my hand I give to you my heart,
> And vow, by all the Gods of hospitality,
> By heaven and earth, and my fair brother's bow,
> By Paphos, Capys, and the purple sea
> From whence my radiant mother did descend,
> And by this sword that sav'd me from the Greeks,
> Never to leave these new-upreared walls
> Whiles Dido lives and rules in Juno's town –
> Never to like or love any but her!
>
> (*Dido* 3.4.42–50)

His promise of love is perhaps amusingly grandiloquent, but it is also a significant addition to Marlowe and Nashe's Virgilian source. Whereas Virgil veils events in the cave, authorising sympathy for Dido without jeopardising Aeneas's moral stature, *Dido Queen of Carthage* provides a scene in which their union is ceremonially confirmed. Aeneas pledges himself to Dido comprehensively, swearing by the gods (43); by heaven and earth (44); by his family (44–6); and by his sword, the symbol of his military and chivalric honour (47). The repetition of 'by' four times within five lines further emphasises the all-encompassing nature of the oath and the mimicking of the repetitious format of a legal oath adds to the sense that it is indeed binding.

Despite the pagan setting and the absence of a priest, it is likely that Marlowe's audience would have regarded Aeneas and Dido's exchange of vows as a marriage ceremony. In Elizabethan England, the essential prerequisite for a legally binding union was not a formal solemnisation of the marriage in church but rather the contract known as spousals or hand-fasting, which required only that a couple should commit to each other as husband and wife using present-tense pronouncements.[191] Although Aeneas does not specifically use the term 'husband', his promise 'never to like or love any but her' constitutes a binding arrangement after the manner of marriage that an Elizabethan audience would most probably have accepted. Dido's words confirm the pact by explicitly appointing Aeneas to a place at her side as joint ruler and husband: 'Sichaeus, not Aeneas, be thou call'd; / The King of Carthage' (3.4.58–9). Finally, visual clues provide further evidence that a marriage is taking place: Aeneas and Dido are hand-fasted for this scene (3.4.42), while Dido's action in presenting her 'wedding-ring' to Aeneas provides the concluding action of the ceremony (3.4.60–1).

These precise details are often overlooked in modern productions; in the 2009 National Theatre production, for instance, the hand-fasting instead took the form of a lovers' clasp with Anastasia Hille's Dido and Mark Bonnar's Aeneas gazing intently into each other's eyes, as in the picture overleaf. Nonetheless, the scene was played seriously and sensitively, providing the tragic crux of a production which interpreted Dido as the vulnerable victim of a nasty divine practical joke; for a modern audience, the almost formal posing of the two actors and the long white dress Dido wore still hinted visually at a wedding or an arrangement akin to marriage.[192] Even if Marlowe's original spectators did not identify Aeneas's promises to Dido as formal wedding vows, the oath he swears to Dido in this scene certainly complicates his eventual departure. In Act 4 Marlowe and Nashe then added another contractual episode involving Dido and Aeneas, in an invented scene which has no basis in the *Aeneid*. The agreement Aeneas and Dido negotiate confirms that Aeneas will stay in Carthage, and that in return Dido will grant him as much power and wealth as he might expect to find in Italy (4.4.56–7). The valuable gifts she offers reinforce the legal status of their pact, since the absolute essence of sixteenth-century contractual theory was reciprocity: for an arrangement to be considered binding under early modern law, each party to it must benefit.[193] Aeneas, having received the material benefits that were legally termed 'consideration', is therefore bound to a reciprocal performance of his promise: once Dido has made him joint ruler of Carthage (3.4.59), given him jewels and 'golden bracelets' (3.4.60–1) and mended his ships 'conditionally that thou wilt stay with me' (3.1.113), he should in return remain at her side.

The legal historian P.S. Atiyah has suggested that, when it is customary to use special ceremonies to create a binding obligation, their very absence may imply that the obligation does not exist.[194] Virgil uses the same strategy in the *Aeneid*: the reader does not witness a wedding ceremony, and so Aeneas owes Dido nothing. Although the Virgilian Dido does attempt to assert her status as bride, asking Aeneas to honour 'our marriage' and 'the wedlock begun', her claims are soon dismissed and she acknowledges that Aeneas bears only 'the *name* of husband' (my italics): the point is made emphatically by Thomas Phaer, who translates Dido's confession as 'husband thee I dare not call'. Aeneas himself consistently denies the legality of the marriage, either upon a point of ceremony ('I never held out the bridegroom's torch') or (in Phaer's words) through a legally viable denial of intention: 'Nor I for wedlock ever came, nor thus did mynd to deale'.[195] For Virgil and the sixteenth-century translators of the *Aeneid*, Aeneas's disavowal of a legal duty to Dido prefaces any reference to the will of the gods in his self-defence.

Conversely, Marlowe and Nashe's *Dido Queen of Carthage* fills in the Virgilian blanks and presents a scene of formally negotiated,

Dido Queen of Carthage, 3.4: Aeneas (Mark Bonnar) and Dido (Anastasia Hille) pledge their love to each other in the National Theatre production of 2009, directed by James MacDonald.

officially contracted union. Since his father often acted as a bondsman for couples about to marry, testifying to the validity of marriage contracts, Marlowe presumably shared with Nashe the clergyman's son a good understanding of the precise legal principles involved in a ceremony of spousals.[196] The legally binding marriage ceremony he and Nashe present in *Dido Queen of Carthage* is thus a significant move away from their Virgilian source, and one that allows them to engage more firmly with the issue of Aeneas's legal obligation to Dido. This emphasis is complemented by their introduction of a second, original scene that reiterates the contractual bonds tying Aeneas to Carthage. These departures from Virgil's epic demonstrate that their absconding hero has a legal obligation to remain with Dido. Indeed, during his first attempt to leave even Aeneas privately admits that he has transgressed 'against all laws of love' (4.2.48); while critics usually interpret this statement in an abstract romantic sense, the conjoining of 'law' and 'love' also economically condenses the elements of a marriage ceremony and reminds readers and spectators of Aeneas's earlier vows. As he departs for good, *this* Aeneas signally fails to refute Dido's claim that 'thy hand and mine have plighted mutual faith!'; he simply states that the decrees of the gods must come first (5.1.122, 126–7).

In *Dido Queen of Carthage*, in contrast to other sixteenth-century versions of the *Aeneid*, legal and religious justifications are no longer united in Aeneas's defence. Instead, Aeneas explicitly prioritises 'the Gods' behest' over his 'spousal rites' (5.1.127, 134). By obeying divine commands rather than the dictates of law, he acts in the manner advocated by sixteenth-century theorists of religious resistance; in fact the messenger-god Hermes, who is dismissive of Aeneas's secular and familial bonds and demands that he 'must straight to Italy' (5.1.51–3), sounds not unlike the Catholic propagandists who urged English subjects to repudiate their secular allegiance to Elizabeth I (as well as any family ties to non-believers). This similarity is strengthened by the fact that, in both cases, the non-performance of religious duties carries spiritual penalties: the papal bull of 1570 threatened excommunication, while Aeneas must 'else abide the wrath of frowning Jove' (5.1.54). Yet there is a casual cruelty about Jove's ultimatum, as well as an indifference to Dido's legal rights; this brutal aspect was emphasised effectively in the 2003 Globe production directed by Tim Carroll, in which Dave Fishley's Hermes impatiently stamped down Aeneas's sandcastle dream version of a reconstructed Troy as he entered to deliver Jove's orders.

By eventually choosing to prioritise religious duty over the claims of secular loyalty, Aeneas might be said to align himself with the Catholic and Protestant proponents of religious resistance. There is perhaps an echo here of Aeneas's alternate medieval and early modern reputation as a traitor who betrayed Troy to her foreign enemies: in John Lydgate's *Troy-Book*, for example, Aeneas is identified as a 'false serpent' who treacherously helped the Greeks to enter the city (l. 6442). This late medieval tradition of Aeneas the traitor was still familiar in the later sixteenth and early seventeenth centuries – in William Alexander's *Julius Caesar* (1607), for instance, Juno condemns 'false Aeneas' as a treacherous usurper (11.125–6); and it sheds an intriguing light upon Marlowe and Nashe's protagonist, who betrays his secular loyalties in the name of religion.[197] Moreover, as usual in Marlowe's writings, Aeneas arguably exploits the play's religious rhetoric to further his own interests; when defending his decision to Dido he blames everything on the stern, unyielding will of the gods, but his previous soliloquy indicated that he is really quite eager to pursue his 'golden fortunes' (4.3.8). Such doubts about the purity of Aeneas's motives are reinforced by the fact that, damningly, his rebuttal of the oath he swore by his paternal and maternal ancestors and his suspect willingness to abandon his own son severely complicates the Roman dynastic project that Jupiter's command ostensibly upholds (1.1.82–108; 3.4.44–6; 4.4.29–30).

Despite Dido's status as queen, the contract Aeneas breaks might be regarded as a domestic rather than state matter, just as the bonds violated by the speaker of *Ovid's Elegies* are marital rather than political. However, this does not negate the relevance of such episodes to Elizabethan concerns about oath-breaking, since religious resistance tracts in fact exploited comparable analogies between marital and political contracts. Radical Catholic propagandists used 2 John 10 to argue that a Catholic people could be divorced from their heretic king in the same way that a marriage between a Catholic and a heretic could be dissolved, while the French Protestant tracts *Vindiciae Contra Tyrannos* and Hotman's *Francogallia* compared the king's power over his domains to a husband's control of his wife's dowry.[198] Perhaps most strikingly, Théodore de Bèze uses the language of marital law to support his justification of resistance in *Du Droit des Magistrats*, and cites Matthew 19.5 to argue that 'the duties of marriage are comparable to the duty of a subject to his superior' – a biblical parallel between marriage and state loyalty that is then extended to justify resistance to a tyrannical ruler.[199]

Marlowe may have known about the analogies that theorists of religious resistance drew between marriage vows and political oaths of loyalty, and perhaps hints at the same connection in his own works. Marlowe's *Elegies* suggestively characterise their speaker's seductive assault upon the bonds of marriage as an act of rebellious, overreaching ambition (2.4.48), while Aeneas's repudiation of his marital obligations in *Dido Queen of Carthage* leads to the political downfall of the Carthaginian monarchy (5.1.312–27). In these works any political connotations remain ambiguous, while the deities who command or are complicit in acts of perjury are pagan rather than Christian. Marlowe's literary fascination with oath-breaking in the name of religion is not always so discreet, however. In plays such as *Tamburlaine Part Two* and *The Jew of Malta* the political significance of oath-taking and oath-breaking is more readily apparent, with Marlowe controversially dramatising acts of perjury that are committed by Christian characters and which entail the treacherous repudiation of political alliances. Thus in *Tamburlaine Part Two*, Marlowe shows the Hungarian emperor Sigismund breaking his truce with the Turkish leader Orcanes in the name of religion, while in *The Jew of Malta* Ferneze similarly breaks faith with his Turkish associates. In both instances, these Catholic oath-breakers cite the notorious 'papist' dictum that 'faith is not to be held with heretics' as they betray their more honourable Turkish allies (*Jew of Malta* 2.3.313). At a time when Protestant England regarded the Ottoman Empire as a potential ally against the encroaching forces of Catholicism, the type of betrayal Marlowe depicts might have provocative implications.[200]

PERJURY AND POLITICAL TREACHERY IN 'TAMBURLAINE PART TWO'

In *Tamburlaine Part Two*, the contractual episode featuring the Hungarian king Sigismund and the Turkish ruler Orcanes is an ahistorical interpolation apparently inspired by historical accounts of the Battle of Varna. Its inclusion suggests that Marlowe deliberately departed from his main sources in order to introduce a notorious example of religiously justified oath-breaking. Certainly, the incident has a disproportionate impact in the first half of the play, raising unfulfilled expectations that either Orcanes or Sigismund will be Tamburlaine's chief adversary in *Part Two*: perhaps for this reason, the episode is almost invariably cut in modern productions. In fact, however, this subplot serves a significant thematic purpose: its prominence reflects Marlowe's continuing interest in the act of oath-breaking, which he now considers in a more formal and ceremonial light. In a play that is preoccupied with military spectacle, Marlowe places particular emphasis on the formal decision made by the two kings to negotiate a peaceful alliance rather than waging war. Orcanes asks his followers, 'What, shall we parley with the Christian, / Or cross the stream and meet him in the field?' (1.1.11–12), while Sigismund uses the symbolic device of a sword to offer Orcanes either 'friendly peace or deadly war' (1.2.3). Though to a modern audience their initial meeting may seem drawn out, the dialogue carefully maps the decision that both characters reach to enter into an alliance. By presenting their early discussions in such detail, Marlowe carefully demonstrates that both Orcanes and Sigismund enter this agreement of their own free will and presumably intend to honour the treaty. The portrayal of the decision-making process also confirms that each party will benefit from the contract by not having to fight a costly battle, and that ''tis requisite to parley for a peace' (1.1.50). Since Elizabethan contractual law took the intention of both parties and the benefit each gained from the agreement into account when evaluating the validity of a promise, this passage demonstrates that Sigismund and Orcanes' agreement is contractually binding.

Marlowe then depicts a lengthy exchange of vows between the two allies, as they pledge their commitment to the new treaty:

> SIGISMUND: By him that made the world and saved my soul,
> The son of God and issue of a maid,
> Sweet Jesus Christ, I solemnly protest
> And vow to keep this peace inviolable.
> ORCANES: By sacred Mahomet, the friend of God,
> Whose holy Alcoran remains with us,
> Whose glorious body when he left the world
> Closed in a coffin mounted up the air
> And hung on stately Mecca's temple roof,
> I swear to keep this truce inviolable
> (*Tamburlaine Part Two* 1.2.56–65)

These vows, packed with religious imagery, are explicitly made 'in sight of heaven' (55). Legal terms such as 'swear', 'vow' and 'solemnly' add weight to the assurances, while Sigismund's use of the verb 'protest' indicates an assertion made 'in formal and solemn terms'.[201] The repetition of the final line across vows, especially the term 'inviolable', further highlights the formal nature of the religious and secular promises the rulers exchange. Finally, Marlowe introduces a visual confirmation of their oath: Orcanes announces that 'each shall retain a scroll / As memorable witness of our league' (1.2.67–8). Since the Turkish leader specifies that the scrolls shall be 'signed with our hands' it is likely these were exchanged on stage, their physical presence testifying to the validity of the oath they record.

Despite Marlowe's careful representation of a formal contractual agreement, however, the Hungarian ruler Sigismund breaks his word only two scenes later. By allowing so little time to elapse,

Marlowe emphasises Sigismund's treachery: the initial vows would still be fresh in an audience's mind, and Orcanes even displays his copy of the scroll they have just signed as a visual testament to this Christian king's perjury (2.2.45–6). In fact Sigismund, who is clearly guilty of breaking his pledged word, exemplifies contemporary English fears about oath-breaking dissidents: he is led into perjury by the persuasive rhetoric of the Catholic lords Frederick and Baldwin, and defends his actions with appeals to religious precedent.

Sigismund's advisor Frederick is the first to counsel him to break the alliance, basing his argument on emotive references to past atrocities committed by the Turks:

> FREDERICK: Your majesty remembers, I am sure,
> What cruel slaughter of our Christian bloods
> These heathenish Turks and pagans lately made
> Betwixt the city Zula and Danubius,
> . . .
> It resteth now then that your majesty
> Take all advantages of time and power
> And work revenge upon these infidels.
> (*Tamburlaine Part Two* 2.1.4–13)

Comparable arguments for revenge were used in contemporary religious resistance tracts. The Jesuit Cardinal William Allen similarly emphasised the persecution of Catholic priests in his *True, Sincere, and Modest Defense* (1584), arguing that many have 'been condemned and put to death, either without all law, or else only upon new laws by which matter of religion is made treason'. Allen argues that such persecution provides justification for rebellion, recounting how King John was, 'for persecution of bishops', 'with his whole land interdicted and brought . . . to yield his crown to the courtesy of the Pope's Legate'.[202] Huguenot writers likewise justified rebellion against the French Catholic regime through reference to the atrocities committed during the St Bartholomew's Day Massacre. In *Tamburlaine Part Two*, Frederick's strategy of using past violence to justify present oath-breaking thus implicitly aligns him with post-Reformation Europe's religious dissidents.

Sigismund initially resists Frederick and Baldwin's advice to betray the Turks, warning them to remember 'the league we lately made with King Orcanes, / Confirmed by oath and articles of peace' (2.1.28–9) – though his rather suspect reference to 'profession' may indicate that he is more concerned about his reputation than the sanctity of his pledged word (2.1.32). The Hungarian lords are undismayed, and continue to urge a policy of oath-breaking in the name of religion. Baldwin next employs the standard distinction in resistance literature between true believers and heretics, arguing that

> with such infidels,
> In whom no faith nor true religion rests,
> We are not bound to those accomplishments
> The holy laws of Christendom enjoin.
> (*Tamburlaine Part Two* 2.1.33–6)

He concludes with a distinctly Machiavellian argument:

> But as the faith which they profanely plight
> Is not by necessary policy
> To be esteemed assurance for ourselves,
> So what we vow to them should not infringe
> Our liberty of arms and victory.
> (*Tamburlaine Part Two* 2.1.37–41)[203]

A half-convinced Sigismund hesitates, protesting weakly that 'those infirmities that thus defame / Their faiths, their honours, and their religion, / Should not give us presumption to the like' (2.1.44–6). But Frederick now provides the clinching argument, assuring him that ''tis superstition / To stand so strictly on dispensive faith' (2.1.49–50). His reasoning convinces the wavering Sigismund, who orders a treacherous attack on the Turks in violation of his sworn word.

Baldwin's argument that promises made to a heretic are not binding is worth noting, since it draws upon a central tenet of religious resistance theory. One of Marlowe's probable sources for *The Massacre at Paris,* the anonymous French tract *Contre-Guyse*, explains that from the fifteenth century onwards Catholics were instructed to

> keepe no faith with the enemies of the faith: by which decree, John Hus and Hierome of Prague were condemned to death, and the Cardinall S. Julian was sent as legate into Hungarie, to breake the treatie of peace made with the Turkes.[204]

As this reference to Cardinal Julian's actions in Hungary suggests, the information reported in the *Contre-Guyse* is highly relevant to Marlowe's portrayal of the oath-breaking Hungarian ruler Sigismund. The same argument recurs in various Catholic resistance tracts, which advocate rebellion against Protestant rulers on the grounds that heresy is sufficient to break the bonds of loyalty between a prince and his subjects. William Allen, for instance, asserts that 'when my Kinge or Prince hathe broken with Christe, by whom and for deffence of whose honor he reigneth, that then I may most lawfully breake with him'.[205]

Such claims are comparatively common in post-Reformation resistance writings, and their use in *Tamburlaine* to justify an act of oath-breaking might well have troubled an Elizabethan spectator. These worrying implications are amplified by Frederick's reference to 'dispensive faith' or papal dispensation. In Elizabethan England appeals to papal dispensation were strongly associated with the spectre of Catholic rebellion, since for Catholic radicals the 1570 excommunication of Elizabeth I had effectively promised salvation to her opponents: indeed, a papal announcement of 1580 confirmed that anyone who assassinated Elizabeth with the 'pious intention of doing God service not only does not sin, but gains merit'.[206]

Since Sigismund's advisors use the same arguments as the sixteenth-century polemicists who advocated rebellion against heretical rulers, his decision to break his word to Orcanes and fight the 'heretic' Turks arguably aligns him with the religious rebels of post-Reformation Europe. At the same time, Frederick's assumption that papal dispensation might be taken for granted or confirmed retrospectively is theologically dubious, implicitly undercutting a central tenet of the Catholic resistance theory he and Baldwin ostensibly promote: it is a pragmatic appeal to Sigismund to reject 'superstition' that ultimately wins the day. In fact, the crusading rhetoric he adopts to excuse this treacherous assault upon his ally lacks the stereotypically Catholic elements a reader or spectator might expect:

> Then arm, my lords, and issue suddenly,
> Giving commandment to our general host
> With expedition to assail the pagan,
> And take the victory our God hath given.
> (*Tamburlaine Part Two* 2.1.60–3)

Sigismund's exculpatory reference to God's divine master plan mirrors Tamburlaine's own claim that he persecutes rulers such as Orcanes because he is the scourge of God. The Hungarian king's defence may also have been inspired by an account in John Foxe's Protestant influential martyrology *Actes and Monuments*, in which Foxe describes Sigismund's war against the Turks as an 'occasion offered him, as it were from heaven, to destroy and utterly to roote out . . . that barbarous nation, and cruell enemies to the name and Religion of Christ'.[207] Yet Sigismund's empty allusions to God's will suggest that even the language of divine providence can be exploited by those who wish to justify politically expedient actions, his own reference to a heavenly master plan complementing Tamburlaine's appropriation of the providentialist rhetoric that is so plentiful in English Protestant propaganda.

Sigismund's religiously justified betrayal of Orcanes reflects but also reassesses Elizabethan concerns about politically threatening acts of oath-breaking. Marlowe's Protestant spectators might have been rather relieved to realise that, for Sigismund, oath-breaking at the behest of Catholic advisors leads not to victory but to defeat and a repentant death: unusually, Marlowe crafts a narrative in which divine providence seems to be at work. Sigismund himself reassuringly acknowledges that his defeat is God's 'vengeance from on high / For my accursed and hateful perjury'

(2.3.2–3). Yet the doubts that Marlowe's works often suggest about providential intervention still creep in, with Sigismund's own conclusion contradicted by Orcanes's general: Gazellus famously avers that the link between Sigismund's perjury and his death is coincidental, noting that ''tis but the fortune of the wars . . . Whose power is often proved a miracle' (2.3.31–2). While the role played by chance in warfare was proverbial, the sceptical emphasis that Gazellus introduces is more unusual and more controversial.

FERNEZE'S SPANISH POLICY: OATH-BREAKING IN 'THE JEW OF MALTA'

Even the slight comfort provided by Sigismund's arguably providential death is absent when, in *The Jew of Malta*, Marlowe returns to the theme of political undertakings broken in the name of religion. In this play he dramatises a fictional alliance between the Catholic Knights of St John and the Ottoman Turks led by Selim-Calymath. Though this political treaty is central to the play's plot, it is not ceremonially confirmed on stage; the agreement between the two parties is already an accepted fact at the start of the play, having been sealed ten years earlier. The long durance of the contract might be said to endorse its validity, despite the absence of a staged undertaking, and Marlowe emphasises the status of this alliance through his use of contractual terminology. Thus, in the play's opening scene, the term 'league' is used three times within six lines (1.1.153, 157, 158), while Barabas's own response to the arrival of the Turkish fleet can be read as a coincidental defence of Marlowe's omission: he asks, 'what need they treat of peace that are in league?' (1.1.157).

Having established the existence of a 'league' between the Turks and the Knights, Marlowe then depicts the meeting of the two parties. The occasion for this meeting is Malta's failure to pay the tribute dictated by the original pact to the Sultan. Ferneze and his companions seem uncommitted to the alliance, describing Calymath's claim as 'hard conditions' (1.2.18); Calymath, in contrast, shows clemency by granting Malta a month's respite in which to pay the debt (1.2.25). His leniency helps to establish him as a comparatively honourable character, but is also significant in a legal sense: Elizabethan contractual theory required that each party to an agreement should gain 'consideration' (benefit). The original consideration received by the Knights from their Turkish allies is hidden in the past, but Ferneze's request that Calymath 'consider us' introduces a verbal echo of the legal term; although Calymath initially states that he 'may not, nay . . . dare not dally' in his father's cause (1.2.10–12), he agrees to give the Knights more time to come up with the money. They are only granted an extension of one month, with the limited nature of the benefit implying that the Knights are not equal partners, but there is no suggestion that the contract itself is invalid. The legal terminology used throughout the scene – 'commission' (22), 'grant' (28), 'conditions' (18) – lends the exchange a formal air despite the lack of a directly reciprocal pledge, and establishes the expectation that Ferneze should keep his promise. When the Turkish Bashaw returns in Act 3 to require of Ferneze 'the performance of your promise passed' (3.5.9), his contractual reference to 'performance' continues this theme: under Elizabethan law, the performance of this promise is rightly due.

Ferneze, however, does not keep his pledged word. On the contrary, he completely repudiates Malta's alliance with the Turks, replying that 'Bashaw, in brief, shalt have no tribute here, / Nor shall the heathens live upon our spoil' (3.5.11–12). By refiguring the league between the Turks and the Knights as one between subject and master through his reference to 'tribute' Ferneze seeks to characterise his oath-breaking as an act of principled resistance, concluding that 'honour is bought with blood and not with gold' (2.2.56). However, Ferneze's stance may indirectly cast the Maltese Knights as rebels against their sworn overlords, while his rejection of his previous promises in favour of a military attack on Malta's former allies might even reflect Elizabethan fears about oath-breaking, which was similarly believed to threaten the political and hierarchical security of the English state.

The possible relevance of Ferneze's oath-breaking to Elizabethan concerns is strengthened by his ostensible reasons for breaking the alliance: he excuses his actions in religious terms, describing the Turks as 'heathens' (3.5.12). Barry Kyle's 1987 RSC production emphasised this hypocritical piety, with the oath-breaking Ferneze flanked by two knights on whose white tunics flamboyantly red Christian crosses were clearly visible – the motif recalling the crusader past and Christian status of Marlowe's Knights of St John, an order symbolised by the Maltese cross, while perhaps also invoking the St George cross of England. For Marlowe's original spectators, the dramatic parallels with the situation in contemporary England were far more urgent and immediate. Ferneze's decision is presumably inspired by his conversation with the Spanish vice-admiral Martin Del Bosco, who contrasts the Knights' political alliance with the Turks with their religious duty as Catholic believers: 'Will Knights of Malta be in league with Turks, / And buy it basely too for sums of gold?' (2.2.28–9). According to Del Bosco the Turkish treaty is a betrayal of the Knights' faith and, like Frederick in *Tamburlaine Part Two*, he cites past instances of Turkish violence against Christians to make his point (*Jew of Malta* 2.2.30–3). Rather than side with the 'heathen' Turks, this Spanish commander proposes that the Catholic Knights should instead transfer their loyalty to his master, the Catholic King of Spain (2.2.37–40). Ferneze is soon convinced, and concludes that Bosco shall 'be Malta's general; / We and our warlike knights will follow thee / Against these barbarous misbelieving Turks' (2.2.44–6). His speech demonstrates the extent to which he has absorbed and learned from Del Bosco's seemingly pious arguments; the coming violence is to be justified by reference to Turkish barbarity and sacrilege.

Ferneze, who follows a Spaniard's advice to break a secular promise in the name of religion, may again realise Elizabethan anxieties about the perceived connection between religious dissidence and political disloyalty. The arguments for resistance which Del Bosco puts to Ferneze suggestively mimic those employed by pro-Spanish Catholic polemicists such as William Allen and Robert Parsons, who recounted the sufferings of Elizabethan England's Catholic martyrs in order to incite English subjects to rebellion: William Allen's 1588 call to arms, for instance, reminds his readers that Elizabeth has constrained 'by greate penalties and extreme punishment many thowsand poore christian soules'. In addition, Del Bosco presents the Catholic King of Spain as a potential ally for the Maltese 'rebels' in the same way that polemicists such as Allen cast Philip II as a saviour who planned to invade England for the 'godly purpose of restoringe the Catholike religion'.[208] Indeed, the characters involved in this episode perhaps strengthen these echoes of Spain's 1588 invasion attempt: Del Bosco introduces himself as 'vice-admiral unto the Catholic king' (2.2.7), while the name Ferneze – probably invented by Marlowe – sounds very similar to that of Alessandro Farnese, Duke of Parma: Philip II's general in the Netherlands, and the military architect of the 1588 Armada expedition. It is moreover possible that the role of Ferneze was doubled with that of Machevill during the play's original performances, as it was in the 1987 RSC production. If so, the associations between Catholic rhetoric, Machiavelli's politic advice about oath-breaking and Ferneze's hypocritical repudiation of an alliance that is no longer advantageous converge provocatively: Marlowe's governor may claim to be motivated by religious considerations, but his own musings suggest a greater interest in the acquisition of personal military glory and, significantly, the opportunity to 'keep the gold' the Turks would otherwise claim (2.2.39).

As in *Tamburlaine Part Two*, oath-breaking in *The Jew of Malta* is predominantly associated with Catholic characters and the stereotypically Catholic dictum that 'faith is not to be held with heretics' (2.3.313). However, Ferneze's treacherous actions are, like Sigismund's, somewhat complicated by his subsequent adoption of a providentialist rhetoric potentially reminiscent of Protestant Elizabethan discourse. After betraying his new ally Barabas in the final act of the play, this time breaking a vow formally confirmed onstage (5.2.102–8), Ferneze ostentatiously attributes his dual victory over the Jew Barabas and the Turk Calymath to divine intervention: 'Let due praise be given / Neither to fate nor fortune, but to heaven' (5.5.122–3). The audience, however, remain aware that this victory was in reality secured by the forsworn governor's deceitful trickery; Ferneze takes advantage of Barabas's plan to outmanoeuvre the Turkish invaders, but then betrays his former ally to his death. As in Sigismund's case, Ferneze's suspect appropriation of providential discourse blurs any straightforward confessional alignment between his perjury and an exclusively Catholic agenda; oath-breaking is instead identified as a practice that surpasses denominational boundaries, with the Jew Barabas and his 'Turkish' servant Ithamore equally guilty of breaking their promises and vows in Marlowe's play.

Marlowe's identification of oath-breaking with rebellion seems to have inspired his contemporaries to explore similar themes in their writings. Thus in Shakespeare's *King Henry VI Part 2*, usually dated to 1592, his audiences would have encountered a charged instance of oath-breaking that leads to rebellion:

> SALISBURY: My lord, I have considered with myself
> The title of this most renowned duke,
> And in my conscience do repute his grace
> The rightful heir to England's royal seat.
> KING: Hast thou not sworn allegiance unto me?
> SALISBURY: I have.
> KING: Canst thou dispense with heaven for such an oath?
> SALISBURY: It is great sin to swear unto a sin,
> But greater sin to keep a sinful oath.
> (*Henry VI Part 2* 5.1.175–83)

Since Salisbury is a noble and fairly positive character, the fact that he voices a theory of conditional allegiance comparable to that espoused by sixteenth-century theorists of resistance is distinctly controversial. The episode has a strong affinity with Marlowe's own fictional representations of oath-breaking: Salisbury's explanatory reference to 'conscience' (177) and his appeal to heavenly precedent is reminiscent of Sigismund's rejection of his peace treaty with Orcanes and Aeneas's abandonment of Dido, while the equation between contractual and secular allegiance also evokes Ferneze's repudiation of his Turkish alliance. Indeed, the parallels with Marlowe's work are so strong that some critics believe

Marlowe collaborated with Shakespeare in writing the *Henry VI* plays. The arguments that Marlowe was involved to some extent are suggestive, though far from conclusive.[209] Certainly, Marlowe remained fascinated throughout his literary career by rebellion in the name of religion, creating episodes in which comparatively positive or charismatic characters argue in favour of conscientious resistance. Yet in Marlowe's plays and poems, unlike in *Henry VI*, there is always a nagging suspicion that such claims are nothing more than self-interested and politic posturing, with no foundation of true belief.

CHAPTER FOUR

FROM REBELLION TO REGICIDE

Elizabethan England assumed a close correlation between oath-breaking and treason, especially when those implicated claimed to be motivated by religious considerations. The connection is important for Marlowe's narratives of political treachery. While oath-breakers such as Aeneas, Sigismund and Ferneze are guilty of betraying legal and political alliances, Marlowe also dramatises various acts of outright rebellion by ambitious and discontented subjects; as they assault established authorities and hierarchies, Marlowe's protagonists cite theological precedents and theories of religious resistance almost identical to those invoked by England's Catholic and puritan dissidents. From Tamburlaine, who consciously patterns his actions on Jupiter's deposition of Saturn, to the military campaigns launched by Catholic Guise and Protestant Navarre in *The Massacre at Paris*, Marlowe represents rebellion in the name of religions variously identified as classical, Catholic and Protestant. The vulnerability of religious rhetoric to politic exploitation is self-evident in these episodes; yet, tellingly, such quasi-spiritual military campaigns are not necessarily condemned. Instead, within a literary framework that treats religious fraud as a near-universal phenomenon, overreaching Marlovian rebels such as Tamburlaine remain popular with audiences despite (or even because of) their defiance of existing social and political mores.

TAMBURLAINE'S REBELLION: THE JUPITER MYTH

Marlowe's rebellious protagonist Tamburlaine is a character of deep contradictions. On the one hand spectators encounter a charismatic conqueror whose glorious victories can be interpreted as a patriotic celebration of English military might: Tamburlaine's popularity with his early audiences was such that by the beginning of the seventeenth century English parents were naming their sons after Marlowe's protagonist.[210] From another perspective, however, Marlowe's Tamburlaine is a cruel, power-hungry thief who usurps the thrones of hereditary rulers and arguably closes his eventful career by embracing atheism. Although Marlowe's *Tamburlaine* plays resist any simple moralistic interpretation, a number of early modern spectators evidently recognised the darker implications of the protagonist's behaviour. As Robert Greene's well-known and perhaps envious attack on 'that Atheist Tamburlan' suggests, Marlowe's fellow writers were alert to the character's ambivalent moral stature – and this awareness informed their subsequent re-workings of Marlowe's phenomenally successful drama.[211] Thomas Lodge, for example, borrowed from Tamburlaine's 'scourge of God' discourse and patterned the political insurgent Scilla's rhetoric on Tamburlaine's vaunting speech in his tragedy *The Wounds of Civil War* (1.1.210–23; 4.1.210–11), while the anonymous Elizabethan drama *Selimus* refers directly to Tamburlaine as an usurper of lawful kings and a 'scourge of nations' (l. 1757).[212]

Tamburlaine is again remembered as a rebel against established authorities in George Peele's *The Battle of Alcazar* (*c.* 1588–9). In Peele's play, the treacherous Muly Mahamet cites the precedent set by Marlowe's Tamburlaine as he appeals to his gods to

> Thunder from heaven damne wretched men to death
> Beare all the offices of Saturnes sonnes,
> Be Pluto then in hell and barre the fiends,
> Take Neptunes force to thee and calme the seas,
> And execute Joves justice on the world,
> Convey Tamberlaine into our Affrike here,
> To chastice and to menace lawfull kings
> (*Battle of Alcazar* ll. 217–23)

Muly Mahamet concludes with the grandiloquent (and unfulfilled) prediction that 'Tamberlaine triumph not, for thou must die / As Philip did, Caesar, and Caesars peeres' (ll. 224–5).[213] The usurping

Moor casts Tamburlaine as the executor of 'Joves justice' (l. 221), but the latter's seditious nature is simultaneously apparent: he is the enemy of the rebel, but also the opponent of 'lawfull' kings (l. 223). Two aspects of Muly Mahamet's speech are particularly intriguing. He identifies Tamburlaine as a scourge sent by Jove, and appeals to the mythological precedents set by Pluto, Neptune and Saturn's rebellious sons to exalt his own achievements: the first allusion echoes the 'scourge of God' status claimed by Marlowe's Tamburlaine, while the second mimics Tamburlaine's claims to model his usurping behaviour on that of Saturn's son Jove. Such details suggest that in *The Battle of Alcazar* George Peele was recollecting and imitating the striking manifesto for rebellion that Marlowe's protagonist outlines in *Tamburlaine Part One*, after betraying the Persian king Cosroe and defeating him in battle.

Tamburlaine is initially Cosroe's ally in a joint rebellion against the latter's brother King Mycetes. While Cosroe's victory is still fresh, however, Tamburlaine decides to overthrow the new king and 'win the Persian crown' for himself (2.5.98). Within the space of forty-seven lines Tamburlaine has achieved his goal – but, before his new status has been formally confirmed, the audience witness the defeated and dying Cosroe reproaching 'bloody' Tamburlaine for his treachery (2.7.1). Tamburlaine, required to defend his actions, does so in one of Marlowe's most famous passages, recounting the story of how Saturn's son Jove expelled his own father from the heavenly throne:

> The thirst of reign and sweetness of a crown,
> That caused the eldest son of heavenly Ops
> To thrust his doting father from his chair
> And place himself in the empyreal heaven,
> Moved me to manage arms against thy state.
> What better precedent than mighty Jove?
>
> (*Tamburlaine Part One* 2.7.12–17)

The analogy of Jove's rebellion is sustained for the rest of the scene, with Tamburlaine's generals appealing to the same authority. Usumcasane explains that

For as when Jove did thrust old Saturn down,
Neptune and Dis gained each of them a crown,
So do we hope to reign in Asia,
If Tamburlaine be placed in Persia.
(*Tamburlaine Part One* 2.7.36–9)

Critical interest in Tamburlaine's striking speech has tended to focus on the closing lines, in which Marlowe's protagonist invokes nature's law and celebrates the 'sweet fruition of an earthly crown' (2.7.29). Indeed, the famous 1951 Old Vic production starring Donald Wolfit actually cut Tamburlaine's account of the deposition of Saturn, while the comparatively recent RSC production of 1992, directed by Terry Hands, retained the speech but diminished its impact by excising Usumcasane's elaboration of the classical motif.[214] Scholarly discussion of this passage has similarly minimised its wider implications: thus Lawrence Danson writes that Tamburlaine takes 'a somewhat sordid family quarrel' as the model for his project of world conquest, adding dismissively that 'the picture of Jove throwing his "heavenly" father out of his chair is neither heroic nor pretty'.[215] However, in Elizabethan England the Jupiter myth was not merely a 'sordid family quarrel'; it was a tale of political deposition. Furthermore, it was a myth that might relate to (and potentially challenge) Elizabeth's own cult of political legitimacy. Mycetes, the first royal victim of Tamburlaine's ambitions, is described as a ruler at whose birth 'Cynthia with Saturn joined', an astrological allusion that aligns Elizabeth's iconographical persona Cynthia with the deposed ruler Saturn and the soon-to-be-deposed Mycetes (1.1.13), while a particularly paranoid spectator might even discern a second damaging allusion to Elizabeth I: Marlowe identifies the mythological father of Diana/Cynthia as a usurper at a time when Catholic propaganda was denouncing Elizabeth's father Henry VIII as an anti-papal rebel and usurper of the English Church.[216]

The classical myth of Jupiter's rebellion against and deposition of his father Saturn was well known during the Renaissance. Lengthy versions of the tale appear in a number of sixteenth-century English works, including William Warner's epic *Albions England*:

> Saturne with his armed troupes into Arcadia went,
> Where Jupiter, forewarned of his fathers ill intent,
> Intreated peace, to him denide: so that perforce he must
> Defend him from his froward Sier, or rather foe unjust.
> There might yee see king Saturne fight like to a Lion wood,
> Whilst Jupiter did beare his blowes, and spares his fathers
> blood:
> And him that foo-like would him sley, he friendlie did
> defend,
> Desiring Saturne to retire, till wordes were to no end.[217]

Warner, who was reportedly a friend of Marlowe's, provides a conventional Elizabethan account of Jupiter's rebellion. According to the standard tradition Jupiter did not actively rebel against his father Saturn, but fought back when forced to protect himself from 'his froward Sier, or rather foe unjust'. Warner's account emphasises Jupiter's reluctance to attack Saturn even in self-defence: his Jupiter 'did beare his blowes, and spares his fathers blood . . . desiring Saturne to retire'. Similar depictions of Saturn as the villainous aggressor are common to most sixteenth-century versions of this myth, and the tradition continued into the seventeenth century. In his classical drama *The Golden Age*, for example, the dramatist Thomas Heywood depicts Saturn as an oath-breaking usurper who launches a pre-emptive strike against Jupiter when his son has just rescued him from the avenging Titans (1.1; 3.1); the narrator Homer emphasises that Saturn initiated the attack and Jupiter 'alone his life defended' (4.1). Intriguingly Heywood, who helped to revive *The Jew of Malta* in 1633, was apparently remembering Marlowe's *Tamburlaine* as he wrote this passage: just three lines after Saturn claims that 'the Gods say he must dy' to excuse a treacherous attack on his own son (3.1), Homer discusses 'the appetite of rule, and thirst of raigne' in an echo of Tamburlaine's famous reference to the 'thirst of reign and sweetness of a crown' (*Golden Age* 4.1; *Tamburlaine Part One* 2.7.12).[218]

Despite these parallels with Heywood's play, however, Tamburlaine's account of Saturn's deposition does not subscribe to the Elizabethan conventions. According to Marlowe's protagonist it was Jove who instigated the conflict, seduced by his ambitious thirst for a crown, and there is no indication that Saturn has threatened Jove. In Tamburlaine's version, he is a 'doting' father: the word 'doting' denotes foolishness or imbecility, possibly hinting at misplaced affection, and Saturn's credibility as a threat to his son is significantly reduced.[219] Marlowe's alterations undercut the tradition that Jove acted in self-defence in order to provide Tamburlaine with a heavenly precedent for his own ambitions. Moreover, since most educated spectators would presumably recognise the discrepancy between the standard sixteenth-century version and Marlowe's account of Jove's actions, the implication is that Tamburlaine's religious justification for rebellion is based upon a consciously manipulated narrative which he alters to suit the rhetorical purposes of the moment.

As a rebel citing dubious divine precedents to justify political treachery, Tamburlaine echoes the religious resistance propagandists who threatened the security of Elizabeth's Protestant regime, often constructing theological and scriptural models for rebellion in the same way that Tamburlaine exploits the mythological example set by Jupiter's rebellion. In a 1587 tract advising Catholics to oppose England's anti-Spanish campaign in the Netherlands, for instance, the Jesuit Cardinal William Allen describes how the biblical ruler Saul was deposed for impiety, arguing that 'after King Saul was by God, and the Prophets sentence, as it were, excommunicated, and deposed, it was no fault for David, or others, either of the Priestes, or people, to revolt from him'.[220] The following year Allen, urging English Catholics to rise up against the 'heretike' queen Elizabeth, returned to the precedent of Saul's deposition:

> For aspiringe to spirituall function, and other disobedience, was by Gods apointment and sentence pronounced

> against him, by the said Samuell deposed of his kingdome, and an other named David anointed by him in the lyfe of the said Saule.

In Allen's tract, scriptural episodes in which priests depose impious and tyrannical kings are used to argue that English Catholics should oppose the excommunicated Elizabeth I.[221] At the same time, these precedents were also being used at the other end of the spectrum by theorists of Protestant resistance. Théodore de Bèze, for example, argued in the *Droit des Magistrats* that since 'it was lawful for David to defend himself against Saul's tyranny', so it is lawful for the French Protestants known as Huguenots to resist the irreligious demands of their Catholic rulers.[222] Finally, Elizabethan clerics interpreted the same biblical analogy from yet another perspective, preaching that David's non-violent resistance to Saul proved that active rebellion against an anointed monarch was sinful.[223] Indeed, any sixteenth-century reader aware of these multiple appropriations of the same theological model might well have experienced the same cross-confessional scepticism that Marlowe's literary representation of rebellion in the name of religion exhibits.

While Allen and Bèze rely on the Christian Bible rather than the Greco-Roman mythologies favoured by Tamburlaine, these sixteenth-century theorists of resistance share with Marlowe's protagonist the tactic of using past religious precedents to excuse a present act of rebellion. In his reliance on the Jupiter myth as a legitimising device, Marlowe's protagonist potentially joins the ranks of the Elizabethan dissidents: as C.L. Barber once observed, it is not such a long way from Tamburlaine to religious rebels such as the Anabaptist John Leyden. Indeed, in Samuel Rowlands' 1605 verse history the 'insolent proude' rebel Leyden even actively models himself on Tamburlaine:

> Have you not heard that Scythian Tamberlaine
> Was earst a Sheepheard ere he play'd the King?
> First over Cattell hee began his raigne,
> Then Countries in subjection hee did bring:

> And Fortunes favours so mayntain'd his side,
> Kings were his Coach-horse, when he pleas'd to ride. [224]

It is possible that the same analogy was also noted by Marlowe's sometime collaborator Thomas Nashe, who gives John Leyden and his fellow rebels a cameo role in *The Unfortunate Traveller* (1593). In Nashe's prose account, however, the glamour of rebellion vanishes; the reader instead encounters a set of heavily satirised 'devout Asses' whose bloody defeat is interpreted by the conservatively hostile narrator as a divine judgement on their seditious behaviour.[225]

Nashe's cautionary tale mocks the futility of Leyden's revolt, but the threat of puritan dissidence was a real concern for the Elizabethan authorities. In this context Tamburlaine's claim to be a 'scourge of God' whose progress is divinely ordained is also potentially problematic, since his providential language is reminiscent of that found in sixteenth-century Protestant propaganda. While Catholic theologians also alluded to divine providence, the historical Tamburlaine or Timur is directly identified as a scourge sent by God in some of the most influential texts of English Protestantism. In his *Actes and Monuments*, for instance, John Foxe describes how Tamburlaine was sent by 'the providence of God' to preserve the Christian city of Constantinople from Turkish conquest. English Protestants such as George Whetstone and Thomas Fortescue followed Foxe's lead, identifying Tamburlaine as a scourge sent by God 'to chastise these Princes, these proud and wicked nations'.[226] Since the same providentialist works and their theories of divine intervention were also central to Elizabeth's own image-making, Tamburlaine's appropriation of 'scourge of God' status in Marlowe's drama arguably invites scepticism about the providential rhetoric used by English Protestant propagandists.

In the providential treatises penned by Foxe and Whetstone Tamburlaine's scourge of God status is announced by the narrator, and Fortescue's account affirms that 'all such cruel and incarnate devils, are instruments wherwith God chastiseth sin'.[227] In Marlowe's *Tamburlaine* plays, however, the protagonist's claims are never upheld by external authority or supported by indications of divine presence. As a number of critics including Paul Whitfield White have suggested, it seems that Tamburlaine may in fact have consciously adopted the identity of a divine scourge to 'give a higher aura of authority' to his political and military actions: certainly, as Daniel Vitkus ironically comments, it is remarkable how often those 'heaven abhors' 'just happen' to be the same characters who impede Tamburlaine's personal ambitions (*Tamburlaine Part Two* 4.1.148).[228] Tamburlaine's linguistic construction of his claim is also somewhat suspect. In *Part One* he presents God's role as a verbal rather than literal contribution, describing himself as 'I, that am termed the scourge and wrath of God' (3.3.44); 'termed' is a particularly elusive verb to use – potentially a synonym for 'designate' or 'affirm', words that imply an identity has been adopted.[229] Such uncertainties persist in *Tamburlaine Part Two*. Tamburlaine, defending his brutal decision to execute his own son, argues that

> since I exercise a greater name,
> The scourge of God and terror of the world,
> I must apply myself to fit those terms
> In war, in blood, in death, in cruelty,
> And plague such peasants as resist in me
> The power of heaven's eternal majesty.
> (*Tamburlaine Part Two* 4.1.152–7)

Yet the verb 'exercise' and noun 'name' may suggest that this is a role Tamburlaine has adopted, rather than a religious duty: to 'exercise' suggests external usage of the 'name' of scourge, but not an internalisation of the reality. Likewise, the term 'apply' suggests an action that must be consciously performed. Whereas a true scourge might be expected to act automatically, guided by God, Tamburlaine must apply himself and study to fit the role.

Such hints that Tamburlaine has hypocritically assumed the 'scourge of God' role to further his own interests render potential parallels with the providential discourse of Elizabeth's Protestant regime especially challenging. When Marlowe's *Tamburlaine* plays first appeared on the London stage in 1586 and 1587, however, Protestant England's most immediate and urgent concern was the threat of imminent Catholic rebellion; Tamburlaine's seditious and hypocritical exploitation of religious rhetoric might well speak to such fears. Especially during the years immediately preceding Spain's 1588 invasion attempt, propagandists openly encouraged English Catholics to revolt against their Protestant monarch: William Allen's *Admonition*, for instance, urged Catholic believers in England 'to pursue the actuall deprivation, of Elizabethe the pretensed Queene' and, on pain of excommunication, 'joine to the said [Spanish] army, with all the powers and aydes they can make'.[230] There was widespread anxiety among Elizabeth's Protestant subjects that such appeals might succeed; though the Armada ultimately came to grief, in 1587 England's queen had good reason to be worried. Against this background, the *Tamburlaine* plays provocatively staged scenes of rebellion against anointed monarchs – while their charismatic and unstoppable protagonist voiced fraudulent religious justifications for his seditious behaviour.

'REBEL CAESAR': RELIGIOUS RESISTANCE AND 'LUCAN'S FIRST BOOK'

In *Tamburlaine Part One* the protagonist's appropriation of a mythological precedent for rebellion is complemented by the way he models his military achievements on those of the Roman rebel Julius Caesar. When challenging the Turkish emperor Bajazeth, for instance, Tamburlaine identifies his army with 'Julius Caesar's host / That never fought but had the victory', and adds that 'nor in Pharsalia was there such hot war / As these my followers willingly would have' (*Tamburlaine Part One* 3.3.152–5). Since Julius Caesar was frequently used to figure monarchical values in early modern literature, Tamburlaine's reference to Caesar's forces complements his new iconographical self-presentation as the reigning King of Persia. However, the comparison may in addition hark back to Tamburlaine's earlier Jupiter-myth rhetoric of rebellion, since references to Caesar also featured prominently in Reformation and Counter-Reformation resistance literature.

Sixteenth-century proponents of religious resistance frequently cited the biblical judgement that 'whosoever do give to Caesar that which is due to God . . . directly do repine against God's ordinance'.[231] In the Huguenot tract *Vindiciae Contra Tyrannos*, for example, it is argued that 'the people follows impious commands . . . by failing to withhold from Caesar those things which are properly God's'. Caesar is subsequently described as a 'tyrant without title' as part of the anonymous author's attack upon the French Valois monarchy and in particular the regime's Catholic councillors.[232] In fact, the Roman Caesars were readily associated with Catholicism in the eyes of early modern Elizabethans. Popes frequently choose classicising names – Pope Julius II adopted his title in conscious reference to Julius Caesar – and emphasised continuity between ancient Rome and papal Rome, while negative depictions of the Caesars and the papacy overlapped in hostile early modern English writings.[233] In addition, and intriguingly for Marlowe's *Massacre at Paris*, the Catholic League leader Guise was often referred to in French pamphlet literature as 'Caesar', a term that might imply either celebration of military prowess or condemnation of Catholic tyranny, or both.[234] Caesar's frequent invocation in the context of civil disobedience and religious resistance is potentially relevant to the Caesar-like Tamburlaine's mythological rhetoric of rebellion, and may also have influenced Marlowe's charcterisation of Julius Caesar in his partial translation of Lucan's *De Bello Civili* (sometimes alternatively called *Pharsalia*).

Even in its original Latin form, Lucan's epic had significant political implications for an Elizabethan reader. Following the example of the much admired Cicero, many early modern readers were fiercely hostile towards Julius Caesar: 'rebel Caesar', as Sir Philip Sidney terms him in *An Apology for Poetry*.[235] These readers would presumably respond to the ironic tone of Lucan's epic, in which Caesar's divine aspirations are consistently mocked and undercut by the sceptical narrator: as the critic John Henderson observes, Lucan's Caesar is 'the ultimate extreme of success-as-futility', a warlord whose cult of aggression leads to a logical end in suicidal implosion.[236] Marlowe, whose own protagonists are restlessly self-driven ever onwards – Tamburlaine, echoing Alexander the Great, weeps for the lands unconquered at his death (*Tamburlaine Part Two* 5.3.150, 158) – no doubt recognised the satiric trend of Lucan's narrative; but his Caesar remains ambivalent, both hypocritical rebel and glamorously charismatic leader.

Edward Paleit perceptively suggests that Marlowe was as much attracted as he was repulsed by Lucan's representation of 'rebel Caesar'. If so, he was far from unique among Elizabethan readers.[237] During the sixteenth century *De Bello Civili* was particularly intriguing to those who considered that Lucan had made a strong case for armed resistance against a tyrannical ruler: the epic is cited approvingly by the Huguenot resistance theorist Théodore de Bèze in *Du Droit des Magistrats*, while in the *Vindiciae Contra Tyrannos* Caesar's campaign is refigured in relation to Huguenot resistance theory.[238] Such Protestant associations were recognised by a number of Lucan's seventeenth-century adaptors. Sir Arthur Gorges's 1614 translation of *De Bello Civili* regularly draws comparisons between Lucan's epic and recent English exploits: for instance, Gorges's rendering of Lucan's Book Two alludes to the English participation in the siege of Antwerp, an episode that Marlowe also refers to in his *Doctor Faustus*.[239] Possibly influenced by Gorges's version or even Marlowe's translation, the seventeenth-century poet Agrippa d'Aubigné interpreted Caesar's rhetoric along comparable politico-religious lines in his fictional account of the French Wars of Religion, *Les Tragiques* (1616): modelled on Lucan's epic, this militantly Protestant poem celebrates opposition to a religiously and politically corrupt Rome and praises England's Queen Elizabeth I as a martyr for the universal Protestant cause.[240] As David Norbrook notes, however, Protestant fears of an international Catholic conspiracy equally coloured the environment in which the first English translations of Lucan were produced: Lucan's rebels, who seek 'neither spoil nor kingdom . . . But Rome at thraldom's feet to rid from tyrants' (ll. 351–2), might easily recall the dissident Catholics and puritans who threatened the security of the Elizabethan regime.[241] Certainly, the English authorities recognised in Lucan's epic a manifesto for treason: in the aftermath of the Earl of Essex's abortive 1601 rebellion, accusations that Essex's supporters had cast the Earl as Caesar and cited *De Bello Civili* to justify their armed revolt featured prominently in the case for the prosecution.[242]

Christopher Marlowe's translation of Lucan's Book One, completed several years before Essex's uprising and published in 1600, exploits the epic's multiple contemporary associations with resistance in the name of religion, international Catholic conspiracy and treason. *Lucan's First Book* was the first successful English adaptation of *De Bello Civili*, and despite a few trifling errors compares favourably with the near-contemporary versions by Gorges and Thomas May (1626);[243] the care and attention that Marlowe lavished on his translation suggest that he, like his contemporaries, took Lucan very seriously. This interest was predominantly political: Lucan's subject – civil war – would have resonated strongly with Marlowe and his contemporaries during a decade that saw the execution of Mary Stuart, the launch of the Spanish Armada and increasing anxiety about the English succession. In early modern England, however, such political anxieties were inextricably associated with the threat of religious resistance. Produced against a background of contemporary paranoia about rebellion in the name of religion, Marlowe's translation is especially alert to the inter-confessional character of the violence Lucan portrays. Indeed, *Lucan's First Book* seems actively to advertise the parallels between Caesar's rebellious advance on Rome and English fears of Catholic and puritan insurgency: when Lucan's narrator discusses the origin of Rome's divisions, Marlowe wryly replaces the original reference to the city's '*asylum*' with the line 'one poor church set them at odds' (l. 97) – an inaccurate and anachronistic, but highly suggestive, revision.[244]

In translating Book One of *De Bello Civili*, Marlowe created a poem that spoke directly to early modern fears of religious resistance. *Lucan's First Book* begins by suggesting that civil war is a threat to imperialist expansionism (ll. 13–14). While England's ambitions to seize territory in the New World were a major factor in initiating the Anglo-Spanish war, in Marlowe's translation his Elizabethan readers would have encountered the following advice about the quest for empire:

> Rome, if thou take delight in impious war,
> First conquer all the earth, then turn thy force
> Against thyself: as yet thou wants not foes.
>
> (*Lucan's First Book* ll. 21–3)

Marlowe's specific use of 'impious' to describe Rome's wars is especially intriguing. Since Lucan's text describes war as '*nefandus*', which can be alternatively rendered as 'abominable', 'unlawful' or 'not to be spoken of', Marlowe's choice of the term 'impious' is potentially telling within an early modern context of religiously inspired civil strife.

Marlowe's rendering of Lucan's sharply demystificatory epic expresses consistent scepticism about the appropriation of religious rhetoric in a political arena. Like the protagonist of *Tamburlaine Part One*, Caesar as depicted in *Lucan's First Book* is not an established ruler but a traitor invading his native land at the head of an army. He frames his seditious campaign with appeals to the gods, including the 'thunderer' Jove and the 'gods of Phrygia and Iulus' line' (ll. 197–9). The latter reference, recalling Caesar's claim to descend from Rome's mythical founder Aeneas, also hints at a possible dynastic argument comparable to those featured in sixteenth-century resistance literature: in the same way that Catholic tracts designated Elizabeth I an illegitimate 'usurper' and French polemicists debated the right of Huguenot and Catholic candidates to inherit the throne, Caesar's religiously inflected allusion to his royal ancestry connects dynastic arguments with the theologically inflected discourse of religious resistance.

Lucan's Caesar is an expert at manipulating rhetoric to his personal advantage, while Marlowe's version of the character can be even more hypocritical in his appropriation of religious discourse. For instance, Caesar characterises the advance on Rome as a patriotic and quasi-divine duty, even though this campaign is in reality a treacherous assault on his homeland that violates his previous vows and 'covenants':

> As soon as Caesar got unto the bank
> And bounds of Italy, 'Here, here,' saith he,
> 'An end of peace; here end polluted laws;
> Hence, leagues and covenants; Fortune, thee I follow,
> War and the Destinies shall try my cause.'
>
> (*Lucan's First Book* ll. 225–9)

Caesar, like other Marlovian oath-breakers including his purported ancestor Aeneas, seeks a religious excuse for abandoning his former promises: by describing Rome's laws as 'polluted' (l. 227), he implicitly passes theological judgement upon the rulers who administer these laws. The discourse of pollution is apparently Marlowe's own – Lucan's term '*temero*' translates more directly as 'dishonoured', although 'defiled' is another possible synonym that may have inspired Marlowe – and might recall the sixteenth-century accusations of 'pollution' exchanged by rival confessional parties.[245]

As the narrative progresses, Marlowe's Caesar proves remarkably adept at reshaping existing events to his own advantage. Even the reproachful figure of the distressed deity Patria ('Rome' in Marlowe's translation), who materialises to bar Caesar's advance towards Rome, cannot throw this rebel off his stride for long; he convinces his followers that her appearance is an omen of victory and argues rather sophistically that the goddess should and will 'aid mine enterprise' since 'he afflicts Rome that made me Rome's foe' (ll. 202, 205). Moreover, Marlowe's translation sometimes actually augments Caesar's skill in introducing politic religious allusions. As his army marches towards Rome, for instance, Marlowe's Caesar assures his men that 'the gods are with us' as they oppose the established 'tyrants' of this polluted city (ll. 350, 352): in the Latin original, Caesar instead states that 'nor will the favour of Heaven fail us'; a much less emphatic and active proclamation of divine support (*Civil War* 1. 349). As these arguments for invasion indicate, Caesar uses religious rhetoric to justify his actions in a way that suggestively recalls the sixteenth-century context of religious resistance. In fact, Caesar's actions might even provide a model for the Spanish king Philip II's campaign against England; as in this 1589 pamphlet, in which the precedent of Caesar's ancient victory becomes an omen of future Spanish success:

> You may reade, how the expedition that Julius Ceaser made into England . . . for that they had aydid the frenche, when he made war against them: came at the first to no effect, yet were those Britaines no whit the more assured of securitie, for the yeare following he returned againe, and gat the victorie.[246]

THE EXCOMMUNICATION OF EDWARD II: MORTIMER'S REVOLT

In *Tamburlaine* and *Lucan's First Book* the discourse of religious resistance is at least ostensibly pagan: Tamburlaine looks to Jupiter and Saturn for divine precedents, while Caesar invokes Fortune and the Roman pantheon. In *Edward II*, on the other hand, Marlowe demonstrates that religious premises which are explicitly Christian can also provide an excuse for rebellion against an anointed monarch. In fact, *Edward II* associates Catholic resistance rhetoric with open insurgency against an English ruler in a manner that potentially recalls the circumstances of Elizabeth's 1570 excommunication, perhaps in response to the urgent anxieties about treason and political allegiance which the play's original spectators would have experienced in the 1590s.

The correspondences between Marlowe's *Edward II* and the politico-religious situation in Elizabethan England are apparent from the play's opening moments, augmented by Marlowe's departures from the historical facts of Edward's reign. Towards the end of the first scene, for instance, King Edward and his lover Gaveston physically attack the Catholic bishop of Coventry in an act of revenge against the priest responsible for the latter's recent exile (1.177–8). The religious rites of baptism and ordination are parodied in their iconoclastic assault: Edward instructs Gaveston to 'christen' the bishop 'in the channel' (1.187); Gaveston mocks the Catholic practice of granting pardons for sins (1.185); and the bishop's ceremonial vestments are 'rent and torn' (2.35). Such violence, specifically directed against the symbols of Coventry's status as a Catholic prelate, invites comparison with the iconoclastic zeal of the sixteenth-century puritans: Martin Marprelate's virulent attacks on the 'ungodly pomp' of the Elizabethan bishops had been published only a year or so previously.[247] Marlowe's Edward II also (ahistorically) instructs his soldiers to confiscate the bishop's 'house' (1.202), a move that evokes both the Henrician Dissolution of the Monasteries and Ferneze's seizure of Barabas's house in *The Jew of Malta*. Edward and Gaveston also excuse their appropriation of church goods in ostensibly spiritual terms when Gaveston asks, 'What should a priest do with so fair a house?', and adds that 'a prison may beseem his holiness' (1.205–6). But, while his hypocrisy is evident, it is likely that at least some of Marlowe's original Protestant spectators might have approved of Gaveston's violent treatment of the Catholic bishop and antagonism towards the papal 'See of Hell' (1.190).

Unlike the early modern chronicle histories, Marlowe's play directly links baronial resistance to King Edward with this assault on the Bishop of Coventry. Although the rebel barons' motives are essentially secular, Edward's persecution of the bishop provides an ostensible justification for their seditious behaviour. Hearing of the attack, the ambitious Lancaster quickly recognises an opportunity for open resistance to his king; as the Archbishop of Canterbury prepares a report of the episode for the papal legate in the next scene, Lancaster enters to demand whether Canterbury will now take arms against Edward (2.39). At first Canterbury avoids committing himself, responding with a pious question: 'What need I? God himself is up in arms / When violence is offered to the Church' (2.40–1). When the lords continue to urge military action, he cautiously advises Mortimer to 'but yet lift not your swords against the King' (2.61). While on the surface his response exemplifies the reasonable attitude of a peaceful clergyman, waiting patiently for divine guidance, the ambiguity of the adverb is intriguing – is Canterbury counselling Mortimer not to oppose the king despite provocation (yet still), or is he simply advising that this opposition should be postponed (not yet)? At this point Marlowe maintains a careful balance between the two possibilities. Canterbury's true meaning is however revealed just two scenes later.

By the end of the fourth scene Edward's opponents, reinforced by Canterbury's promotion to papal legate, abandon subtlety. The rebel leader Mortimer is the first to unleash the spectre of religious resistance: demanding that Edward banish Gaveston, he openly urges Canterbury to 'curse him if he refuse, and then may we / Depose him and elect another king' (4.54–5). Canterbury, nothing loath, now formally threatens Edward II with excommunication:

> Remember how the Bishop was abused;
> Either banish him that was the cause thereof,
> Or I will presently discharge these lords
> Of duty and allegiance due to thee.
>
> (*Edward II* 4.59–62)

Marlowe's king responds angrily, but to no avail. Assuming that papal excommunication equals deposition, Edward eventually accepts that he must either banish Gaveston or lose his crown: 'The legate of the Pope will have it so, / And thou must hence, or I shall be deposed' (4.109–10).

This episode is strongly evocative of the Elizabethan context in which Marlowe's play was written and performed. In particular, the triple repetition of the phrase 'legate of the Pope' in this scene emphasises the Catholic nature of Canterbury and Mortimer's threats and potentially recalls Elizabeth I's own excommunicate status (4.51, 64, 109). Proclaimed at the request of England's rebellious Northern Earls in 1570 and reiterated in time for the Armada invasion of 1588, Elizabeth's excommunication was attributed by some Catholic writers to her persecution of the clergy – a sin of commission that England's queen shares with Marlowe's Edward II. Yet in Marlowe's play the barons who accuse Edward of oppressing the English clergy prove as self-seeking and politic as the brutally anti-clerical Gaveston. Though Lancaster enters loudly bemoaning the way that Edward and Gaveston 'tyrannise upon the Church', the Mortimers are unconvinced by his pious rhetoric and inquire further into the true cause of his discontent – which is soon revealed to be his material jealousy of Gaveston (2.3–11).

Although England weathered both the Northern Rebellion and the Spanish Armada, fears of Catholic invasion and internal treachery remained intense throughout the 1590s. When the nobles of *Edward II* request a papal excommunication to endorse their uprising, an anxious English Protestant audience might easily have been reminded of the contemporary Catholic threat, particularly since Mortimer proceeds to adopt another rhetorical register associated with resistance literature. As the rebel baron besieges the English king, he subtly likens his present campaign to the religious crusades of the Christian past:

> This tattered ensign of my ancestors,
> Which swept the desert shore of that dead sea
> Whereof we got the name of Mortimer,
> Will I advance upon these castle walls.
>
> (*Edward II* 7.21–4)

Mortimer's reference to past crusades may mimic early modern Catholic propaganda: polemicists sometimes represented Philip II's campaign to invade England as a religious crusade against the heretical Protestants, denouncing Elizabeth and her councillors as 'Turkes'.[248] Moreover, Mortimer's words indicate that he may have carried a 'tattered ensign' onstage, hinting at a visual reinforcement of the parallels between his fictional campaign and the Northern Rebellion of 1569; during the latter revolt, the English rebels bore the traditional crusade emblem of 'a crosse with a banner of the five wounds' to demonstrate their loyalty to 'the old Romish religion'.[249]

In Marlowe's play, Edward II initially defies the threat of excommunication with proto-Protestant rancour:

> Why should a king be subject to a priest?
> Proud Rome, that hatchest such imperial grooms,
> For these thy superstitious taper-lights,
> Wherewith thy antichristian churches blaze,
> I'll fire thy crazèd buildings and enforce
> The papal towers to kiss the lowly ground
> (*Edward II* 4.96–101)

This attack on the Catholic clergy would presumably appeal to sixteenth-century Protestant and puritan spectators. However, the iconoclastic threats of church reform are ineffectual and, when Lancaster and Mortimer enter into an alliance with the Catholic Archbishop, Edward faces a humiliating challenge to his royal authority. Even the fleeting victories he achieves are belittled by his opponents: for instance, the captured rebel Warwick proudly declares that, 'tyrant, I scorn thy threats and menaces; / 'Tis but temporal that thou canst inflict' (13.21–2). By distinguishing between Edward's earthly power and the implied spiritual authority of his Catholic opponents, Warwick undermines the king's declared intent to reduce the power of the clergy; his uncompromising separation of the secular from the spiritual also arguably echoes the arguments of England's Catholic martyrs, who denied the state's authority in matters of faith.

By the end of Marlowe's tragedy Edward loses even his temporal power, being defeated in battle by Mortimer, his adulterous wife Queen Isabella and their French army. The triumph achieved by Edward's opponents, who ally themselves with Catholic bishops and are supported by a foreign invasion force, might have resonated ominously in Elizabethan England. While Edward's deposition was historical fact, the emphasis placed on his opponents' resistance rhetoric is Marlowe's innovation – perhaps even an alteration inspired by contemporary polemic. Analogies between Edward II's reign and the religious politics of the sixteenth century had been noted as early as 1556 by English Protestant exiles writing against Mary I: John Ponet, for example, defended opposition to tyrannical kings as 'just and consonaunt to Goddes judgement' and cited in evidence the example of Edward II, who was deprived of his throne 'bicause without lawe he killed his subjectes, spoiled them of their goodes, and wasted the treasure of the Realme'.[250] After Mary's death and Elizabeth's accession, the same precedent of Edward's deposition was eagerly claimed by Catholic polemicists. Thus in 1592, the year in which Marlowe's play was first performed, the Jesuit Robert Parsons compared Elizabeth's Protestant councillors to Edward's self-seeking favourites 'pierse of Gauerston, and the Spencers', and warned Elizabeth

> not to suffer her self to be caried away, or to be made a pray to one mans ambition only, who will not be able to remedy the calamities, that now he soweth, but will leave them all on his Princes backe . . . as the pittifull examples of King Jhon, King Edward the second . . . and others driven into miseries by such evill Councellours do wel declare.[251]

REBELS AND TRAITORS IN 'THE MASSACRE AT PARIS': FROM GUISE TO NAVARRE

The nightmare of rebellion in the name of religion again haunts Marlowe's *The Massacre at Paris*, a 'history' play in which the real-life occurrences dramatised are shockingly recent. The last event it depicts, the murder of Henry III, took place just four years before Marlowe's death in 1593, and this direct engagement with recent political affairs was almost unprecedentedly daring. Although the play seems to have slipped through the censor's net, perhaps by virtue of its aggressively (and ultimately self-subverting) patriotic tone, state censorship subsequently discouraged the staging of such potentially inflammatory material; as Park Honan notes, Marlowe risked offending the Revels Office even as he intrigued and titillated his audiences.[252] In these circumstances, it is especially striking that the *Massacre* depicts – and gives the starring role of charismatic Marlovian overreacher to – one of Elizabeth I's most feared enemies: the Catholic League leader, the Duke of Guise.

Guise was implicated in several plots against Elizabeth during the 1580s, including the 1581 D'Aubigny conspiracy in Scotland and the Spanish-funded Throckmorten plot to land a Guizean army in Sussex. Though Guise's motivation was probably more dynastic than religious, at least until his niece Mary Stuart's death in 1587, he was consistently denounced by contemporary writers as an inflexible and ruthless opponent of English Protestantism. In *The English Myrror*, for instance, George Whetstone places the blame for the French civil-war violence against the Huguenots firmly upon Guizean shoulders, following a convention that dated back to the 1560s; in Whetstone's analysis, which draws on common anti-Catholic tropes, the Cardinal and Duke of Guise were motivated not by genuine religious zeal but the desire for revenge against their personal enemy, Admiral Coligny. An anonymous French pamphlet of 1589, *The Contre-Guyse*, similarly accuses the Guises of inciting the St Bartholomew's Day Massacre to 'feede the warre that was hatched in their fathers and unckles ambition', adding that 'to colour their warres they have propounded . . . the rooting out of heresie'.[253] In these accounts the Duke of Guise's animosity towards Protestants is neither pious nor disinterested, but instead akin to that of the Marlovian protagonist whose 'policy hath fram'd religion' (2.62).

When *The Massacre at Paris* was first performed in 1593, barely a decade had passed since the real Duke of Guise had attempted to invade England and overthrow Elizabeth I. In Marlowe's play Guise is initially content to win the king with his words (2.70), but his early soliloquies also reveal his secret ambition to usurp the French throne: 'Then, Guise, since thou hast all the cards within thy hands / To shuffle or cut, take this as surest thing: / That, right or wrong, thou deal thyself a king' (2.85–7). The flippancy of the card-game metaphor demonstrates that Marlowe's Duke sees the crown as a prize to be seized by a skilled competitor, and also plays upon Guise's real-life reputation: the *Contre-Guyse* critiques the resistance theory of royal election, which used contractual theories of monarchy to suggest that subjects might have a say in appointing their ruler, and denounces the ambition of 'these Guizians' to make the 'realme' 'elective'.[254] The discourse of election is indeed often associated with sedition in Elizabethan drama: Marlowe's rebellious baron Mortimer similarly plots to replace Edward II with a 'new-elected king' (*Edward II* 20.78), while in the anonymous drama *Selimus* the atheist protagonist plans to 'deale about' and 'shuffle out my selfe a king' (ll. 1539–44).[255]

In *The Massacre at Paris* Marlowe's Guise habitually uses religious rhetoric to shape his political ambitions, secure in the knowledge that 'what he doth the Pope will ratify' (1.39). As a beneficiary of papal 'largess', he also enjoys the more concrete benefits of a 'religious' campaign:

> For this, have I a largess from the Pope,
> A pension and a dispensation too;
> And by that privilege to work upon,
> My policy hath fram'd religion.
>
> (*Massacre at Paris* 2.59–62)

Marlowe's Guise, cataloguing the rewards of piety on the early modern stage, might well have reminded early modern Elizabethan spectators of the much-feared Catholic and puritan dissidents. The same textual and ideological networks nourished French and English Catholic resistance during this period, and Marlowe's Guise openly celebrates his role in promoting such insurgency. Guise notes in particular his involvement with the Douai-Rheims seminary, a Catholic college which was notorious in England as the training-ground of the Jesuit missionaries who secretly infiltrated the realm. Marlowe describes these missionaries as a 'sort of English priests' drawn by Guise to Rheims 'to hatch forth treason 'gainst their natural queen', and stresses Guise's personal role in promoting these conspiracies (21.100–2): his eloquent protagonist is a mentor to the Catholic priests so feared and hated by Elizabethan Protestants.

Although Guise's Catholic rhetoric is hardly heartfelt, he subsequently fulfils the seditious promise of these early scenes by rebelling against his former ally Anjoy, the new king of France. However, Marlowe's *Massacre at Paris* unexpectedly downplays Guise's revolt by condensing the violent events of May 1588 into one spoken challenge; perhaps, as Julia Briggs suggests, Marlowe had misgivings about presenting a full-scale Catholic revolution on the public stage.[256] Nonetheless, Marlowe's protagonist still launches a direct attack upon Henry III's royal authority, as the new king's response indicates:

> Guise, wear our crown, and be thou King of France,
> And as dictator make or war or peace
> Whilst I cry *placet* like a senator!
> I cannot brook thy haughty insolence
>
> (*Massacre at Paris* 19.55–8)

Though Guise then decides to 'dissemble' rather than launch an outright rebellion (19.61), the point has been made. Indeed, Guise's violent opposition to Henry is specifically characterised as a form of religious resistance, with the Duke boasting that 'the Pope will sell his triple crown . . . ere I shall want' and ascribing his enmity towards the king to 'religious zeal' (19.44–9). Such exculpatory allusions to his faith are central to Guise's strategy of resistance, as his defensive statement to Henry III's councillor Epernoun illustrates: 'Why, I am no traitor to the crown of France: / What I have done, 'tis for the Gospel sake' (19.21–22). Epernoun's response, however, displays a scepticism that Marlowe's audience seem likely to share: 'Nay, for the Pope's sake, and thine own benefit' (19.23).

The Protestant prince Navarre, condemning the Duke of Guise in the next scene, displays the same cynicism about his motives:

> That wicked Guise, I fear me much, will be
> The ruin of that famous realm of France,
> For his aspiring thoughts aim at the crown,
> And takes his vantage on religion,
> To plant the Pope and popelings in the realm
> And bind it wholly to the see of Rome.
>
> (*Massacre at Paris* 20.20–5)

Yet Navarre's ringing denunciation proves distinctly ironic. Having spent six lines censuring Guise for taking 'his vantage on religion'

(23), in the next four lines the Huguenot leader develops a manifesto for resistance that relies upon providential theory and references to divine favour (26). Navarre's appropriation of the very tactics he has so recently criticised lays him open to charges of hypocrisy, as Marlowe's play dramatically implicates its main Protestant protagonist in an act of religious rebellion.

The first hints that Navarre intends to oppose the new French king Henry III emerge in Scene 13. Following the previous ruler Charles IX's death, Navarre abandons the political naivety he has previously displayed and prepares for military action:

> And now, Navarre, whilst that these broils do last,
> My opportunity may serve me fit
> To steal from France and hie me to my home,
> For here's no safety in the realm for me;
> And now that Henry is call'd from Poland,
> It is my due by just succession;
> And therefore, as speedily as I can perform,
> I'll muster up an army secretly.
>
> (*Massacre at Paris* 13.30–7)

Navarre presents himself as a rightful heir raising an army to defend his 'just' rights to 'it' – and since the subsequent battles occur in France, 'it' in this passage is presumably either the French crown or, more moderately, Navarre's position as Henry's heir. Comparable appeals to dynastic right were common in Huguenot resistance literature, especially by the later 1580s. However, several factors undermine Navarre's claim to be justifiably defending himself against a ruthless enemy. Most importantly, there is little doubt that Henry III is the rightful king of France. Raising an army on the occasion of his accession is rather precipitate, since Navarre is at best the heir presumptive and in reality did not even have that status: at the time when this episode takes place Henry III's younger brother and Elizabeth I's real-life suitor the Duke of Alençon and Anjou was still alive, and Marlowe refers to him using the nickname 'Monsieur' in the following scene (14.64). Navarre's campaign is primarily an act of resistance to a 'heretical' Catholic regime and, while many English spectators might have approved of his militant Protestant agenda, portraying rebellion in the name of religion on the Elizabethan stage could still be a controversial move. Moreover, the credibility of Navarre's cause is problematised by his secretive behaviour. In particular, his declared intention to 'steal from France' before mustering his army indicates that he will effectively invade France with a foreign force: Protestant England was particularly sensitive to threats of this nature, after suffering a number of invasion scares during the later years of Elizabeth's reign.

Even Navarre's linguistic choices in this speech have negative implications, with the recurrence of terms such as 'steal', 'perform', and 'secretly' potentially cancelling out his protestations of justice and 'due' right. The emerging impression of Machiavellian intrigue is strengthened by Navarre's statement that the current 'opportunity' may 'serve' him well, which mimics the advice given by Marlowe's villain Spencer in *Edward II* that 'you must be proud, bold, pleasant, resolute, / And now and then, stab, as occasion serves' (5.42–3).[257] Navarre's words suggest that he is motivated as much by self-interest or political ambition as by religious duty, and his appeal to God's will in this soliloquy is a palpable afterthought (*Massacre at Paris* 13.40–1). Moreover, his request a few lines later that God 'so prosper me in all / As I intend to labour for the truth / And true profession of His holy word!' raises the challenging possibility that Navarre's 'professed' faith is merely an external pose or fabrication (13.49–51); in *The Jew of Malta*, Marlowe puns on the term 'profession' in a way that suggests he associated it with deceit and religious fraud. While it is always possible that certain problematic features such as Navarre's mimicry of Spencer's advice are attributable to textual corruption, for a character regularly identified by critics as a pious Protestant hero Navarre certainly adopts the language of Marlowe's hypocritical villains to a surprising and suggestive extent.

Marlowe's portrayal of Navarre as a religious rebel culminates in a speech saturated with references to Huguenot resistance theory:

My Lords, sith in a quarrel just and right
We undertake to manage these our wars
Against the proud disturbers of the faith –
I mean the Guise, the Pope, and King of Spain,
Who set themselves to tread us under foot
And rent our true religion from this land
(But for you know our quarrel is no more
But to defend their strange inventions,
Which they will put us to with sword and fire) –
We must with resolute minds resolve to fight
In honour of our God and country's good.
(*Massacre at Paris* 16.1–11)

Navarre seeks to characterise his campaign as a defensive response to religious persecution and the treacherous machinations of evil councillors. In 1562 the dissident Huguenots had similarly claimed to be protecting the monarchy from the 'seditious' Guises, and for much of the sixteenth century their propaganda characterised active political resistance as a necessary and hence legitimate act of self-defence against a tyrannical government.[258] Indeed, Navarre's reference to the persecution 'with sword and fire' (9) inflicted by the Catholics perhaps indirectly (or even directly) echoes the anonymous Huguenot treatise *Vindiciae Contra Tyrannos*, which announced in 1579 that 'cruel flames' are 'triumphing everywhere over sacred things'. The terms in which the *Vindiciae* advocates defensive resistance – arguing that 'piety commands us to keep the law of God and to protect the church; justice bids us to check tyrants and overthrowers of right and the commonwealth' – are certainly in keeping with Navarre's rhetoric; for instance, the *Vindiciae*'s emphasis on a subject's duty to defend the 'commonwealth' (*polita*) closely resembles Navarre's appeals to our 'country's good' (11).[259]

In Marlowe's play, however, Navarre's pious rhetoric cannot completely disguise the fact that his militant 'defence' involves a direct rebellion against the French monarch. Navarre may assert, perhaps correctly, that 'the Guise . . . hath incens'd the King / To levy arms and make these civil broils' (16.32–3); but, nonetheless, it is the *king*'s army that is dispersed by Navarre's victory (18.1). Since the royal commander slain in this battle has been introduced as a favourite of Henry III in a scene that showed the king personally ordering the attack on 'rebellious King Navarre' (17.1–3), Marlowe's play seems to highlight the extent of Navarre's sedition. In *The Massacre at Paris* it is not only the Catholics who are dangerous subjects, but also the 'sectious Puritans' (19.46).

Though Navarre's adoption of resistance rhetoric is historically accurate it is also potentially controversial when portrayed on the Elizabethan stage, as the Protestant leader formulates an elaborate argument that justifies military rebellion against an anointed monarch. Navarre might be Henry III's future heir and eventual successor, but that was hardly reassuring at a time when Elizabeth's own heir presumptive, Mary Queen of Scots, had been executed a few years earlier for plotting her royal cousin's death. Even Navarre's Protestant credentials might not have been enough to neutralise the impact of his insurgency: for an Elizabethan audience, the Huguenots were not merely persecuted co-religionists but also rebels against their lawful kings, and French Protestant rebellion was never a simple or clear-cut issue. English Catholics encouraged this uncertainty, contrasting their own patient acceptance of Elizabeth's rule with the rebellious behaviour of the French Huguenots. Even the government's own propagandists were uncomfortable with the idea of Protestant resistance: in a St Paul's Cross sermon of 1588/9, the Bishop of London Richard Bancroft attacked Huguenot resistance tracts as 'rebellious propositions' and argued that Protestant theories of rebellion were as dangerous as Catholic ones, reminding his audience that England's near neighbour Scotland had recently suffered a puritan revolt against King James VI.[260]

The potential ideological overlap between Protestant and Catholic rebellion ultimately renders Navarre's religiously justified dynastic campaign nearly as suspect as Guise's treacherous scheming. Navarre as depicted in *The Massacre at Paris* is as willing as Guise to manipulate religious rhetoric for his own ends, even when this amounts to a direct rebellion against the French king. By eliding the distinction between Protestant and Catholic radicalism, Marlowe's play follows the drift of Bancroft's conventional governmental propaganda while also coming close to the arguments of the 'sort of English priests' *The Massacre* denounces; that the 'sectious' Protestants are as likely as Catholics to conclude that 'subjectes are not bound to obey their Princes for conscience sake'.[261]

KILLING THE KING: REGICIDE IN 'EDWARD II' AND 'THE MASSACRE AT PARIS'

The dual threat of Catholic and puritan rebellion was a terrifying prospect for loyal English subjects. In Marlowe's plays the military campaigns conducted by Tamburlaine, Mortimer, Guise and Navarre brought such dangers to life upon the public stage, while his translation of Lucan's *De Bello Civili* familiarised his early modern readers with a classical account of a civil war shaped by religious rhetoric. Yet sixteenth- and seventeenth-century rebellion was not only about armed opposition to the authorities and the deposition of an established monarch. At the most radical fringes of resistance theory an Elizabethan reader might have encountered tracts by Protestant and Catholic writers that actively advocated the killing of heretical rulers, and Marlowe's works also respond imaginatively to this contemporary discourse of regicide.

The extension of religious theories of resistance to justify the assassination of a heretical ruler is particularly evident in the writings of the Marian English Protestant exiles. John Ponet's *Shorte Treatise of Politike Power* (1556) includes a lengthy section explaining why it is lawful to kill a tyrant and outlines various scriptural precedents for regicide including Jehu, who killed Joram for his 'idolatrous tyrannie and evil governement', and Moses, who executed the idolatrous Princes of Israel upon God's command.[262] Ponet regularly quotes biblical instances of tyrannicide in support of his arguments, and this emphasis upon religious precedents endured as the theories of the Marian exiles were appropriated and adapted by their Catholic opponents. By the later decades of the sixteenth century, regicide in the name of religion was most notoriously associated with Europe's Catholics, and particularly the Jesuits. Catholic arguments in favour of tyrannicide permeated the early modern French polemic with which Marlowe was familiar: in 1589 the Catholic League writer Jean Boucher published a defence of regicide entitled *The Just Renunciation of Henry III*, while Guillaume Rose proclaimed the same theme more stridently in *The Just Authority of a Christian Commonwealth over Impious and Heretical Kings* (1590). Indeed the very act of king-killing advocated by these two writers, the murder of Henri III, takes centre stage in Marlowe's *Massacre at Paris*.

Across early modern Europe Catholic radicals put their tyrannicidal doctrines into practice. Including Henri III, three European rulers were killed between 1584 and 1610: the Dutch leader William of Orange was assassinated by the Catholic fanatic Balthazar Gerard on 10 July 1584; Henri III was stabbed by the Dominican monk Jacques Clément in 1589; and King Henri IV suffered more than twenty attacks on his life between his excommunication in 1585 and his murder in 1610. From the 1580s onwards, fears that Elizabeth I might suffer a similar fate were rife in Marlowe's England. Pope Pius V's 1570 bull of excommunication had already put Elizabeth's throne in jeopardy, and in 1580 a papal proclamation announced that anyone who assassinated Elizabeth with the 'pious intention of doing God service not only does not sin, but gains merit'.[263] The Jesuit Cardinal William Allen's 1588 call for English Catholics to support the Spanish Armada additionally confirmed that 'charge was given expressly in Deutronomie, to slei all false Prophetes and their followers . . . Princes and rulers no more excepted, but muche more punishable in this case then the people'.[264]

The same decade also witnessed a series of conspiracies against Elizabeth's Protestant regime, including the 1583 Throckmorten plot and the Babington conspiracy of 1586. Both intrigues potentially threatened Elizabeth's life: the Babington plotters reportedly planned Elizabeth's death 'by secret treacherie', while a colourful rumour held that the intended Throckmorten assassin John

Somerville had been taught Jesuit theories of tyrannicide by a priest disguised as a gardener.[265] Intriguingly for Marlowe's fictional representations of regicide, Somerville's assassination attempt was supported by the Duke of Guise; indeed, Guise began offering an open reward for Elizabeth's murder from 1582 onwards, apparently on the advice of the Jesuit priest Robert Parsons.

Protestant England was deeply paranoid about Catholic plots against Elizabeth's life. In the *Censure of a Loyal Subject* (1587), for instance, George Whetstone's speaker Walker accuses the Jesuit missionaries of seeking to 'entertain murtherers, theeves, Atheists and all maner of discontented persons, into the service of the pope, to the intent that they should murther the Q[ueen's] majestie'.[266] Such fears were exacerbated by the known involvement of radical Catholic priests in previous conspiracies against Elizabeth, and by the successful assassinations carried out in contemporary Europe by friars, monks and priests. The authorities also acknowledged as a minority threat the danger posed by puritan radicals. In 1591, for instance, the extreme puritan William Hackett's attempt to establish himself as the new Messiah and England's monarch was regarded as a treacherous attack against Elizabeth I's life; a government-sponsored account of this rebellion, written by the repentant conspirator Henry Arthington, was published in 1592.[267] Fears of political assassination continued to loom large throughout the 1580s and 1590s. 'I am not so void of judgement as not to see mine own peril', Elizabeth I informed representatives of Parliament in 1586, 'nor so careless as not to weigh that my life daily is in hazard.'[268] Such alertness to the threat of regicide also encouraged a number of early modern dramatists to stage episodes of royal assassination. Thus in Marlowe's works Tamburlaine's relentless military campaign of king-killing is complemented by the scenes of literal regicide that Marlowe depicts in *Edward II* and *The Massacre at Paris*, with the carefully plotted assassinations of English and French monarchs shown in the latter two plays reflecting the theoretical premises and sixteenth-century experience of regicide.

In *Edward II* the English king's murder is secretly arranged by a man who claims to rule only as regent for Edward's young son:

the former rebel and newly appointed Lord Protector Mortimer. While Mortimer employs Catholic theories of religious resistance during the baronial rebellion against Edward II, as discussed earlier, as Lord Protector he adopts the role of 'bashful Puritan' in order to secure his new political position (23.54–62). His decision to murder the imprisoned king Edward is announced in the same scene, in which this 'Puritan' transformation may have been visually signalled by Mortimer's costume or mannerisms. Yet the actual plan is framed by a linguistic trickery perhaps more reminiscent of England's Catholic dissidents: the warrant Mortimer provides for Edward's death is deliberately obscure, employing the type of syntactical ambiguity outlined in the Jesuit manual *A Treatise of Equivocation* (23.6–16).[269] Mortimer also uses a parodic religious terminology to control his accomplice Maltravers, couching a threat to murder his repentant partner in crime in the language of Catholic confession:

> Maltravers, if thou now growest penitent
> I'll be thy ghostly father; therefore choose
> Whether thou wilt be secret in this,
> Or else die by the hand of Mortimer.
>
> (*Edward II* 25.3–6)

These Catholic allusions are complemented by his choice of murderer. Lightborne, whose name suggests the devil of medieval morality drama, is also characterized as an Italianate and presumably Catholic assassin: his catalogue of the elaborate poisoning techniques he learned in Naples exploits early modern stereotypes of the Italian, recalling Thomas Nashe's description of Italy as 'the sporting place of murther, the Apothecary-shop of poison for all nations'.[270]

Mortimer's regicidal plans are thus framed by both puritan and Catholic rhetoric, with a bias towards the latter. In 1592, when *Edward II* was probably first performed, extreme Protestant and Catholic radicals might equally be regarded in Elizabethan England as potential regicides: William Hackett's 1591 rebellion threatened the queen's life, while the turn of the year saw a security scare about a specialist Italian 'executioner' supposedly on his way from the Low Countries to assassinate Elizabeth.[271] Yet Marlowe's Mortimer uses the religious rhetoric of these confessions almost indiscriminately, suggesting his ultimate indifference to its spiritual implications: he orders Edward's murder out of self-interest rather than religious zeal, quickly deciding that 'the King must die, or Mortimer goes down' (23.1). His subsequent willingness to parody the language of Catholic confession while threatening Maltravers further exposes his indifference to the theological theories that supposedly underpin his campaign of resistance and regicide. In *Edward II* Marlowe explores the implications of a politic royal assassination framed by the language and imagery of religious faith but in reality motivated by the self-interested ambitions of a hypocritical and sceptical rebel.

Nonetheless, Mortimer's career as a regicide is restrained in comparison to the murderous Catholics of Marlowe's *Massacre at Paris*, in which two of the play's three royal assassinations are framed by direct appeals to religious duty while the third also hints at the influence of resistance literature. The confessional emphasis is now more closely focused on the murderous potential of Catholic subjects: all three royal victims are ostensibly killed for their connections to Protestantism by killers who use Catholic rhetoric to further their political agendas. From Queen Navarre to Charles IX to Henry III, the rulers murdered are victims of Catholic assassination plots – or, at least, of killers who purport to uphold the Catholic faith.

The first royal victim in *The Massacre at Paris* is Navarre's own mother Queen Navarre, who is murdered on Guise's orders towards the start of the play. Whereas the Queen of Navarre Jeanne D'Albret historically died several months before the wedding of Navarre and Marguerite de Valois, Marlowe transposes her demise to immediately after this wedding and the associated exchange of vows between Navarre and Charles IX; an alteration that underscores Marlowe's murderer Guise's villainy, as he kills Navarre's mother on the heels of his king's peace treaty with her son. Marlowe's decision to treat the queen's death as suspicious makes good dramatic sense, but also reflected the rumours circulating in sixteenth-century Europe. One of Marlowe's sources, François Hotman's *Furious Outrages*, reports that when the queen died of a sudden sickness 'the suspition was great that she died of poyson': Hotman adds that 'it hath bene found that she was poysoned with a venomed smell of a pair of perfumed gloves'.[272] Poisoned gloves are similarly used to kill Queen Navarre in *The Massacre at Paris* but, whereas Hotman attributed the real-life murder to the Queen Mother Catherine de Medici, in Marlowe's play her death is arranged by the Duke of Guise (2.10–6). In addition, Marlowe's version emphasises Guise's cruelty: the Duke, arranging for the delivery of the poisoned gloves, gloats that 'every savour' will 'breed a pang of death' (2.14).

Marlowe's callous killer attributes his brutal action to religious duty, instructing his Italian accomplice to poison Queen Navarre because 'she is that huge blemish in our eye/ That makes these upstart heresies in France' (2.21–2). Thus an apparently gratuitous murder is justified in terms of confessional difference, with Marlowe's protagonist claiming that he executes Queen Navarre because she has treacherously introduced her 'heretical' Protestant faith into France. Similar charges of promoting heresy were used to justify attacks against Elizabeth I's English Protestant regime, and Guise's confessional justification of murder in Marlowe's play also pre-empts his appropriation of religious rhetoric during and after the St Bartholomew's Day Massacre. Subsequently, Guise claims to be opposing heresy as he launches an attack on the Protestant royal house of Bourbon, whose members ruled Navarre and later France:

> My brother Guise hath gather'd a power of men
> Which, as he saith, to kill the Puritans –
> But 'tis the house of Bourbon that he means.
> Now, madam, must you insinuate with the King
> And tell him that 'tis for his country's good,
> And common profit of religion.
>
> (*Massacre at Paris* 14.54–9)

Guise's allies in this assault on the Bourbons are his brother the Cardinal of Guise and the Queen Mother, Catherine de Medici. At the Cardinal's request Catherine agrees to persuade the new king, her son Henry III, to approve Guise's violent plan:

> Tush, man, let me alone with him
> To work the way to bring this thing to pass;
> And if he do deny what I do say,
> I'll despatch him with his brother presently.
>
> (*Massacre at Paris* 14.60–3)

Catherine's declared willingness to 'despatch' her son Henry is striking, and seems to confirm the earlier hints that she was responsible for Charles IX's death. In the 1594 edition of *The Massacre*, indeed, this speech discussing the possible murder of Henry III is duplicated almost exactly in Scene 11, where it becomes a plan to kill Charles IX (11.37–44; 14.60–8); although the transposition is presumably an error, it suggests that the play's original readers associated Catherine with regicide and even filicide.[273] These hints recur in Scene 14. The 'brother' with whom Henry will be dispatched cannot be his younger sibling, since Catherine plans that 'Monsieur' shall succeed him (14.64); instead, the Queen Mother apparently alludes to her responsibility for Charles IX's suspicious death.

Historical accounts of Charles's death often hint that his mother was guilty of his murder. Jean Boucher, for example, suggested that 'the queen mother said on parting from Henry, "Go boldly, my son, you will not be away long"'; Boucher adds provocatively that 'however that may be, King Charles was poisoned'.[274] Though Marlowe's Charles IX himself tentatively suggests that his death is a divine punishment for perjury (13.8–12), the action of *The Massacre at Paris* subtly confirms that Charles is in fact brought low by poison. In Marlowe's play as in Boucher's account Anjoy accepts the Polish crown in the suspiciously confident expectation that God will soon 'take my brother hence' (10.19); certainly, it is implied, before Charles can have sons of his own to inherit. Catherine's words to Guise also hint at her involvement in her son's death:

> Catherine must have her will in France:
> As I do live, so surely shall he die,
> And Henry then shall wear the diadem;
> And if he grudge or cross his mother's will,
> I'll disinherit him and all the rest;
> For I'll rule France, but they shall wear the crown,
> And, if they storm, I then may pull them down.
> (*Massacre at Paris* 11.38–44)

Charles's death just two scenes after Catherine confidently predicts that 'surely shall he die' is suggestive, while the correspondence between Queen Navarre's symptoms and the 'sudden pang' that seizes Charles's heart signals that both have been poisoned (13.3). The scene becomes one of apparent regicide, its shocking impact augmented by the eagerness with which the onstage witnesses of Charles's death anticipate replacing him: Catherine passes in just four lines from lamentation to appointing Anjoy to 'his brother's crown and dignity' (13.22), acting as soon as she believes Charles no longer 'hears nor sees' 'what we do' (13.18).

There seems a strong implication that Marlowe's Catherine had murdered her own son. If so, there is little doubt about her motive. Her antagonism towards Charles is ostensibly linked to his recent confessional *volte-face*; her son reportedly regrets the radical Catholic violence committed during the St Bartholomew's Day Massacre and now conspires with the Protestant prince Navarre 'to revenge their deaths' (11.30–6). Yet although Catherine claims to oppose her son's new Protestant sympathies and pays lip service to religious considerations, the real cause of her antipathy is pointedly secular. Charles dies, not because his Catholic faith is weak, but because 'Catherine must have her will in France' (11.38).

Marlowe's implication that Catherine poisons her son to secure her own political position is alarming, but Charles IX's death is never openly identified as murder. With Henry III, on the other hand, Marlowe depicts virtually every stage of the king's assassination, from the Catholic friar's original plan to kill him to the French monarch's lingering death. Marlowe's version emphasises the exculpatory religious rhetoric used by the conspirators, whose claims to be motivated by religious zeal were often noted in historical accounts of Henri's murder. As the Protestant Antony Colynet reports, the Catholic League sought an assassin 'covered with the cloake of hypocrisie' and so chose a friar; this friar, Jacques Clément, was told 'what a good deed he might doo to deliver holy Church from the tiranny of Henry the third, who was become an heretike'.[275]

Marlowe's version of Henry's death makes much of Catholic arguments for regicide. In *The Massacre at Paris* it is the murderous friar who makes the first approach; convinced by the League propaganda justifying Anjoy's assassination, he explains that

> I am a friar of the order of the Jacobins, that for my conscience' sake will kill the king . . . [for] I have been a great sinner in my days, and the deed is meritous.
> (*Massacre at Paris* 23.23–8)

The friar's belief that killing Henry is 'meritous' presumably refers to the claims made in contemporary League propaganda. After Henri III ordered the deaths of the Duke and Cardinal de Guise the Catholic theologians of the Sorbonne effectively excommunicated him, casting his murder as a religious duty; indeed, the sentence passed upon Henri might have reminded Elizabethan spectators of their own queen's excommunicate state. Religious rhetoric continues to frame Marlowe's depiction of the French king's murder. When Henry's favourite Epernoun expresses reservations about the friar's intentions, for instance, it is the latter's sanctimonious appearance that secures his success; Henry replies that 'our friars are holy men / And will not offer violence to their King / For all the wealth and treasure of the world' (24.21–5). Underlining the fact that the 'wealth and treasure' his Catholic friar expects to receive is not material but heavenly, Henry's response highlights the role that religious rhetoric plays in justifying his murder.

Marlowe's *Massacre at Paris* was not the only play of the 1590s to stage the assassination of a ruler, or even the only play to associate regicide with religious controversy. Shakespeare's histories regularly feature royal murders, and his 1590s history play *King John* even shows the English king being excommunicated and murdered by a monk. The actual act of excommunication is more central to Shakespeare's narrative than it was in Marlowe's *Massacre at Paris*; unlike Henri III, the real King John was formally condemned by papal decree. In Act 3, the wicked Cardinal Pandulph announces that

> meritous shall that hand be call'd,
> Canonised and worshipp'd as a saint,
> That takes away by any secret course
> Thy hateful life.
>
> (*King John* 3.1.102–5)

In comparison with Marlowe's staging of Henry's death, however, Shakespeare's depiction of the murder itself is heavily truncated. The poisoning of John by the monk takes place offstage, and the implied connection between the murderer's Catholic faith, Pandulph's sentence of excommunication and the assassination of King John is not fully articulated: Hubert's report of John's death draws a more generic connection between Catholic villainy and murderous violence (5.6.23). Moreover, Shakespeare's play carefully emphasises the operation of providential justice. Hubert describes how the murderous monk's bowels 'suddenly burst out' after he poisons King John (5.6.28–31), details an early modern spectator would presumably have recognised from the Protestant author John Foxe's influential account of King John's murder in his *Actes and Monuments*, where Foxe describes how the murderous monk, 'being absolved of his Abbot for doyng this acte', poisoned John's cup of wine – but was immediately punished by divine providence, his bowels suddenly bursting out of his body.[276] Though the Abbot's role is cut, Shakespeare's dramatic narrative otherwise follows Foxe's conservative providential narrative closely.

In contrast, Marlowe's *Massacre at Paris* lacks a clear providential structure – Henry III's assassin dies when the wounded king physically stabs him – and, unlike Shakespeare's history, prominently stages the very recent murder of a sixteenth-century monarch. While episodes of regicide were common enough in early modern drama, Marlowe's contemporary setting, graphic presentation and explicit association of regicide with religious theories of tyrannicide ensure that his depiction of Henry III's death is more provocative than most. Marlowe's portrait of Catholic regicide brought to the public stage a recurrent Elizabethan nightmare, and Henry III's dying words acknowledge the relevance of his own fate to the dangers facing England's queen:

> Sweet Epernoun, all rebels under heaven
> Shall take example by his punishment
> How they bear arms against their sovereign.
> Go call the English agent hither straight.
> I'll send my sister England news of this,
> And give her warning of her treacherous foes.
> (*Massacre at Paris* 24.46–51)

Comparable addresses to the English queen were relatively common in early modern drama, and usually serve a conservative and patriotic purpose. However, Marlowe's character's signal failure to allude reassuringly to Elizabeth's predicted longevity or God's protective care for England strikes a more unusual note. In 1590s England, when the queen was perceived to be under threat of assassination from all sides, the correlation Marlowe establishes between religious conflict and the violent assassination of an anointed king is not at all reassuring. In fact, despite the sop of Navarre's ringing anti-papal rhetoric, this final scene perhaps edged towards the limits of what early modern censorship would permit – especially since Navarre himself converted to Catholicism just a few months after Marlowe's death, in a pragmatic and politic move perhaps anticipated in *The Massacre at Paris*.

CHAPTER FIVE

'DOCTOR FAUSTUS': A CRISIS OF CONSCIENCE?

Edward II, Mortimer, Guise and Henry III pay with their lives for their failure to outdo their enemies in pious deceit. In the fictional worlds Marlowe creates, success and even survival depend upon an ability to deceive others and cloak seditious ambitions in the language of faith; his protagonists compete with and are often eventually outmanoeuvred and defeated by opponents who similarly seek to appropriate religious precedents and allusions. For such self-seeking opportunists, religious rhetoric has little or no spiritual value; it is prized as a politic tool that can be exploited to secular advantage. Focused on the earthly present, Marlowe's protagonists pay little heed to the supernatural implications of the religious syntax they commandeer, and are indeed rarely required to face up to the consequences of their actions. Divine justice is represented as apathetic, indifferent or arbitrary, and the threat of retribution after death seems minimal: when these characters fail, their punishment is the 'but temporal' death suffered by the rebellious barons of *Edward II* (13.22). This pattern holds true across almost all of Marlowe's plays and poems with one crucial exception: *Doctor Faustus*, in which the protagonist loses his soul to the devil who outwits him.

I began this book by suggesting that in Marlowe's tragedy *Doctor Faustus* both Faustus and Mephistopheles seek to control and manipulate religious rhetoric. While Mephistopheles misleads Faustus with equivocating phrases, for instance, Faustus simultaneously twists scriptural language into his own flawed justification for repudiating God. Marlowe's play also incorporates episodes of pseudo-conversion, oath-taking and oath-breaking, and politically inflected usurpation, drawing together the various strands of politic religion that recur so persistently in Marlowe's plays and poems. However, there is one significant distinction that sets *Doctor Faustus* apart from the rest of his writing. Whereas Marlovian protagonists from Tamburlaine to Guise operate within a firmly secular universe, and classical characters such as Aeneas and Leander interact with obviously pagan deities, Faustus inhabits a supernatural Christian universe which harks back to the Heaven-and-Hell duality of late-medieval morality drama. Within this recognisably Christian framework, Faustus's politic appropriation of religious rhetoric to negotiate with angels and devils takes on a unique resonance. This chapter explores the impact the play's supernatural setting has on Faustus's efforts to manipulate religious rhetoric, and considers how Faustus's tragic fate relates to Marlowe's broader literary engagement with the demands placed upon the individual conscience in post-Reformation England.

SELLING SOULS: FAUSTUS'S REBELLION AGAINST GOD

Marlowe's protagonists often resist secular authority, but Faustus takes this one step further when he rebels against his God. He is not the only character in Marlowe's writings to launch such an attack: Aeneas is aggressively ready to furrow Neptune's glassy fields and 'cut a passage through his topless hills' in his pursuit of 'golden fortunes' (*Dido* 4.3.7–12), while Tamburlaine threatens to assault the heavens and boasts in *Tamburlaine Part One* that 'Jove viewing me in arms looks pale and wan, / Fearing my power should pull him from his throne' (5.2.390–1). Faustus shares Tamburlaine's ambition to be more than mortal, and this desire motivates his defiance of God: whereas Tamburlaine uses Jove's example to justify rebellion against a secular ruler (*Tamburlaine Part One* 2.7.12–29), the Evil Angel fosters Faustus's ambition to be 'as Jove is in the sky', urging him to defy God and 'try thy brains to gain a deity' (1.1.63, 76). Marlowe's contemporaries also associated Faustus's demonic magic with Tamburlaine's seditious progress, perhaps because both protagonists invoke the classical precedent set by Jove's usurpation of the heavenly throne. In Barnabe Barnes's *The Devil's Charter*, for instance, the protagonist Pope Alexander conjures after Faustus's example and explains that through his alliance with the devil his sons will 'mount in equall parallel / With golden majesty like Saturnes sonne' (ll. 368–9). Alexander even admits that he has used the 'name of Christian' as a 'stale' or cloak for his 'Arcane plots' (ll. 363–4): Barnes follows the innovative precedent set by Marlowe's *Doctor Faustus*, locating his own representation of demonic magic and religiously inflected deceit within a Christian framework.[277]

The precedent set by Marlowe's Faustus is particularly provocative since despite his classical allusions it is not the pagan deities that Faustus opposes. Instead, Marlowe's protagonist rebels against a recognisably Christian and most probably Calvinist God. Faustus's defiant audacity often appeals to modern readers and spectators. Various influential twentieth-century scholars including Frederick Boas have identified Faustus as a heroic Renaissance Prometheus, suffering eternal torment for the sake of enlightenment, while various theatrical productions have explored his actions from a heroic or martyrological perspective: in Jerzy Grotowski's 1963 Theatre Laboratory production, for instance, Faustus's re-baptism in a river following his renunciation of God invited iconoclastic comparisons with Jesus Christ.[278] More recently, the 2011 Shakespeare's Globe production of *Doctor Faustus* used humour to make the audience complicit in Faustus's denial of his God: while citing 1 John 1.8 to justify summoning Mephistopheles, Paul Hilton's Faustus looked down his nose at the Bible in an exaggerated fashion, bidding 'divinity adieu' in a comically airy manner that had the audience laughing along with him (B-text 1.1.50).[279]

Faustus's regular and lengthy soliloquies suggest that Marlowe's protagonist also addressed audiences directly in the Elizabethan and Jacobean theatres, again involving the play's spectators in his decision to repudiate God. In Marlowe's day, however, this suggestion of complicity could have been very uncomfortable for the audience. Faustus's pact with the devil is particularly problematic, and the desires that inspire him were equally condemned by Elizabethan moralists as transgressive and blasphemous. Even Marlowe's possible collaborator Thomas Nashe criticises the quest for earthly power in terms that recall *Doctor Faustus*: in his 1593 tract *Christs Teares* Nashe attacks those who 'will be Gods and Monarchs in our lyfe, though we be devils after death', adding that 'the spyrite of monarchising in pryvate men is the spyrite of Lucifer'.[280]

Nashe's reference to the dissidents who seek to be both 'Gods and Monarchs' suggests that Faustus's revolt against God might also have echoed Elizabethan fears of secular disobedience, at a time when religious and secular concepts of treason often converged. Marlowe was almost certainly familiar with the suggestive comparison that the 1570 'Homily against Disobedience' drew between political resistance to Elizabeth and Lucifer's rebellion 'against the majestie of God'; in the 1590s collaborative drama *The Book of Sir Thomas More* the title character similarly argues (in a section sometimes attributed to Shakespeare) that civil disobedience is 'a sin / Which oft th'apostle did forewarn us of', adding that since to the king 'God hath his office lent', rebellion is equivalent to rising 'gainst God' (6.105–21).[281] In addition, Marlowe's Elizabethan and Jacobean contemporaries were highly alert to the subversive political implications of magic: in the Old Testament, rebellion is described as 'the sin of witchcraft' (1 Samuel 15.23), and Faustus's rebellion against God may respond to this conventional association of conjuring and treason. In an early passage in Marlowe's tragedy, he muses that

> emperors and kings
> Are but obeyed in their several provinces,
> Nor can they raise the wind or rend the clouds;
> But his dominion that exceeds in this
> Stretcheth as far as doth the mind of man.
> (*Doctor Faustus* 1.1.59–63)

Two scenes later, Faustus declares that 'the Emp'ror shall not live but by my leave, / Nor any potentate of Germany' (1.3.112–13).

His quasi-divine ambitions acquire a secular dimension as, like Tamburlaine, he aspires to supplant hereditary monarchs; indeed, the sixteenth-century rulers of Christian Europe were often described as God's representatives on earth.

As a rebel against God and God's representatives, Faustus follows Marlovian usurpers from Tamburlaine to Mortimer by using religious rhetoric to justify treachery. In Chapter One I discussed how he uses scriptural quotations to 'prove' that 'the reward of sin is death', basing his decision to summon Mephistopheles upon a mangled misinterpretation of the Bible (1.1.41). Once he adopts magical practices that are specifically demonic, Marlowe's protagonist then changes tack and introduces a classical precedent for rebellion. The play's prologue compared Faustus to the doomed Icarus, whose 'waxen wings did mount above his reach' (Prologue, 21); the idea that 'melting heavens conspired his overthrow' has certainly caught the eye of those who see Faustus as a doomed hero destroyed by a tyrannical God (Prologue, 22).[282] However, Marlowe's Faustus seems to have little interest in exploiting a precedent that admittedly speaks of failure rather than success. Instead, he favours the classical precedents established by ancient Greek and Roman philosophers such as the Greek thinker Epicurus and his Roman disciple Lucretius, who discredited providential arguments and denied the immortality of the soul.

Faustus seems eager to impose a Greco-Roman veneer on the Christian cosmography he inhabits. He refers to his Judeo-Christian God as 'Jove' (a conventional practice in early modern drama) and, more controversially, refuses to accept the Protestant bipartite model of Heaven and Hell: instead, he announces that he 'confounds hell in Elysium' (1.3.61). Faustus builds his rejection of God upon a classicised reimagining of the play's spiritual framework, a rhetorical strategy that enables him to repudiate the Christian model of judgement in the afterlife and so act without fear of retribution. Initially inspired by his misreading of the Christian Bible, Faustus's dismissive attitude towards damnation is predominantly indebted to the 'old philosophers' and perhaps in particular to the sceptics who denied the immortality of the soul

(1.3.60–2). Lucretius wrote for instance in *De Rerum Natura* that 'when the body has perished, you must confess that the spirit has passed away', a remark which anticipates Faustus's own sceptical remark that 'think'st thou that Faustus is so fond / To imagine that after this life there is any pain? / Tush, these are trifles and mere old wives' tales' (2.1.136–8).[283] Lucretius's arguments, based on the teachings of Epicurus, were notorious in the sixteenth and seventeenth centuries and condemned as damnable atheism: thus Marlowe's puritan detractor Thomas Beard scathingly condemned the 'voluptuous Epicures . . . that deny the providence of God, beleeve not the immortality of the soule, think there is no such thing as life to come, and consequently impugne all divinity'.[284] But even Aristotle, whose works lay at the heart of the Tudor education system, was known to have denied the immortality of the soul; Faustus, who previously declared that he would 'live and die in Aristotle's works', has a wealth of classical precedents for denying his soul's immortality (1.1.5).[285]

As Faustus's denial that there is any pain after death suggests, Marlowe was apparently familiar with the 'atheist' concept that death is an eternal sleep free from pain or punishment (2.1.137). In *Tamburlaine Part One*, for example, the doomed Agydas welcomes death with the words:

> Go wander free from fear of tyrant's rage,
> Removèd from the torments and the hell
> Wherewith he may excruciate thy soul.
> And let Agydas by Agydas die,
> And with this stab slumber eternally.
>
> (*Tamburlaine Part One* 3.2.102–6)

Like Agydas, Faustus embraces the classical philosophy that denied the existence of 'torments' or 'hell' after death; in his case, as an escape from the threat of eternal punishment. Faustus may even believe in his own arguments. Though he expresses regret and fears divine retribution after selling his soul to the devil, it is the finality of death that preoccupies him; he regularly blames Mephistopheles for depriving him of heaven's immortal joys, but it is not until the end of the play that he explicitly associates the loss of heaven with eternal damnation. Despite the onstage presence of a devil whose existence seems to affirm the reality of hell, Faustus spends much of the tragedy dreading the 'temporal' death Marlowe's protagonists more commonly experience. Even in his final scene, Faustus's pleas indicate that he regards the ending promised by Lucretian philosophy as a possible alternative to hell. Lucretius held that nature, which forms all living things from the elements, divides them back into the elements once they are 'dissolved' by death: 'O soul', Faustus pleads, 'be changed into little waterdrops / And fall into the ocean, ne'er be found!' (5.2.118–19).[286]

Although modern spectators do not usually note Faustus's refusal to associate hell with eternity, Marlowe's original audiences may have recognised parallels between the 'wanton' Faustus who scales Mount Olympus and the Renaissance Epicurus, who was said to have 'exalted' men as 'high as heaven' but was accused by sixteenth-century moralists of gluttony and lechery (*Doctor Faustus* 2.1.144).[287] At least one of Marlowe's fellow-writers apparently appreciated the significance of Faustus's classically inspired scepticism: in the anonymous late Elizabethan play *Selimus*, which is heavily indebted to Marlowe's *Tamburlaine*, the protagonist's dismissal of belief in 'hell and a revenging God' as 'schoole conditions' echoes Faustus's own rejection of such concepts as 'trifles and old wives' tales' (ll. 418–20). Selimus's scepticism inspires him to rebel against his father, since 'in death nothing shall to us fall, / Here while I live, Ile have a snatch at all' (ll. 366–7), in the same way that Faustus bases his rebellion against God upon a denial of his soul's immortality.[288] Yet Marlowe's protagonist also embraces a range of alternative rhetorical strategies, and simultaneously seeks to vindicate his rebellion against God in Christian terms: casting himself as a hero of the Protestant cause, Faustus controversially characterises his demonic magic as a necessary defence against the encroaching forces of international Catholicism.

Faustus first lays claim to a militant Protestant purpose in the play's opening scene, when he describes his magical aspirations:

> I'll levy soldiers with the coin they bring
> And chase the Prince of Parma from our land,
> And reign sole king of all our provinces;
> Yea, stranger engines for the brunt of war
> Than was the fiery keel at Antwerp's bridge
> I'll make my servile spirits to invent.
>
> (*Doctor Faustus* 1.1.94–9)

Faustus's fantasy of military triumph recalls England's involvement in the sixteenth-century conflict between the provinces of the Netherlands and their Catholic Spanish overlords. Several of the rebellious states were motivated by a desire for religious freedom, and Elizabeth I grudgingly agreed to assist her Protestant co-religionists in the struggle against Spain. Such support usually took the form of 'coin' to 'levy soldiers' (94), but in 1585–6 English forces were sent to the Netherlands in significant numbers to ward off the threat of Spanish victory: this intervention was a response to the recent capture of Antwerp, after the Spanish commander Parma almost miraculously managed to blockade the city by building a bridge across the river Scheldt. Faustus's reference to 'Antwerp's bridge' presumably recalls Parma's 1585 success (98); he also alludes to the 'fiery keel', a flotilla of fire-boats launched by the besieged city that nearly succeeded in destroying the bridge.

Faustus's desire to align his own conjuring with the international Protestant cause is apparently recognised by his companions Valdes and Cornelius, who claim that their magic will bring 'from America the golden fleece / That yearly stuffs old Philip's treasury, / If learnèd Faustus will be resolute' (1.1.133–5). Valdes's promise perhaps exploits the contemporary fame of the Elizabethan privateers who attacked and seized Spanish vessels with the informal approval of the English government. The reference might also recall a more specific instance of militant Protestant aggression: in 1586 Sir Francis Drake had led an expedition to the Indies where, by threatening the treasure galleons returning from Spain's New World colonies, he forced the Spanish admiral Santa Cruz to divert the Armada fleet and delayed the attack on

England until 1588. The episode is an especially likely one for Marlowe's play to invoke since the Lord Admiral Charles Howard, patron of the playing company that first staged *Doctor Faustus*, had been personally involved in this English victory. Either way, Valdes's words indicate that magic can be used against Catholic Spain in a way that supports Faustus's proclaimed Protestant purpose and recalls England's real-life activities abroad.

By presenting himself as a champion of Protestant values Marlowe's Faustus appeals to the sympathies of the play's original, predominantly Protestant, London audiences. His objectives, whether realised or not, accord closely with contemporary English foreign policy, while his admittedly trivial victories over a pompous pope, arrogant nobles and foolish clowns are likely to have delighted many of his Elizabethan spectators. As in Marlowe's probable source *The English Faust-Book*, Faustus combines the qualities of the medieval folk hero with those of a champion of European Protestantism; indeed, the patriotic magician seems to have been a familiar sight on the early modern stage. Other prominent examples include Robert Greene's Friar Bacon, who uses his demonic magic to ward England from harm and (by defeating a rival German magician) affirm English superiority (9.165–6); and Anthony Munday's John a Kent, who disguises himself in 'ffryers gray' in order to reunite a pair of young lovers (ll. 303–4).[289] Kent remains a positive character in Munday's romance despite the accusations of his enemy John a Cumber that he deceives others 'by pollicye' (ll. 671–9); in early modern drama, it seems that it was easy enough to reconcile the practice of magic with a positive and arguably proto-Protestant agenda.

Unlike his fellow-playwrights, however, in *Doctor Faustus* Marlowe emphasises that the magical champion of international Protestantism has made a deal with the devil. Faustus's conjuring is explicitly demonic: he summons 'devils' as well as elemental spirits (1.3.6, 17), conjures in the name of Beelzebub and refers to spirits who must 'rise' from below, suggesting their hellish origins (13). Although he uses militant Protestant rhetoric to characterise his magic as a weapon against the threatening forces of

Catholicism, the overlapping of these claims with Faustus's appeals to the classical precedent of Epicurean and Lucretian scepticism subtly raises doubts about his commitment to the Protestant cause. In addition, and perhaps even more problematically, Faustus conducts and seals his agreement with the devil in the style of Catholic ritual: his statement that he has 'prayed and sacrificed' to Lucifer recalls Protestant accusations that Catholics had warped the sacrament of the Eucharist into a bloody literal sacrifice (1.3.7); he conjures using 'the breviated names of holy saints' (10); and Mephistopheles' role as an intermediary between Lucifer and Faustus mimics the hierarchy of priests and saints who intervened between the Catholic worshipper and God. Overall, the magic that Faustus supposedly embraces for the sake of the Protestant cause is based upon an 'atheistic' denial of his soul's immortality, and riddled with the terms and gestures of Catholic ceremony.

The discrepancy between Faustus's claim to be a champion of European Protestantism and the demonic, proto-Catholic magic he practises is particularly relevant when he visits Rome. To berate the Pope without fear of retribution was a typical Protestant fantasy: Anthony Munday, for instance, describes the idealised heroism of the English traveller who

> would tell the Pope of his lascivious and unchristian life, the Cardinals of their Sodomiticall sinnes, the Friers of their secret jugling with the Nunnes, and the Pre[i]estes of their painted Purgatorie, their wafer God, and their counterfeit blood in the Challice.[290]

Marlowe's protagonist, protected by the devil, is in the perfect position to fulfil this fantasy: he steals the Pope's food and boxes his ears, humiliating the head of the Catholic Church by subjecting him to the same treatment as the play's clowns. While this comic anti-papal assault no doubt appealed to Marlowe's Protestant spectators, however, in the 1604 A-text edition Faustus's actions in no way further the political Protestant agenda that he outlined in the play's opening scene. In fact, Faustus does not even initiate this papal encounter: his first impulse is to go sightseeing in Rome, and it is Mephistopheles who must remind him that 'I know you'd fain see the Pope' (3.1.50). Faustus's response remains lukewarm: he answers that he is 'content' to 'compass then some sport' (3.1.54), the casual reference to 'sport' implying that he intends to enjoy an entertainment planned by the devil rather than actively pursue his militant Protestant campaign.

Faustus's apparent neglect of his Protestant agenda during the A-text encounter with the Pope is illuminated by comparison with the 1616 B-text edition, in which the scene has been adapted to enhance its theological and political significance. Thus in the 1616 version the dialogue exposes the hypocrisy behind the flawed doctrine of papal infallibility (B-text 3.1.149–52), while Faustus's role in rescuing the German anti-Pope Bruno from captivity is actively political. In the B-text it is Faustus who initiates the attack on the Pope, telling Mephistopheles that

> Thyself and I may parley with this Pope,
> This proud confronter of the Emperor,
> And, in despite of all his holiness
> Restore this Bruno to his liberty
> And bear him to the states of Germany.
> (*Doctor Faustus* B-text 3.1.117–21)

Faustus subsequently enters into an alliance with the Holy Roman Emperor (B-text 4.1.1–64), and his role in securing the independence of the German Church accords with his self-proclaimed status as the champion of militant Protestantism. However, it remains unclear how far such evidence of Faustus's active contribution to the Protestant cause was present in the version of the play that was performed during the 1590s. In fact, the unusually marked use of rhyming couplets and adjectives ending in -al in this part of the B-text indicate that the Bruno episode was probably added by Samuel Rowley as part of the revisions commissioned by Philip Henslowe in 1602; as critics have noted, the anti-Catholic material added by Rowley and his co-writer William Birde may reflect a perceived need to enhance Faustus's status as a patriotic Protestant hero.[291]

In the A-text, Faustus's initial lack of interest in meeting the Pope and subsequent clowning suggest that he has lost interest in the militant Protestant ideals he previously laid claim to; ironically, it is Mephistopheles who is the driving force in this encounter, and meeting the Pope becomes another comic show to delight and distract Faustus. Faustus's apparent neglect of his Protestant agenda once he has achieved the alliance with Mephistopheles his militant rhetoric was designed to justify is intriguing. Indeed, Faustus's behaviour perhaps hints that he, like Marlowe's other politic protagonists, is perfectly willing to exploit religious rhetoric in pursuit of his own selfish ends. Faustus appears less hypocritical in the 1616 B-text, since he does challenge the political power of the papacy, but the change in emphasis is arguably attributable to the play's 1602 revisers. Moreover, the B-text raises the problematic possibility that Faustus's Protestant agenda may be tainted by association with the devil; though Marlowe's magician ostensibly advances the Protestant cause, he is aided by Mephistopheles and Lucifer, the demonic Father of Lies. Either Faustus is a hypocrite who consciously appropriates the language of militant Protestantism to justify his self-serving pact with the devil, or Mephistopheles is a cunning deceiver who pretends to support the Protestant cause as he tempts Faustus deeper into damnation: in both scenarios the credibility of Marlowe's protagonist, and of his cause, is threatened. Indeed, a couple of years later the Catholic polemicist Robert Parsons linked militant Protestantism with demonic conjuring practices reminiscent of Faustus's magic as part of his own efforts to discredit the pro-war Elizabethan councillor Sir Walter Ralegh. Parsons accused Ralegh of organising a 'schoole of Atheisme', wherein 'the olde, and new Testamente are jested at, and the schollers taught amonge other thinges, to spell God backward'; intriguingly, the Jesuit writer identified the chief 'Conjurer' of this school of atheism as Marlowe's friend Thomas Harriot.[292]

Parsons's account is pure propaganda, and should not be taken too seriously. However, several modern critics have also claimed that *Doctor Faustus* exposes the flaws in the militant Protestant enterprise. Leah Marcus argues that Faustus 'both reflects and hideously violates' the militant sentiments held by English audiences in the 1590s, since his anti-Spanish rhetoric conceals vast personal ambition, while Stephen Orgel describes Faustus as an illusory 'Protestant hero' whose dreams of power and glory are exposed as so much hot air.[293]

This attack on militant Protestantism cannot have been *too* obvious to the play's original audiences: it is unlikely that the Lord Admiral's Men would have performed *Doctor Faustus* twenty-four times between September 1594 and January 1597 if the play was considered incompatible with their patron's Protestant ideals. Nonetheless, it seems that Marlowe's contemporaries may have sometimes associated Faustus's magic with militant Protestantism, to the potential discredit of the Protestant cause. For instance, Marlowe's fellow writer Gabriel Harvey alludes to Faustus in an attack on the Protestant propagandists who sought to refute the subversive puritan arguments of Martin Marprelate: Harvey's particular target is the playwright John Lyly, whose pseudonym in the anti-Marprelate tract *Pappe with an hatchet* was 'double V.':

> As for that new-created Spirite, whom double V. like an other Doctour Faustus, threateneth to conjure-upp at leisure . . . were that Spirite disposed to appeare in his former likenesse, and to put the Necromancer to his purgation, he could peradventure make the conjuring wisard for sake the center of his Circle, and betake him to the circumference of his heeles.[294]

The title page to the 1616 edition of *Doctor Faustus* suggests that this image of Faustus drawing an elaborate magic circle on the stage had a significant impact in performance. Harvey's highly visual analogy thus draws on his readers' memories of Marlowe's foolish and misguided magician to critique a mainstream Protestant propaganda campaign, while implicitly associating the seditious puritans with the devil Mephistopheles. Harvey's taunt may also imply that Faustus's rhetoric is susceptible to appropriation by propagandists such as 'double V.', in the same way that Faustus himself invokes militant Protestant ideals for his own suspect purposes.

Marlowe's fellow writers seemingly recognised in *Doctor Faustus* a consistent interest in the appropriation of religious rhetoric by opportunistic characters: be it the political claims of militant Protestantism, lines from the scriptures, or the classical precedents of Epicurus, Lucretius or Aristotle. The fact that Faustus uses such questionable religious rhetoric to justify the treasonous repudiation of his God aligns him with Marlovian rebels such as Tamburlaine – save that Faustus acts within an explicitly Christian spiritual framework, betraying the very Protestant God whose cause he claims his demonic magic will advance.

FAUSTUS'S 'UNLAWFUL' CONTRACT: RELIGION VERSUS SECULAR LAW

Faustus's affinity with Marlowe's other protagonists is again evident in the way that his rebellion against his God involves an act of oath-breaking, followed in Faustus's case by the confirmation of a treacherous alliance with the devil. In the same way that Faustus's repudiation of God is both a political betrayal and an act of religious apostasy, his acts of oath-taking and oath-breaking unite Elizabethan concepts of the secular and the spiritual. In particular, Marlowe's characterisation of Faustus as an oath-breaker who fails in his duty to God seems to have been influenced by the idea of the heavenly covenant. Based on the old Jewish notion of a contract through which God provided temporal and spiritual benefits to believers as a reward for loyalty, the theory that a heavenly covenant existed between God and humanity was revived in Chriatian teaching during the early years of the Reformation and gained prominence in Elizabethan England from the late 1580s, particularly in extreme Protestant or puritan preaching.

In the *English Faust-Book*, Marlowe's probable source for *Doctor Faustus*, there is no suggestion that John Faustus has a prior agreement with God. In this prose version the protagonist seems inherently sinful: for instance, the narrator describes how Faustus, while studying divinity, 'would throw the Scriptures from him as though he had no care of his former profession'.[295] In contrast,

Marlowe's Faustus may have originally been a faithful believer. During the opening chorus the term 'graced' is associated with the protagonist twice within the space of two lines, and there is no mention of any reprobate behaviour committed in his childhood (Prologue, 16–17). The decision Faustus reaches in Act 1, to abandon God by selling his soul to Lucifer, is thus a more startling act of rebellion. Moreover, it necessitates the Protestant scholar Faustus's repudiation of his original baptismal contract with God. This oath-breaking aspect is emphasised in Marlowe's tragedy, which presents Faustus's contract with Mephistopheles as a demonic inversion of his prior covenant with God.

Critics often note the commercial implications of Faustus's agreement with Lucifer: Simon Shepherd argues that Faustus follows an intellectually stunted economic logic, while for David Riggs 'the sinner's discovery that he possesses a market value underlies the Faustian pact'.[296] Commercialised references – 'affords' (1.1.9), 'gold' (14), 'bills' (20) – abound in Faustus's opening soliloquy as he debates the value of his soul, while the chorus's previous comment that Faustus 'profits in divinity' introduced an association between souls and profit that Marlowe's protagonist now seeks to exploit (Prologue, 15). Assuming that his soul is a personal possession he is free to trade at will, Faustus expresses surprise when this sale runs into difficulties, asking, 'is not thy soul thy own?' (2.1.68). His supposition that the soul is a chattel which can be distinguished from the inner self may sound at odds with Protestant belief, but in fact Faustus's commercialised relationship with his soul relates suggestively to the sixteenth-century theory of the heavenly covenant. Indeed, the puritan clergy of Elizabethan England regularly drew attention to the economic implications of this covenant, with its connotations of exchange and reciprocity: sermons of the period explained doctrinal tenets and pastoral precepts in terms of commercial undertakings and seals, while the heavenly covenant itself was compared to bills or bonds of debt.[297]

The parodic parallels between the heavenly covenant and Faustus's demonic pact continue as Marlowe's magician summons

Mephistopheles using phrases and gestures associated with Christian baptism. The Elizabethan Thirty-Nine Articles emphasised that baptism was the outward seal of the heavenly contract with God, the means through which 'the promises of forgiveness of sin, and of our adoption to be the sons of God by the Holy Ghost, are visibly signed and sealed; faith is confirmed, and grace increased by virtue of prayer unto God'.[298] Faustus, however, inverts the traditional ceremony to repudiate his original contract with God and negotiate a new deal: rather than increasing his grace by prayer to God, Marlowe's protagonist has 'prayed and sacrificed' to the devil (1.3.7). Faustus goes on to write and sign his new demonic contract in his own blood, an action that parodies the Christian view that blood had confirmed God's covenant with his chosen people: it is reported in Exodus that 'Moses took the blood, and sprinkled it on the people, and said, Behold the blood of the covenant, which the LORD hath made with you' (Exodus 24.8). John Foxe's influential martyrology *Actes and Monuments* similarly characterises the blood shed by the Marian martyrs as a testimony to the validity of the Elizabethan Church and a confirmation of God's covenant with the English nation.[299]

The sight of Faustus's blood and his verbal mimicry of Christ's famous line '*Consummatum est*' evoke in addition the covenant of Christian mercy established by Christ's sacrifice on the cross – a covenant that Marlowe's protagonist rejects. Instead, Faustus bequeaths his soul to Lucifer through a 'deed of gift' (2.1.90) – the contractual terminology used by Protestant and puritan preachers to describe the gift of divine grace which Christ's sacrifice had secured. References to Christ's merciful undertaking as a 'deed of gift' are especially common, as in this early Jacobean sermon:

> As the Lands and goods of one man are made over unto another by deed of gift, sale, exchange or some like conveyance of Law, both for title and use: even so, the righteousnesse of Christ, by vertue of the free gift of God, according to the tenure of the Covenant of Grace, is truely and really conveyed unto us and made ours.[300]

This shared terminology of the 'deed of gift' again emphasises the extent to which Faustus's demonic contract is an inverted version of the heavenly covenant. Indeed, Faustus's contractual betrayal of his Protestant God can be regarded as a form of conversion: he summons Mephistopheles by praying to the devil, uses magical rites that parody the Elizabethan ceremony of baptism, promises to build Lucifer 'an altar and a church' and even offers to sacrifice the 'lukewarm blood of new-born babes' to his demonic master (2.1.13–14). Yet the contract that frames Faustus's 'conversion' is not purely spiritual in its significance; instead, Marlowe places significant emphasis on the legal status of the demonic contract. As with Faustus's rebellion against God, spiritual and secular concepts overlap and combine in the contract he subscribes to, and the question of whether or not the demonic pact is valid and Faustus must be damned becomes the driving force of Marlowe's tragedy.

In the *English Faust-Book* the contract between Faustus and Mephistopheles is a formal affair. Faustus's demands are set out in numbered lists, and followed by the demonic spirit's pledge that 'all this should be granted him and fulfilled, and more, if he would agree unto unto him upon certain articles'.[301] These legal elements are preserved and elaborated upon in Marlowe's drama. He even incorporates the reading of the legal contract into his play, despite the unusually lengthy recitation that is required; Faustus's list of his five 'conditions' is followed by the pledge that:

> I, John Faustus of Wittenberg, Doctor, by these presents, do give both body and soul to Lucifer, Prince of the East, and his minister Mephistopheles; and furthermore grant unto them that twenty-four years being expired, the articles above written inviolate, full power to fetch or carry the said John Faustus, body and soul, flesh, blood, or goods, into their habitation wheresoever.
>
> By me, John Faustus.
>
> (*Doctor Faustus* 2.1.105–113)

As in the *EFB* the structure and language of this statement emphasise its legal status, with terms such as 'the said', 'grant' and 'articles' mirroring the legal syntax of sixteenth-century secular contracts. In comparison with the *EFB*, however, Marlowe's version of the Faustian pact seems to highlight the possibilities for debate. Thus Faustus gives the devil's right to claim his soul greater prominence in the original agreement, but cautiously adds the explicit proviso that the articles must remain 'inviolate' for Mephistopheles to enforce this claim; then complicates the legal significance of his proviso by characterising the agreement as a 'deed of gift' rather than an explicitly reciprocal contract. The complexity of these additions suggests that, rather than strengthening or weakening the contract overall, Marlowe is introducing legal points which invite his audience to speculate about the validity of Faustus's agreement.

It is likely that there was no shortage of informed spectators in Marlowe's day: Elizabethan sources indicate that law students from the Inns of Court regularly attended theatrical performances, while other spectators would have had personal experience of contractual disputes during a highly litigious age in which formal commercial bonds were increasingly common. Such informed spectators might have noted several possible loopholes in Faustus's agreement with Mephistopheles. Firstly, it is unclear if Faustus's articles do remain 'inviolate', since Mephistopheles refuses to obey one of Faustus's commands almost as soon as he receives the deed of gift (2.3.64–9); Mephistopheles' proviso that he will only tell and perform what 'is not against our kingdom' might or might not be regarded as a valid legal defence by spectators (2.3.71). Since Elizabethan law took the intentions of oath-takers into account when determining the validity of a contract, it is also worth noting that the devil's commitment to the undertaking is somewhat dubious: Mephistopheles blandly swears to 'effect all promises between us' before he even hears Faustus's conditions (2.1.94). Finally, there is the crucial issue of whether or not Faustus's soul is his to sell: anticipated by his early reference to a legal case in which one object is willed to two parties (1.1.27–9), Faustus's attempt to bequeath to Lucifer the soul he previously pledged to God invites legal and spiritual debate about who really holds the title deed. These are important questions that potentially challenge the legal validity of Faustus's contract; yet Marlowe's protagonist, having previously dismissed the legal parallel to his own situation as 'a pretty case of paltry legacies!' (1.1.30), is equally oblivious to the potential loopholes in his demonic pact.

We cannot be certain if an Elizabethan spectator would have regarded Faustus's contract with the devil as legally binding, but it is likely that Faustus's lengthy recitation of his contract and the existence of a handwritten deed of gift would have carried some degree of conviction: as the notorious Niccolò Machiavelli put it, 'nothing is more likely to convict you than is your own handwriting'.[302] Faustus himself believes that the evidence is decisive: in Act 5 he admits despairingly that 'I writ them a bill with mine own blood. The date is expired, the time will come, and he will fetch me' (5.2.41–3). A few lines later, an apparently suicidal Faustus confirms that Hell has a legal right to claim his soul: 'Hell calls for right, and with a roaring voice / Says, "Faustus, come! Thine hour is come." / And Faustus will come to do thee right' (5.1.50–2). Later in the same scene, after trying but failing to repent, he seeks a means to 'extinguish clean / Those thoughts that do dissuade me from my vow, / And keep mine oath I made to Lucifer' (5.1.86–8). While Faustus's determination to 'keep mine oath' wavers when he thinks he glimpses an alternative, it remains a default position he consistently returns to. And, although Marlowe's protagonist vacillates wildly between stoic announcements that he will keep his word and desperate appeals to God to save him, he does not deny what he has done: however close to despair Faustus comes, he regards the sale of his soul as a legally valid transaction.

Acknowledging that his soul is pledged to Lucifer, Marlowe's protagonist does not attempt the sustained contractual chicanery that other stage magicians seek (often unsuccessfully) to practise. For instance, in Barnabe Barnes's *The Devil's Charter*, a play heavily influenced by *Doctor Faustus*, the villainous magician Pope Alexander tells his son the Duke of Candy that 'it is not alwaies needfull to keepe promise' (l. 447), quoting almost directly from Machiavelli's *Discourses*.[303] Yet Faustus's unwillingness or inability to engage in comparable secular trickery has intriguing implications. Crucially, Faustus's vacillations between stoic adherence to his pledged word and panicked appeals to God polarise the spiritual and legal imperatives Faustus faces: his religious duty is to repent and try to secure God's forgiveness, but his legal duty, at least as he sees it, is to keep to the terms of the demonic pact.

Faustus's distinction between legal and religious imperatives is deeply significant in Elizabethan terms, and links to Marlowe's wider interest in post-Reformation confessional polemic. Faustus does not look for legal loopholes, but that does not mean that he is content to let Lucifer claim his soul. Instead, Faustus repeatedly tries to escape by citing his opposed religious duty to God; the dilemma of the soul that belongs to two masters is introduced, not as a legal case, but as a religious appeal. The Good Angel and the Old Man advise Faustus to pursue the same course, ignoring the legal implications of the demonic contract and assuring him that God's forgiveness alone can release him from his promise to the devil: though in the event their tactics apparently fail, Faustus's damnation perhaps owes more to his failure to repent than to any triumph of legal 'right' over spiritual claims. Certainly, though Lucifer and his assistants airily claim that 'none but I have int'rest' in Faustus's soul (2.3.85), the fact that Mephistopheles and the Evil Angel so consistently disrupt his efforts to repent implies that they do not have as much confidence in their contractual right to his soul as they pretend.

It is perhaps unlikely that an Elizabethan audience would have seen anything wrong in Faustus's efforts to escape a pact with the devil by repenting and turning to God. Early modern legal manuals even added explicit provisos explaining how to proceed in cases where secular obligations conflict with divine law: the standard Elizabethan law text, St German's *Doctor and Student*, makes it quite clear that 'the law is to be left aside in favour of conscience in such particular cases . . . which are excepted from the general rules of English law by equity, the law of reason or the law of God'.[304] St German, however, was writing in the early sixteenth century. By the time *Doctor Faustus* was performed, oath-breaking in the name of religion was associated with urgent and immediate debates about political loyalty. In particular, as discussed in Chapter Three, the Elizabethan authorities were wary of the argument that secular oaths of loyalty could be broken in the name of a paramount spiritual duty to God. Such theories were initially associated with Catholic dissidents, but by the late 1580s instances of seditious puritan oath-breaking were also being publicised in sermons and printed tracts. The contemporary reality of religious conflict, invoked by Faustus's militant Protestant allusions, might equally have informed the way Elizabethan spectators responded to Faustus's treacherous oath-taking and his subsequent efforts to break his demonic vow in the name of religion.

The possibility that Marlowe's Elizabethan spectators would have perceived these connections is strengthened by the language used to describe Faustus's attempts at oath-breaking. Like the Catholic and puritan dissidents of Elizabethan England, Faustus is frequently identified as a rebel and a traitor. For a Christian spectator his treachery lies in his original rejection of his spiritual allegiance to God; yet Faustus's later efforts to repudiate his demonic pact and reaffirm his loyalty to God are equally termed betrayal by the devil he seeks to abandon. As Lucifer points out, Faustus breaks his earlier pledge to Mephistopheles when he asks for God's forgiveness: 'Thou talk'st of Christ, contrary to thy promise. / Thou shouldst not think of God. Think of the devil' (2.3.91–2). Yet Marlowe's spectators would have known that Faustus must break this particular promise; to have any chance of salvation, he must call on Christ. Given Faustus's dilemma, torn between two conflicting allegiances, there is a suggestive irony in Mephistopheles' subsequent conviction of Faustus for treachery: in Act 5, the devil declares, 'Thou traitor, Faustus, I arrest thy soul / For disobedience to my sovereign Lord. / Revolt, or I'll in piecemeal tear thy flesh' (5.1.67–9). While 'revolt' in this context ostensibly means that Faustus must reaffirm his allegiance to Lucifer, it also puns on 'revolt' as political disobedience; the epithet 'traitor' takes on the double resonance of traitor to Lucifer and traitor to God, as well as potentially reminding spectators of the real-life Elizabethan rebels who broke their secular oaths of loyalty in the name of religion.

By contrasting Faustus's legal duty to the devil with his spiritual duty to God, *Doctor Faustus* stages a conflict of allegiances that would have had a charged significance for Elizabethan audiences. As far as Faustus, the Good Angel and the Old Man are concerned, it seems that the loopholes in the demonic contract cannot provide Faustus with an acceptable legal defence: the only way for him to get out of the contract is to prioritise his purely spiritual duty of allegiance to God. Yet while breaking his bond to Lucifer would presumably increase Faustus's chances of salvation, it would also potentially align him with the oath-breaking Catholic and puritan rebels who haunted the imaginations of loyal Englishmen; as Marlowe's audiences were aware, salvation was the prize these rebels and assassins expected to earn. Moreover, as Luke Wilson argues, 'the problematic instrumentality of the demonic pact – what can it possibly mean? how could it possibly be binding? – reveals the ideological basis of all contractual obligation – in what sense is *any* contract binding?';[305] the potential implications for a state fearful of oath-breaking rebels are certainly intriguing.

The debate may even continue past the *ad terminus* of Faustus's death: while the display of Faustus's scattered limbs in the 1616 B-text imposes a 'hellish' judgement that suggestively mirrors the fate of England's convicted traitors, dismembered on the stage of the scaffold, the apparent omission of this final spectacle from the 1604 A-text arguably allows the audience to reach their own 'judgements' (Prologue, 9). Indeed, in both editions the play's closing lines revitalise the ongoing debate between the competing claims of law and religion: when the epilogue didactically instructs Marlowe's audiences to regard Faustus's 'hellish fall, / Whose fiendful fortune may exhort the wise / Only to wonder at unlawful things' (Epilogue, 4–6), the term 'unlawful' becomes double-edged. Faustus's contract is of course unlawful in the theological sense – but from a strictly legal perspective perhaps even his salvation might be unlawful, if it denies Mephistopheles his due right to Faustus's soul.

AN ATHEIST'S TRAGEDY: 'DOCTOR FAUSTUS' AND THE FAILURE OF DISBELIEF

Doctor Faustus shares with the rest of Marlowe's plays and poems a close interest in religiously inflected hypocrisy and fraud, as various characters appropriate religious rhetoric to justify their own self-interested agendas. Yet *Doctor Faustus* also differs significantly from Marlowe's other works. *Edward II* shares the focus on a protagonist who is less successful in manipulating religion than his plausible opponent, and in *The Massacre at Paris* rival characters similarly compete for ownership of the play's religious rhetoric. *Doctor Faustus*, however, remains the only play in which such rhetoric is employed in an actively Christian spiritual setting. Thus Faustus experiences an unusual problem: whereas the politic appropriation of religion in Marlowe's writings usually operates on the premise that such 'religion' is a secular fraud, Faustus seeks to exploit spiritual phenomena whose reality is visually and aurally apparent to the play's spectators. The only other Marlovian protagonists to experience a comparable tension between the spiritual rhetoric they manipulate and genuine religious experience are Hero's lover Leander, in his encounter with Neptune; Caesar, who in *Lucan's First Book* meets the goddess Rome on the banks of the Rubicon; and Aeneas, who speaks to Hermes and his mother Venus face to face and receives instructions about oath-breaking from Jupiter himself. But these three protagonists inhabit a classical universe peopled with Greco-Roman gods; Faustus's interaction with the literal angels and devils of the Christian cosmos is unique in Marlowe's writings.

Faustus occupies a spiritually orientated world in which supernatural episodes abound. But at the beginning of Marlowe's tragedy he is largely oblivious to this reality; even as he repudiates his God and prepares to summon the devil, Faustus shows little awareness of the genuine religious implications. Instead, he announces that he will 'be a divine *in show*' before deciding to 'perform' magic (1.1.3, 138; my italics) – an emphasis on the performative implications of his actions that prioritises external appearance above inner truth, and hints at Faustus's belief that both the divine authority he repudiates and the demonic power he intends to wield are primarily illusory. He is perfectly willing to manipulate religious rhetoric to defend his ambitions, twisting and misquoting scripture to provide a biblical rationale for his actions; defending his decision to repudiate God as a means to advance the international Protestant cause; and patterning his undertaking to Lucifer upon the Christian covenant so as to confer a feigned religious status on his apostasy. As far as Faustus is concerned, however, it seems that such claims are the linguistic equivalent of being a divine in show. Ultimately, his willingness to repudiate God and forge a contract with Mephistopheles is based on disbelief; Faustus, who accepts only the evidence of his own senses, refuses to accept the existence of hell and is sceptical about heaven's power to intervene on earth.

Faustus's reliance on the sceptical arguments of 'old philosophers' such as Epicurus, Lucretius and Aristotle is however complicated by his encounter with the devil's representative Mephistopheles. Forced to believe in the existence of the supernatural *after* he has signed his soul away, Faustus spends the rest of the play alternating between sceptical denial of the soul's immortality, indulging a stereotypically 'Epicurean' appetite for worldly pleasures, and fierce crises of conscience in which he appeals for divine redemption. Again, however, Faustus's new-found alertness to the spirituality of his world puts him at a disadvantage. The fact that the miraculous signs he witnesses are presumably real may even hinder his efforts to break his secular contract; he remains too conscious of his legal duty to Mephistopheles and too mindful of the initial sin he committed against God to try and interpret or appropriate a genuine sign from heaven. Instead, Faustus takes refuge in a blinkered disbelief that rejects the reality of all divine portents and denies the existence of hell. In consequence, the power in this play rests not with the protagonist but with his devilish companion Mephistopheles, who excels at adopting deceitful rhetorical poses and staging demonic shows.

Mephistopheles' authority over Faustus is provocative, potentially implying that the fraudulently 'miraculous' spectacles he fabricates are more effective than the genuine item. Barbara Traister suggests that the play's restrained signs of heavenly presence, so small as to be visible only to Faustus, hardly balance the many visual wonders provided by the devils, and it is certainly true that the shows arranged by Mephistopheles are almost always the most spectacular element in modern productions.[306] Yet Faustus's inability to exploit either these demonic spectacles or the signs sent by heaven to his own advantage may be equally to blame for his damnation; after all, he never manages to compose a convincing excuse to repent and return to his God. Indeed, when we compare him to Marlowe's more successful protagonists we might even wonder if Faustus is destroyed not only by his initial lack of faith in God, but also by his failure to commit fully to disbelief: Marlowe's magician is neither sceptical enough to interpret religious spectacle to his own advantage and justify abandoning the devil; nor enough of a true believer to trust without question in divine mercy. Caught between belief and disbelief, religious loyalty and secular duty, and unable to commit to either side, Faustus's experiences reflect the tragic failure of politic religion in the hands of a man who is forced to believe; in this sense, Marlowe's play might be described as the tragedy of an atheist whose scepticism fails him. Yet it is also the tragedy of a man, torn between two conflicting allegiances, who stays caught in the middle, unable to commit fully to either side.

Marlowe's play suggests that Faustus has made foolish decisions, but within this tragedy there is no straightforward condemnation of his original desires and ambitions. Contemporary spectators noted the actor Edward Alleyn's impressive build as well as his powerful voice and his Faustus must have physically dominated the stage; spoken by the same actor who played mighty Tamburlaine, Faustus's divine aspirations may not have seemed as disproportionate to Elizabethan spectators as a modern reading might suggest. The tragic note struck by the play is deepened by this intense awareness of the heights that Faustus aspires to but fails to hold. Even in his final moments, as he pleads for God's forgiveness in wildly passionate terms, Faustus's refusal to deny his fatal deed bestows a certain stoic dignity upon his actions: 'God forbade it indeed, but Faustus hath done it' (5.2.39). Marlowe's protagonist acknowledges his actions, and his tragedy is that such acceptance offers no solution. He believes that Lucifer has a legal right to his soul and, having been forced to accept the spiritual reality of the Christian cosmos he inhabits, equally believes that he betrayed his religious duty to God by signing a contract with the devil. His early efforts to manipulate scriptural precedents and militant Protestant polemic come to nothing once he recognises that the Christian framework such religious rhetoric invokes surrounds him in its fearsome reality. Only the exculpatory precedent of classical scepticism is left – and then only because he so desperately longs to believe that his soul will dissolve away in death. Too much of an atheist to truly repent, and too embedded in belief to skilfully manipulate religion, Marlowe's Faustus is trapped between his spiritual and secular allegiances; divided in his conscience, he suffers accordingly, and in the 1616 B-text at least is physically 'torn asunder', his limbs scattered across the stage (B-text 5.3.6–7).

THE DIVIDED CONSCIENCE: BELIEF AND SUFFERING IN MARLOWE'S WORKS

Lisa Hopkins believes that Faustus's indecision touched a culturally crucial chord with Marlowe's original audiences and readers, forced to choose between Catholicism and Protestantism.[307] Faustus, weighing the conflicting demands of a Calvinist Good Angel and a devil dressed in Catholic robes, certainly experiences a confessional quandary that would be familiar to Elizabethan and Jacobean spectators. In Marlowe's tragedy, however, the psychomachia expressed in Faustus's soliloquies stems less from a choice between Catholicism and Protestantism than from the incompatibility of his spiritual duty to God and his contractual obligation to the devil; it is the struggle to balance these opposing obligations, rather than to choose between rival confessions, that preoccupies Marlowe's protagonist. The conflicting religious and legal imperatives that divide Faustus's conscience might equally have struck a chord with his sixteenth- and seventeenth-century spectators.

Thus in *Doctor Faustus* Marlowe's protagonist must prove either a traitor to God or a traitor to Lucifer, having pledged his soul to both; this concept of dual allegiance and opposed loyalties recalls the situation of England's Catholic and puritan dissidents, torn between their allegiance to the state and their perceived religious duty to oppose a heretical regime. Thus, behind Marlowe's literary depiction of a protagonist who struggles to reconcile opposed loyalties, his audiences might perhaps have heard echoes of the painful question framed by the Catholic priest Robert Parsons: 'Must everye man be an enymie to the state, which lykethe not that religion whiche is favoured bye the State?'.[308]

Few of Marlowe's protagonists would recognise the dilemma Parsons's words express between faith and secular loyalty. In his plays and poems most characters prioritise their own interests above the claims of either, adopting the rhetoric of whatever confession or faith seems most likely to bring secular advantage at a given moment. These expert practitioners of politic religion are, unlike Parsons's imagined readership of Catholic recusants, prepared to feign a false outward conformity to avoid persecution or gain material advantage; in contrast to Faustus, they have no qualms about breaking contracts the moment an alliance threatens their position, and readily attribute such oath-breaking to a paramount religious obligation. Faustus on the other hand becomes trapped by belief in the course of Marlowe's tragedy, offering an unusual though not entirely unique example of a Marlovian character who actively suffers the pangs of conscience.

Although it is rare for Marlowe's characters to make even the slightest reference to conscience, the tragic trajectory of *Doctor Faustus* demonstrates Marlowe's ability to dramatise the intense suffering the conflicting demands of religious and secular loyalties might generate. Indeed, Marlowe's depiction of Faustus's dilemma places considerable emphasis on the emotional torments the protagonist experiences: in this respect, it is reminiscent of Nathanial Woodes's Protestant morality drama *The Conflict of Conscience*.[309] A comparably sensitive portrayal of the struggle to reconcile Catholic religious loyalties with a proto-Protestant legal demand can be found in the history play *Sir Thomas More* (*c*. 1600). In this drama, the pivotal issue is the refusal of the Catholic More and the Bishop of Rochester to subscribe to Henry VIII's Act of Supremacy: unlike Faustus, More refuses to sign the act until his 'conscience' can 'parley with our laws', and concludes with the Bishop that 'subscribing so, I were an hypocrite' (10.73–8). This play's daring engagement with questions of divided loyalty in an English political context is striking, rivalling Marlowe's own alertness to and engagement with the politico-religious controversies of his day – except that More and the Bishop react to the genuine pangs of conscience that Marlowe's politic protagonists rarely pause to acknowledge.

A similar though less explicitly religious sensitivity to the torments of a divided conscience can be seen in *Tamburlaine Part One*. As Tamburlaine wages war against his lover Zenocrate's father the Sultan of Egypt, and her former fiancé Arabia, she laments her inability to reconcile her opposed loyalties:

> Now shame and duty, love and fear, presents
> A thousand sorrows to my martyred soul.
> Whom should I wish the fatal victory
> When my poor pleasures are divided thus,
> And racked by duty from my cursèd heart?
>
> (*Tamburlaine Part One* 5.2.321–5)

The loyalties Zenocrate attempts to reconcile are political and familial in nature, but her reference to her 'martyred soul' also implicitly relates her experience to the confessional divisions of Elizabethan England. Potentially invoking the 'racked' and 'martyred' English Catholics forced to choose between their church and their country as Spanish forces threatened 1580s England, Zenocrate's moving words again invite a comparatively sympathetic response. The moment was especially poignant in Terry Hands's 1992 RSC production, in which Claire Benedict's Zenocrate spoke these lines in a broken voice while kneeling as if at prayer; as she reached the end of the speech, a mortally wounded Arabia entered to die in Zenocrate's arms.[310] Though Marlowe's writings more frequently centre on the hypocritical manipulation of religious rhetoric by characters who repudiate their secular loyalties for personal advantage, his renderings of Zenocrate's dilemma and Faustus's tragic fate demonstrate that he was not oblivious to the pain endured by those who suffered for their consciences.

The crises of allegiance experienced by Faustus and Zenocrate reflect a tension in Marlowe's writings between genuine faith and the sceptical appropriation of religious rhetoric; a conflict in which true belief rarely if ever proves compatible with earthly advancement. Faustus is the only Marlovian protagonist who fails because he cannot exploit religion successfully within a spiritual Christian universe, but he is not the only character to suffer for conscientiously adhering to religious or secular loyalties. In *The Massacre at Paris*, the Huguenot victims of the 1572 massacre die because they refuse to conform outwardly to the Catholic faith; the efforts of their Catholic murderers to demarcate the limits of acceptable prayer through violence are epitomised by Gonzago's order that the dying Admiral Coligny 'pray unto our Lady; kiss this cross' (5.28), an instruction that puns on the shape of his bloody dagger. By contrasting the conscientious deaths of Huguenot martyrs such as Coligny with the sceptical dissimulation practised by their killers Guise and Anjoy, *The Massacre at Paris* responds to Elizabethan concerns about the gap between outward display and inner reality, especially insofar as this pertains to religious conviction. Yet, problematically, the characters who achieve success in Marlowe's drama are those who are willing to embrace religious hypocrisy; characters who listen to the urgings of their consciences become silenced victims, often killed within a few short lines.

This contrast between conscientious suffering and politic achievement is equally evident in Marlowe's *Edward II*. King Edward and his enemy Mortimer follow structurally opposed trajectories, with the rise of one mirroring the fall of the other: thus the rebellious Mortimer's growing skill at appropriating religious rhetoric is inversely paralleled by Edward's sincere if arguably immature efforts to trust in God. The contrast is especially apparent at the moment of Edward II's death. Mortimer is at the height of his powers, having exploited first Catholic and then puritan religious rhetoric to establish himself as Lord Protector, while his imprisoned royal victim has experienced a religious epiphany that he clings to in the face of physical degradation. Edward's conscientious spirituality does not place him in danger directly, but his new-found faith is most evident in the moments before his hideous death. Realising that he is about to die, Edward asks that the assassin 'let me see the stroke before it comes, / That even then when I shall lose my life, / My mind may be more steadfast on my God' (24.75–7); virtually his last words are an appeal to heaven to 'assist me, sweet God, and receive my soul' (24.108). Marlowe's king is perhaps more sympathetic as he dies than at any other point in the play, and the language and imagery surrounding his death may even have encouraged Elizabethan spectators to associate him with a tradition of religious martyrdom: the handkerchief that Edward tells his queen to dip in his blood recalls the holy relics Elizabethan Catholics gathered when the English authorities executed missionary priests such as Edmund Campion (20.118–20), dipping their handkerchiefs into the dying men's blood. While the handkerchief motif is not exclusively Catholic, it may serve to link Edward's fate visually with that of the English men and women who died for prioritising religious duty above secular allegiance.

Marlowe acknowledges the genuine suffering experienced by characters who listen to their consciences, rather than embracing religious hypocrisy. In his plays and poems, however, such characters are the losers in a secular arena – and, unlike many of his fellow dramatists, Marlowe provides no authoritative external commentary or glimpses of an afterlife to correct this impression. Despite the standard Christian expectation that those who suffer for their faith on earth will be rewarded in heaven, Marlowe offers his audiences and readers little assurance of celestial recompense. On the contrary, such conventional assumptions are undercut by the nature of the characters who experience crises of conscience in his writings. Since sixteenth-century moralists and theologians were adamant that only true martyrs would be rewarded in heaven, and that those of an opposed 'false' confession or faith did not qualify, many of those who suffer for their consciences in Marlowe's work would presumably not count as martyrs in Protestant England: Zenocrate is a pagan who prays to Mahomet and Jove; Edward II is a spoilt and gullible ruler who ruins the realm; and Faustus ultimately fails to repent even though he acknowledges his religious duty to do so, falling instead into despair. Only the Huguenot victims of *The Massacre at Paris* have any real claim to be considered martyrs of Protestant conscience, and in the play text as it survives their quick deaths lack significant theatrical impact.

However, even the tentative and problematic crises of 'conscience' experienced by characters such as Faustus and Edward II are emphatically at odds with earthly advancement in Marlowe's drama. Throughout his plays and poems the terminology of 'conscience' never appears in contexts where it is compatible with secular profit: in *The Massacre at Paris*, for instance, 'conscience' is used only twice, and on both occasions in a context of religiously inflected violence (4.12; 23.24). Within a literary framework that polarises conscientious belief and politic hypocrisy, only one option brings literal success in the course of Marlowe's narratives. There is little indication that the faithful will be rewarded after death; instead, the practical godlessness so dreaded by both the Elizabethan authorities and their confessional opponents starts to seem like the only route to success, even survival, within fictional environments in which religious fraud and hypocrisy is universal. Reducing religious rhetoric to a tool of political and financial advancement, Marlowe's plays and poems thus reflect the scepticism that informed Elizabethan attitudes towards the external performance of religious conviction in a post-Reformation context of inter-confessional antagonism.

CODA

MARLOWE'S LEGACY

In Marlowe's writings the politic exploitation of religion is the norm – a near-universal phenomenon, not limited to those of one confession or faith. The scope of such religious fraud is one of Marlowe's most significant innovations, and one that is central to the way his literary works explore the realities of scepticism. While Marlowe's precursors and contemporaries also portray characters who manipulate religious rhetoric to their own ends, they do so within a moral framework that Marlowe dispenses with. In most Elizabethan texts, the hypocritical exploitation of religion is associated exclusively with villainous characters, and the religion or confession in question is almost invariably one considered false or heretical by the author. In contrast, virtually every character in Marlowe's plays and poems appropriates religious rhetoric at one point or another and the rhetoric ranges widely across confessional divides: Greco-Roman, Catholic, Jewish, Islamic and Protestant discourses prove equally ripe for exploitation. Characters of all denominations deceive and are deceived by equivocating rhetoric: the youthful lover Leander uses religious precedent to mislead as eagerly as the demonic Mephistopheles, while Mortimer and Anjoy's proto-Protestant posturing is as untrustworthy as the conversions to Catholicism enacted by Barabas and his daughter Abigail. Throughout his literary career Marlowe engages with religious fraud in cross-confessional episodes that negate religious difference, presenting characters of all confessional allegiances and faiths as uniformly willing to exploit religion for politic ends.

The prevalence of politic religion in Marlowe's writings enables the questions they raise about the appropriation of religion to extend beyond a simplistic demonisation of the religious other.

At the same time, much of the conventional moral structure that surrounds the discussion of politic religion in contemporary discourse is lost. Instead, Marlowe's second innovation was to deconstruct the moral determinants of religious fraud by creating fictional universes that are effectively immune to providential judgement; even in works such as *Doctor Faustus* and *Dido Queen of Carthage* which feature the active participation of gods, angels and devils, divine authority is discredited or rendered problematic. The sustained uncertainty in Marlowe's writings about divine providence, the immortality of the soul and life after death means that secular success becomes the primary standard of achievement. Within this predominantly earthbound context, it is the politic exploitation of religion that most readily ensures success; in contrast, those who take religious faith and allegiance too seriously become the suffering victims.

Fired in the melting pot of post-Reformation polemic, Marlowe's literary representation of politic religion was provocative, strikingly innovative and influential. This coda explores the impact that Marlowe's scepticism had on the subsequent representation of religious themes by seventeenth-century writers. In particular, Marlowe's literary heirs responded to his morally ambivalent vision of politic religion by allowing positive and even heroic characters to manipulate religious rhetoric for the sake of earthly success in their own plays and poems. Although Marlowe's literary scepticism continued to inform the dramatic and poetic representation of religion during the seventeenth century, however, his radically sceptical conclusions were ignored by more pious or conservative contemporaries; it was not until the late seventeenth and early eighteenth centuries that Marlowe's characteristically cross-confessional approach was mirrored in the writings of mainstream thinkers. By then, the upheavals of the English Civil War had led to a renewed emphasis on the monarch's authority over the church and reinvigorated debates about secular and spiritual allegiance, while over the next few decades freethinkers such as Charles Blount and John Toland pointed to the similarities between religions in order to discredit the priesthood. The latter group's attacks on popular superstition could also be interpreted as a more general condemnation of organised religion; pious readers reproachfully defined the model of civic faith these writings outlined as 'politick religion'.[311]

The cross-confessional perspective adopted by seventeenth- and eighteenth-century freethinkers also shaped the literary scepticism Marlowe expresses in his plays and poems, which themselves edge towards outright disbelief; in Marlowe's writings, the recognition that religious belief is an ideology susceptible to near-universal appropriation provokes the contempt of the protagonists who so skilfully exploit its 'simple sound' (*Massacre at Paris* 2.65). With nearly eighty years separating Marlowe's intuitive and imaginative engagement with the metaphysical anxieties of post-Reformation Europe from the cross-confessional scepticism voiced in works such as Charles Blount's *Oracles of Reason*, the Elizabethan author remains an important figure in the intellectual history of disbelief. Marlowe's literary response to the doubts and uncertainties engendered by the religious conflicts of post-Reformation Europe and his open acknowledgement of the cross-confessional value of hypocrisy, which took more than half a century to be paralleled in English non-fiction, established him as one of the pioneers of early modern religious scepticism, as well as a literary inspiration for writers from William Shakespeare to John Milton.

MARLOWE'S INFLUENCE: POLITIC RELIGION AFTER 1593

During Marlowe's own lifetime, only one other English playwright seems to express a similar degree of scepticism in his writings: Thomas Kyd, who in 1593 bore witness to his former room-mate Marlowe's 'atheist' beliefs after being imprisoned on charges of heresy. Kyd may not have received the same university divinity training and consequent exposure to classical traditions of scepticism as Marlowe, but he did share his colleague's experience of the virulent religious controversies of the 1570s, 1580s and 1590s, which also strongly influenced Kyd's depictions of politic religion. *The Spanish Tragedy*, Kyd's most famous and influential work, displays an almost Marlovian interest in the appropriation and manipulation of religious rhetoric. The military conquest of Portugal is for instance credited by the King of Spain to 'heaven, and [the] guider of the heavens' (1.2.10); his providentialist discourse may be inspired by Tamburlaine's 'scourge of God' rhetoric in Marlowe's roughly contemporary drama. Similarly, the King's villainous nephew Lodowick uses linguistic equivocation and visual deceit to trick the unhappy murderer Pedringano into playing the role of scapegoat, assuring Pedringano that he will 'mount' for Serberine's murder (3.2.93); the pun on mounting as promotion and mounting the scaffold again recalls Marlowe's characteristic style. Moreover, Kyd's tragedy seems as devoid of a Christian providential framework as Marlowe's plays and poems. The most prominent representative of the divine pantheon is the sleepy Revenge (3.15.1–10), Kyd's hero Hieronimo is notably sceptical about divine justice (3.2.5–11; 3.7.10–18), and the only character to refer consistently to a Christian belief system is his wife Isabella (2.5.57–9) – who runs mad with grief for her dead son and kills herself when the heavens apparently ignore her pleas for justice.[312] Kyd's interest in pious deceit is less politically engaged than Marlowe's and his characters rarely use religious rhetoric to justify their dishonest and murderous behaviour, preferring to appeal to considerations of revenge and honour. Yet Kyd, depicting a dramatic universe in which divine justice is arbitrary and even positive characters must embrace deceit to survive, perhaps comes closer to the preoccupations of his one-time roommate than any other author of the 1590s.

After Marlowe's death, his arresting message that the politic appropriation of religion is a near-universal practice began to influence his literary successors. During the course of the seventeenth century playwrights and poets gradually moved closer to representing religious hypocrisy after the fashion set by Marlowe, creating episodes that owe a strong debt to the latter's writings. William Shakespeare and Ben Jonson were especially haunted by his legacy, while a literary scepticism reminiscent of Marlowe pervades the tragedies of John Webster.

Shakespeare's early drama often features instances of religious hypocrisy, but it is with his late-Elizabethan and great Jacobean plays that such hypocrisy acquires a more morally ambivalent edge. From the mid-1590s, Shakespeare apparently began to absorb and respond to Marlowe's notion that even characters who are generally pious and heroic may manipulate religious rhetoric for politic ends. Several critics have explored this shift in Shakespeare's thinking with reference to Machiavelli's political theories: Hugh Grady for instance notes that the histories and tragedies written after 1595 seem to take for granted a secular understanding of political power as a force for both good and evil, while John Roe, in *Shakespeare and Machiavelli*, demonstrates that even predominantly positive characters such as Henry V and Duke Vincentio in *Measure for Measure* use religiously inflected deceit to attain their ends.[313]

Popular Elizabethan associations between Machiavellianism and religious fraud were no doubt a factor in Shakespeare's representation of politic religion, but such episodes also show signs of Marlowe's literary influence. For instance, Henry V's striking attempt to displace responsibility for his French wars on to God recalls the providential rhetoric used by such Marlovian warmongers as Navarre and Tamburlaine (*Henry V* 1.2.303–9; 4.1.165–84), while Hamlet's struggles with his conscience and gradual decision to take action rather than waiting for a divine judgement that may never materialise arguably reflect the doubts Marlowe's characters express about providential intervention. Moreover, Hamlet draws attention to the prevalence of religious deceit in Shakespeare's fictional Denmark: he recognises in the looks of Rosencrantz and Guildenstern a 'kind of confession' that they 'have not craft enough to colour' (2.2.245–6), and sees through Ophelia's efforts to 'sugar o'er' deceptive behaviour 'with devotion's visage' and 'pious action' (3.1.46–7). This preoccupation with religious hypocrisy is reflected in the play's vocabulary: Hamlet is the first character to use the term 'equivocation' in Shakespeare's writings (5.1.130).

Linguistic deceit is also a central theme in Shakespeare's Jacobean tragedy *Macbeth*: the equivocation practised by the three witches may recall Marlowe's elusive devil Mephistopheles. The witches' linguistic trickery is explicitly associated with 'th'equivocation of the fiend, / That lies like truth'; like Mephistopheles, with his misleadingly truthful description of hell, Shakespeare's witches rely on a series of prophecies that are literally true in one sense, but which Macbeth interprets wrongly (*Macbeth* 5.5.43–4). As Banquo warns Macbeth, 'oftentimes, to win us to our harm, / The instruments of Darkness tell us truths; / Win us with honest trifles' (1.3.123–5):[314] the strategy of 'honest' dissimulation again recalls Mephistopheles' use of plain rhetoric, as well as Iago's tactics in *Othello*. The equivocation portrayed in *Macbeth* perhaps responds to Jacobean anxiety about Catholic deceit, just as Marlowe's episodes of politic religion spoke to urgent contemporary concerns. Thus critics often suggest that Shakespeare is mimicking the linguistic tricks used by the Catholic conspirators who plotted to blow up the Houses of Parliament and kill King James I in 1605, while Macbeth's arguments for killing King Duncan seem conversely to rely on the Protestant monarchomach George Buchanan's theories of elective monarchy and constitutional resistance; his appropriation of Protestant resistance rhetoric echoes the practice of Marlovian murderers such as Mortimer in *Edward II*, and suggests the influence that Marlowe's cross-confessional representation of politic religion had on Shakespeare's own dramatic imagination.[315] In addition, and as in *Hamlet*, equivocation is not exclusively associated with the villains of *Macbeth*. In Act 4 Macduff's wife and son describe Macbeth's nemesis as a 'traitor' and a liar, suggesting that in Shakespeare's Jacobean tragedies loyal heroes, murderous usurpers and demonic witches can be equivocators (4.2.44-58).

Shakespeare's late-Elizabethan and early Jacobean plays show an increased willingness to depict sympathetic characters such as Ophelia adopting religious poses for deceitful ends; in *Hamlet* and *Macbeth*, religious hypocrisy even becomes a near-universal trait. However, Shakespeare's fictional worlds retain an overarching moral framework. While heroic characters occasionally manipulate religion, such conduct seems to be a necessary aberration rather than an actively desirable quality; elsewhere in Shakespeare's writings religiously inflected fraud remains the preserve of the villain, while in later Jacobean plays such as *Pericles* and *The Winter's Tale* Shakespeare develops a revitalised providentialist structure whereby final resolution is achieved through supernatural intervention. But despite his greater commitment to providential narratives, Shakespeare was strongly influenced by Marlowe's literary representation of politic religion: in the Jacobean histories and tragedies that he wrote which built upon and refined Marlowe's formulae for commercial success, religion is almost universally acknowledged as a tool of policy.

Shakespeare's contemporary Ben Jonson was similarly influenced by Marlowe's literary scepticism. There are many episodes in his plays in which characters manipulate religious rhetoric, and these scenes often bear the marks of Marlowe's influence; like Shakespeare, Jonson apparently recognised the politic appropriation of religion as a significant theme. In the unfinished play *Mortimer His Fall*, modelled on Marlowe's *Edward II*, Jonson's Mortimer for instance shares his Marlovian predecessor's belief that conscience is incompatible with earthly achievement:

> There is a Fate, that flies with towring spirits
> Home to the marke, and never checks at conscience.
> Poore plodding Priests, and preaching Friars may make
> Their hollow Pulpits, and the empty Iles
> Of Churches ring with that round word: But wee
> That draw the subtile, and more piercing ayre,
> In that sublimed region of Court,
> Know all is good, we make so, and goe on,
> Secur'd by the prosperity of our crimes.
>
> (*Mortimer His Fall* 1.1.11–19)

The Bishop of Worcester, one of the main voices of baronial opposition in Jonson's draft, is even explicitly described as 'politique' (Arguments, 3); and while we cannot know how this play would have developed, Jonson's outline suggests an almost Marlovian fascination with exploring the dangers and advantages of politic religion in an English political context.[316]

Jonson never finished his tale of 'subtile' Mortimer, but instances of religious manipulation are common in Jonson's writings. In *Catiline His Conspiracy*, for example, Catiline models his desire to rebel against Rome upon the mythological precedent set by the seditious Titan Atlas; his rhetoric echoes Marlowe's great Tartar/Titan Tamburlaine's use of classical precedent to justify his seditious campaigns (*Catiline* 1.83–93).[317] Catiline's co-conspirator Lecca similarly uses religious rhetoric to inspire their rebel army, presenting the eagle standard to the soldiers as a 'sacred' symbol that will consecrate their cause – an image of men vowing sedition on a religious symbol perhaps echoing the Catholic villains of Marlowe's *Massacre at Paris*, who swear 'by the argent crosses' to kill all that they suspect of heresy (5.1–3). Furthermore, Jonson's play follows Marlowe's example in that the manipulation of religious rhetoric is not a tactic confined to the villainous usurper Catiline and his allies. The orator Cicero invokes abstractions of divine justice and omnipotence in an attempt to conceal the sordid truth about his intelligence-gathering activities (3.2.1–4, 211–12),[318] while the Roman general Petreius urges his soldiers to 'trust the Senate's and Rome's cause to heaven' and fight:

> For the rais'd temples of th'immortal gods,
> For all your fortunes, altars, and your fires,
> For the dear souls of your lov'd wives and children,
> Your parents' tombs, your rites, laws, liberty
>
> (*Catiline* 5.1.15–18)

Jonson also responded to Marlowe's literary scepticism in his comedies. In these plays politic religion becomes a target for Jonson's satiric pen, as he builds upon the mockery already implicit in Marlowe's darkly ironic narratives. In *Volpone*, for instance, Jonson lampoons puritan conversions in a comic masque:

NANO: but I
Would ask, how of late, thou hast suffered translation,
And shifted thy coat, in these days of reformation?
ANDROGINO: Like one of the reformèd, a fool, as you see,
Counting all old doctrine heresy.

(*Volpone* 1.2.28–32)

Androgino's ridicule of the 'precise, pure, illuminate brother', 'by some writers called an ass' (1.2.42–3), reflects not only Jonson's distaste for extreme Protestantism but also perhaps his contempt for those that abandon 'all old doctrine'. Yet despite Jonson's real-life experience of religious persecution and his possibly forced submission to the Jacobean state church in 1610, the mood of such exchanges is lighthearted. Whereas Marlowe's comedy is often distinctly macabre, Jonson's writing modifies the sinister implications of the religious hypocrisy he depicts. His predominantly humorous engagement with themes of politic religion is facilitated partly by his mastery of satiric comedy, partly by changing historical circumstances that rendered the polemical discourse of the 1580s and 1590s less immediately threatening, and perhaps most of all by his retention of an overarching providential framework. While this providential framework is often gently challenged or even lightly mocked, it is not abandoned; serendipitous last-minute conversions and attacks of conscience remain a common plot device in Jonson's plays (*Volpone* 5.12; *Bartholomew Fair* 5.5.102–6).

The retention of a loosely providential framework in Shakespeare's and Jonson's drama suggests that these authors shied away from the more extreme implications of Marlowe's literary scepticism, even as they absorbed and responded to his concept that religion is manipulated by heroes and villains alike. Other seventeenth-century writers similarly emphasised an overarching divine justice to neutralise the impact of the politic religious fraud their plays depicted: thus the prolific Thomas Heywood regularly crafts scenes in which religious rhetoric is manipulated for suspect ends, but just as consistently shows those who sin against spiritual and social mores repenting of their behaviour.[319] Nonetheless, the influence of Marlowe's literary scepticism continued to be felt. Throughout James I's reign writers who shared Marlowe's vision of a fictional universe in which divine justice is erratic and unreliable, or were intrigued by the idea that religious fraud might be morally neutral, introduced their own versions of literary scepticism into print and on to the stage.

John Webster's bleak Jacobean tragedies represent a particularly extreme engagement with such questions, as like Marlowe before him Webster places characters who practice religious hypocrisy within a fictional world in which there is no clear sense of an afterlife; no certainty that true piety will be rewarded after death. Thus Webster's characters share Faustus's obsession with the fearful idea that death might be final, but arguably surpass Faustus when it comes to appropriating religious rhetoric in the struggle to survive. For instance, the heroine of *The Duchess of Malfi* turns to religious deceit in desperation when her life is threatened, fleeing to Ancona under cover of a feigned pilgrimage (3.2.306–17). Although the Duchess's mistaken trust in her treacherous servant Bosola means that this venture fails, spectators and readers of Webster's play seem more likely to blame Bosola's skill at deception than recognise a providential judgement on the Duchess's hypocritical piety. While her unsuccessful pretence does parallel the excuse used by the equally doomed Julia to facilitate her visits to her lover in Rome (2.4.1–5), any simplistic moral verdict that attributes both their deaths to the sin of using religion as their 'riding-hood' is complicated by the fact that the same pious condemnation is passed by Webster's Cardinal; this same hypocritical villain persecutes his sister the Duchess, seizes her possessions with a suspect church decree, and murders his mistress Julia (3.3.59). Moreover, apparently providential patterns are not always reliable in Webster's drama. As the revenger Bosola, having accidentally stabbed his intended ally, mourns: 'We are merely the stars' tennis-balls, struck and banded / Which way please them' (5.4.53–4).

Webster's tragedy may not encourage his audience to see the politic appropriation of religion as a particularly successful survival tactic, but his characters certainly seem to treat religion as a practical tool. This theme is even more evident in Webster's *The White Devil*, a play saturated with references to 'policy' and politic action. In Act 3 the ambitious villain Flamineo, feigning madness, delivers a commentary on the connection between such policy and religion that is worthy of Marlowe's Guise at his most sceptical, exclaiming: 'Religion; oh how it is commeddled with policy' (3.3.338–9). Flamineo's concluding remark – 'Would I were a Jew' (3.3.40) – also signals a possible affinity with Marlowe's politic villain Barabas; this connection is perhaps strengthened by Flamineo's punning references to the value of jewels in the context of his sister's tryst with Bracciano, arguably echoing Barabas's risqué description of Abigail to her suitor Lodowick as a 'diamond' that 'ne'er was foiled' (*Jew of Malta* 2.3.57). Webster's debt to *The Jew of Malta* is however most strongly suggested in Act 5 of *The White Devil*, when the suggestively named revenger Lodovico, now acting as an intelligence agent for the Pope, dons the armour of a Maltese Knight of St John to murder Duke Bracciano (5.1.13–27); intriguingly, a ghost character named Farnese or Ferneze (Lodowick's father in Marlowe's play) is identified in the stage directions as Ludovico's accomplice. The religious implications of the disguise adopted by the murderers are strongly emphasised: Bracciano's killers claim to have travelled to Padua to 'settle themselves here in a house of Capuchins' (5.1.22–3); swear a secret vow 'sealed with the sacrament' to murder the duke (5.1.64); and perform a fraudulent ritual of feigned confession and absolution at his deathbed (5.3.132–52). This vicious parody of the Catholic sacrament reaches its height when, as Bracciano draws his last breaths, the two 'monks' abandon their religious posturing to taunt and then strangle the dying duke.

As this episode indicates, there are suggestive traces of Marlowe's *Jew of Malta* in Webster's tragedy. Flamineo's subsequent vision of an afterlife in which he might 'resolve to fire, earth, water, air, / Or all the elements' may in addition recall the Lucretian model invoked in the opening and closing moments of *Doctor Faustus* (*White Devil* 5.6.111–12), while his sceptical comment likening 'lovers' oaths' to 'mariners' prayers' perhaps invites comparison with the speaker of *Ovid's Elegies*, who casts his own false vows in 'Carpathian seas' (*White Devil* 5.1.176; *Ovid's Elegies* 2.8.19–20). While such allusions are perhaps less direct than Shakespeare's response to Marlowe in his early Jacobean tragedies, the sceptical tone of Webster's drama is strongly reminiscent of Marlowe's previous fictional engagement with a politic religious hypocrisy depicted as both a near-universal practice and an indispensable quality for anyone wishing to succeed (or survive) in a world stripped of providential security. Thus Marlowe's legacy of a scepticism deeply rooted in the Elizabethan discourse of politic religion lived on in the drama of Shakespeare, Jonson and Webster, though in an ever-changing and evolving fashion.

In a more diluted form, Marlowe's writings continued to influence the writers of the later seventeenth century. The eloquent Satan of John Milton's *Paradise Lost*, who tempts his listeners with 'seeming' truth (9.738), is sometimes compared to Marlowe's equally persuasive Mephistopheles: indeed, the poet William Blake once famously declared that Milton was 'of the Devil's party', while William Empson and A.D. Nuttall have speculated whether Milton perhaps follows Marlowe's lead to imply that disobedience to God is a positive act.[320] In fact, however, it seems more probable that Milton (unlike Marlowe) was genuinely concerned to 'justify the ways of God to men' (1.26), depicting the type of religious fraud that Marlowe delights in only to decisively refute it. Similarly, the speaker of Milton's *Lycidas* experiences a loss of faith following the death of his friend that potentially mirrors the scepticism of Marlowe's *Elegies*, in which the speaker announces that 'when bad fates take good men, I am forbod / By secret thoughts to think there is a god' (3.8.35–6); in Milton's poem, however, such doubt is ultimately overcome by the speaker's new-found faith in the promised resurrection of his friend Lycidas's soul.[321]

If Milton's poetry explored instances of religious doubt reminiscent of Marlowe's writings with the intention of confirming his reader's faith, Milton's seventeenth-century editor and biographer John Toland was a rather different prospect. Toland was a political and religious radical who, influenced by Thomas Hobbes's arguments in *Leviathan* (1651), developed a model of civic religion that cast belief as a tool of political control. Such theories were common enough during the later seventeenth century, but Toland's method of argument is more intriguing: in *Nazarenus* (1718), he illustrates his model of civic religion through cross-confessional examples that stress the continuity of Judaic, Christian and Islamic theology, even introducing the conflated concepts of 'Mahometan Christianity' and 'Jewish or Gentile Christianity'.[322] This correlation in Toland's writings between the blurring of denominational divisions and a civic or 'politic' model of religion is intriguingly reminiscent of the literary approach adopted by Marlowe more than a century earlier.

The extent to which the cross-confessional scepticism expressed by late seventeenth- and eighteenth-century freethinkers is comparable to that which informs and energises Marlowe's plays and poems is shown by the writings of Christopher Blount. Arguably more radical than Toland, Blount similarly explored the concept of civic religion by comparing different confessions and faiths in his *Religio Laici* (1683). His declared intention was 'to study with an impartial mind, not only all the several Religions; but likewise the Controversies amongst them in divers Ages, Languages and Countries' – an aim relating back to Marlowe's fictional representations of pagan, Christian, Jewish and Islamic characters and their various conflicts and 'Controversies'. Blount's interest is like Marlowe's sparked by specific historical circumstance, and he claims to be reacting to the way that 'the Name of Christ is made use of to palliate so great Villianies and Treasons, under the Pretext of God's Cause, against both King and Government'. In a prefatory letter to Blount's treatise, his colleague Charles Gildon expands on this contemporary experience of religious controversy and strikingly concludes that the accusations exchanged by polemicists of rival confessions, 'their Practice and Doctrin being so Contradictory, gives a more effectual Blow at Religion, than all the Attempts of professed Atheists; for when these clash, they give too great Grounds to suspect a trick in the whole'.[323]

Gildon's critique of religious polemic might almost serve as a manifesto for Marlowe's earlier fictional response to the confessional conflicts of post-Reformation Europe; Gildon goes on to argue that, were religion 'meerly a political Trick for the Convenience of Government and human Life', 'then indeed it would be something pardonable in these Gentlemen, that Patronise the Fire and Faggot so vehemently, to strive with so much Ardor for the reducing all to their own Fancy'.[324] Gildon's sceptical assumption that the quest for political control lies at the root of all religious controversy is one Marlowe would have recognised, having demonstrated his own awareness that arguments for religious uniformity might be used to justify self-interested secular policies in plays such as *The Jew of Malta* and *The Massacre at Paris.* Ninety years after Marlowe's death English freethinkers were beginning to express in a non-fictional context the type of cross-confessional scepticism his plays and poems communicate, their theoretical arguments laying the foundation for the outspoken atheism associated with the radical Enlightenment.[325]

This is not to suggest that Marlowe's writings were an exclusive inspiration for seventeenth-century expressions of doubt, although Blount and Toland did move in literary circles that might have familiarised them with the work of Marlowe and his contemporaries. Even if these seventeenth-century freethinkers never read a line of Marlowe's work, however, the cross-confessional scepticism his plays and poems express is closely analogous to that explored by writers such as Toland, Blount and Gildon, as well as by literary contemporaries such as the notorious John Wilmot, Earl of Rochester. Marlowe's scepticism, mediated through his fictional narratives, thus anticipated the religious radicalism of the seventeenth-century freethinkers by several decades, even as his poetic and dramatic model of a politic religion freed from moral constraints continued to inspire and enrich the work of his literary heirs – though perhaps none of his immediate successors raised the fictional expression of religious doubt to such heights as did Christopher Marlowe, Elizabethan England's most notorious literary sceptic.

NOTES

PREFACE

1. Thomas Beard, *The Theatre of Gods Judgements* (London, 1597; STC 1659), Sig. K5r–K5v.
2. Richard H. Popkin, *The History of Scepticism: From Savonarola to Bayle* (Oxford and New York, 1960, rpt with revisions 2003).
3. Philippe de Mornay, *A woorke concerning the trewnesse of the Christian religion* (London, 1587; STC 18149), Sig. A6v.
4. William M. Hamlin, *Tragedy and Scepticism in Shakespeare's England* (Basingstoke, 2005), p. 2.

INTRODUCTION: MARLOWE THE ATHEIST

5. Baines, 'Note'.
6. Kyd, 'Unsigned Note'.
7. During Marlowe's 1592 visit to Flushing, Richard Baines accused him of treason out 'of malice' towards him, as reported by Sir Robert Sidney. See Charles Nicholl, *The Reckoning: The Murder of Christopher Marlowe*, 2nd edn (London, 1992), pp. 279–80.
8. Roy Kendall, 'Richard Baines and Christopher Marlowe's Milieu', *ELR* 24 (1994), pp. 511–20.
9. Robert Greene, *Perimedes the blacke-smith* (London, 1588; STC 12295), Sig. A3r; Robert Greene, *Greenes, groats-worth of witte* (London, 1592; STC 12245), Sig. E4v–F1r; Gabriel Harvey, *A new letter of notable contents* (London, 1593; STC 12902), Sig. D4r.
10. Thomas Beard, *The theatre of Gods judgements* (London, 1597; STC 1659), Sig. K5r–K5v.
11. David Riggs, *The World of Christopher Marlowe* (London, 2004), p. 4.
12. Michael Hattaway, 'Christopher Marlowe: Ideology and Subversion', in Darryll Grantley and Peter Roberts (eds), *Christopher Marlowe and English Renaissance Culture* (Aldershot, 1996), p. 215; G.E. Aylmer, 'Unbelief in Seventeenth-Century England', in Donald Pennington and Keith Thomas (eds) *Puritans and Revolutionaries: Essays in Seventeenth-Century History Presented to Christopher Hill* (Oxford, 1982), p. 27; Riggs, *World of Christopher Marlowe*, p. 4.

13. Marlowe's firm statement lacks Ovid's conciliatory framework; compare Ovid, *Heroides and Amores*, trans. Grant Showerman, ed. G.P. Goold, 2nd edn, Loeb Classical Library (Cambridge, Mass., 1977), 3.9.35–6.
14. Lucien Febrve, *The Problem of Unbelief in the Sixteenth Century: The Religion of Rabelais*, trans. Beatrice Gottlieb (Cambridge, Mass. and London, 1982), p. 460. Febvre's arguments are refuted by Aylmer, 'Unbelief', pp. 22–46; Nicholas Davidson, 'Christopher Marlowe and Atheism', in Grantley and Roberts (eds), *Christopher Marlowe and English Renaissance Culture*, pp. 129–47.
15. Baines, 'Note'.
16. PRO Privy Council Registers (Eliz.) 6, 381b. See Park Honan, *Christopher Marlowe: Poet and Spy* (Oxford, 2005), pp. 120–55; Nicholl, *Reckoning*, pp. 109–95.
17. David Riggs, 'The Poet in the Play: Life and Art in *Tamburlaine* and *The Jew of Malta*', in Takashi Kozuka and J.R. Mulryne (eds), *Shakespeare, Marlowe, Jonson: New Directions in Biography* (Aldershot, 2006), p. 217.
18. Robert Southwell, *An humble supplication to her Majestie* (England, 1595 [printed 1600]; STC 22949.5), Sig. C1r–C8r; Thomas Nashe, *Have with you to Saffron-Walden*, in Nashe, *Works*, III, p. 106.
19. See Davidson, 'Atheism', pp. 133–5.
20. See Richard H. Popkin, *The History of Scepticism: From Savonarola to Bayle* (Oxford and New York, 1960, rpt. with revisions 2003), pp. 1–43; William M. Hamlin, *Tragedy and Scepticism in Shakespeare's England* (Basingstoke, 2005), pp. 29–71.
21. Harvey, *New letter*, Sig. D1r.
22. Greene, *Groats-worth*, Sig. E4v–F1r.
23. Scott, Edward John Long (ed.), *Letter-book of Gabriel Harvey* (London, 1884), pp. 79–80; N.W. Bawcutt, 'The "Myth of Gentillet" Reconsidered: An Aspect of Elizabethan Machiavellianism', *MLR* 99 (2004), p. 867.
24. Niccolò Machiavelli, in *The Discourses*, ed. Bernard Crick, trans Leslie J. Walker (London, 1970; rpt. with revisions 2003), pp. 139–43; Niccolò Machiavelli, *I discorsi di Nicolo Machiavelli* (London, 1584; STC 17159), Sig. D3v–D6r.
25. John Leslie[?], *A treatise of treasons* (Louvain, 1572; STC 7601), Sig. 4r.
26. Sir John Davies, *Sir Martin Mar-people* (London, 1590; STC 6363), Sig. A2v–A3r; Thomas Bilson, *The true difference betweene Christian subjection and unchristian rebellion* (Oxford, 1585; STC 3071), Sig. E2v.
27. William Charke, *An answere to a seditious pamphlet* (London, 1581; STC 5006), Sig. C3r.
28. Richard Hooker, in W. Speed Hill (ed.), *Of the Laws of Ecclesiastical Polity: Book V*, in *The Folger Library Edition of the Works of Richard Hooker*, 7 vols (Cambridge, Mass. and London, 1977), II, p. 22, pp. 25–6.
29. William Allen, *An apologie and true declaration of the institution and endevours of the two English colleges* (Rheims, 1581; STC 369), Sig. E2r–E2v.

30. Debora Kuller Shuger, *Habits of Thought in the English Renaissance: Religion, Politics, and the Dominant Culture* (Berkeley, Los Angeles and London, 1990), p. 151.
31. Robert Southwell, *An epistle of comfort* (London, 1587[?]; STC 22946), Sig. L6r.
32. Michel de Montaigne, 'An apology for Raymond Sebond', in M.A. Screech (trans. and ed.), *The Essays of Michel de Montaigne* (London, 1991), II.12, p. 494, p. 497. See Tullio Gregory, 'Pierre Charron's "Scandalous Book"', in *Atheism from the Reformation to the Enlightenment*, ed. Michael Hunter and David Wootton (Oxford, 1992), pp. 87–109; Michael Hunter and David Wootton (eds), 'Introduction', in *Atheism from the Reformation*, pp. 5–6.
33. William Cecil, Lord Burghley, *The Execution of Justice in England*, in *'Execution' and 'Defense'*, ed. Kingdom, p. 9.
34. William Allen, *A True, Sincere, and Modest Defense of English Catholics*, in *'Execution' and 'Defense'*, ed. Kingdom, p. 57.
35. Jonathan Burton, *Traffic and Turning: Islam and English Drama, 1579–1624* (Newark, 2005); Matthew Dimmock, *New Turkes: Dramatizing Islam and the Ottomans in Early Modern England* (Aldershot, 2005); James Shapiro, *Shakespeare and the Jews* (New York, 1996); and Daniel Vitkus, *Turning Turk: English Theater and the Multicultural Mediterranean, 1570–1630* (New York and Basingstoke, 2003).
36. Raphael Hallet, '"Vile Interpretations" and "Devilish Supplements": Jewish Exegesis and Linguistic Siege in Martin Luther's "On the Jews and Their Lies" (1543)', in Matthew Dimmock and Andrew Hadfield (eds), *The Religions of the Book: Christian Perceptions, 1400–1600* (Basingstoke, 2008), pp. 89-109; Dimmock, *New Turkes*, p. 44.
37. Henry Blount, *A Voyage to the Levant* (London, 1636; STC 3136), Sig. Q1r. Noted by Shapiro, *Shakespeare and the Jews*, p. 35.
38. Shapiro, *Shakespeare and the Jews*, p. 138.
39. Alexandra Walsham, *Church Papists: Catholicism, Conformity and Confessional Polemic in Early Modern England* (Woodbridge, Sussex, 1993), pp. 105–7; Sir Francis Bacon in Brian Vickers (ed.), *The Essays or Counsels Civil and Moral* (Oxford, 1999), p. 38.
40. George Whetstone, *The English myrror* (London, 1586; STC 25336), Sig. P6r; Thomas Nashe, *Christs teares over Jerusalem*, in Nashe, *Works*, II, pp. 117–8, pp. 121–2.
41. See J.H.M. Salmon, 'Politiques', in Hans J. Hillerbrand et al. (eds), *The Oxford Encyclopedia of the Reformation*, 4 vols (New York and Oxford, 1996), III, pp. 291–2; Paul Strohm, *Politique: Languages of Statecraft between Chaucer and Shakespeare* (Notre Dame, Ind., 2005), pp. 1–17.
42. Robert Parsons, *An advertisement written to a secretarie of my L. Treasurers* (Antwerp, 1592; STC 19885), Sig. B3v–B4r; John Fielde, *A caveat for Parsons Howlet* (London, 1581; STC 10844), Sig. F1r.

43. See Howard S. Babb, 'Policy in Marlowe's *The Jew of Malta*', *ELH* 24 (1957), pp. 85–94.
44. Strohm, *Politique*, esp. pp. 1–17.
45. Robert Wilson, *The Three Ladies of London*, in Lloyd Edward Kermode (ed.), *Three Renaissance Usury Plays* (Manchester and New York, 2009), pp. 79-163.
46. Seneca, *Hercules Furens*, in *Seneca: Six Tragedies*, trans. Emily Watson (Oxford, 2010), pp. 139–77.
47. George Peele, *The Battle of Alcazar*, in John Yoklavich (ed.), Peele, *Works*, II, pp. 213–373.
48. George Peele, *The Araygnement of Paris*, in R. Mark Benbow (ed.), Peele, *Works*, III, pp. 1–131.
49. Robert Greene, *Alphonsus King of Aragon*, Malone Society (Oxford, 1926).
50. See Ruth Lunney, *Marlowe and the Popular Tradition: Innovation in the English Drama before 1595* (Manchester, 2002), p. 139.
51. Philippe de Mornay, *A woorke concerning the trewnesse of the Christian religion* (London, 1587; STC 18149), Sig. L6v.
52. Thomas Heywood, in Robert K. Turner (ed.), *The Fair Maid of the West, Parts I and II* (London, 1968).
53. See for instance David Riggs, 'Marlowe's Quarrel with God', in Paul Whitfield White (ed.), *Marlowe, History, and Sexuality: New Critical Essays on Christopher Marlowe* (New York, 1998), pp. 15–38; Hamlin, *Tragedy and Scepticism*, pp. 144–54.
54. On the date of composition, see Millar Maclure (ed.), Christopher Marlowe, *The Poems* (London, 1968), pp. xx, xxxii, xxxiv. It seems possible that Marlowe later revised his Lucan translation, perhaps during the Armada period of 1587–9: *Lucan's First Book* was first published in 1600.
55. A post-1588 date has been posited by Margo Hendricks and Martin Wiggins, but the current critical consensus still favours a 1585–6 date. See Margo Hendricks, 'Managing the Barbarian: *The Tragedy of Dido, Queen of Carthage*', *Renaissance Drama* 23 (1992), pp. 165–88; Martin Wiggins, 'When Did Marlowe Write *Dido, Queen of Carthage*?', *RES* 59 (2008), pp. 521–41.
56. See Christopher Marlowe, in J.W. Harper (ed.) *Tamburlaine the Great* (London, 1971), p. viii.
57. See Christopher Marlowe, in David Bevington and Eric Rasmussen (eds), *Doctor Faustus: A- and B-texts (1604, 1616)* (Manchester and New York, 1993), pp. 1–3.
58. For a summary of the various dating arguments, see respectively Christopher Marlowe, *The Jew of Malta*, ed. James R. Siemon, 2nd edn (London, 1994), p. xi; Christopher Marlowe, *Edward the Second*, ed. Martin Wiggins and Robert Lindsey, 2nd edn (London, 1997), pp. xiii–xv; and Christopher Marlowe, *'Dido Queen of Carthage' and 'The Massacre at Paris'*, ed. H.J. Oliver (London, 1968), pp. li–lii.

1: EQUIVOCATION, DISSIMULATION AND DECEIT

59. *OED*, 'frame', *v.* 1, 5c, 5e, 8a.
60. Thomas Wilson, *The arte of rhetorique* (London, 1553; STC 25799), Sig. A4r.
61. Baines, 'Note'.
62. Anthony Munday, *A discoverie of Edmund Campion* (London, 1582; STC 18270), Sig. G1r–G2r.
63. John Foxe, *Actes and monuments* (London, 1583; STC 11225), Sig. §6v.
64. Sir Thomas More, *The second parte of the confutacion* (London, 1553; STC 18080), Sig. D2r.
65. *Elizabethan Casuistry*, ed. P. J. Holmes, *Catholic Record Society*, 67 (1981), p. 52.
66. 'The Confession of Leonard Romseye delivered unto me Thomas Barwicke minister with his owne hand', in Joan Dietz Moss, 'Variations on a Theme: The Family of Love in Renaissance England', *RenQ* 31 (1978), p. 191.
67. *Doctor Faustus*, Manchester Royal Exchange (2010), dir. Toby Frow; *Doctor Faustus*, Shakespeare's Globe, London (2011), dir. Matthew Dunster.
68. *The English Faust Book: A critical edition based on the text of 1592*, ed. John Henry Jones (Cambridge, 1994), p. 94. In future references, this edition is abbreviated as the *EFB*.
69. Théodore de Bèze, *A tragedie of Abrahams sacrifice*, trans. A.G. (London, 1577; STC 2047), Sig. B5r.
70. Peter Stallybrass, 'Worn Worlds: Clothes and Identity on the Renaissance stage', in Margreta de Grazia, Maureen Quilligan and Peter Stallybrass (eds), *Subject and Object in Renaissance Culture* (Cambridge, 1996), pp. 305–6.
71. Foxe, *Actes*, Sig. 5F2r.
72. Henry Ainsworth, *An apologie or defence of such true Christians as are commonly (but unjustly) called Brownists* (Amsterdam, 1604; STC 239), Sig. §4v.
73. Samuel Harsnett, *A declaration of egregious popish impostures* (London, 1603; STC 12880), Sig. A2v, M4v.
74. *OED*, 'conjure', *v.* 5a and 7. Noted by Gareth Roberts, 'Marlowe and the Metaphysics of Magicians', in J.A. Downie and J.T. Parnell (eds), *Constructing Christopher Marlowe* (Cambridge, 2000), p. 59.
75. Sara Munson Deats, '"Mark this show': Magic and Theater in Marlowe's *Doctor Faustus*', in Sara Munson Deats and Robert A. Logan (eds), *Placing the Plays of Christopher Marlowe: Fresh Cultural Contexts* (Aldershot, 2008), pp. 18–19.
76. Baines, 'Note'.
77. *EFB*, p. 119.
78. Claire Armitstead, *Guardian*, 18 November 1993; Charles Spencer, *The Daily Telegraph*, 20 November 1993. Reprinted in *Theatre Record*, 13.23 (1993), p. 1324.
79. Douglas W. Hayes, *Rhetorical Subversion in Early English Drama* (New York, 2004), p. 81.

80. Henry Peacham, *The Garden of Eloquence*, ed. William G. Crane (Ann Arbor, Mich., 1977), Sig. M3r–M3v.
81. Hayes, *Rhetorical Subversion*, pp. 81–2.
82. Charles Spencer, *Daily Telegraph,* 19 March 2002. Reprinted in *Theatre Record*, 22.6 (2002), p. 341.
83. Noted by Kenneth J.E. Graham, *The Performance of Conviction: Plainness and Rhetoric in the Early English Renaissance* (Ithaca and London, 1994), pp. 12–13.
84. Martin Luther, 'Romans, Chapter Thirteen', in *Lectures on Romans*, trans. and ed. Wilhelm Pauck, 2 vols (London, 1961), II, p. 365.
85. The 1616 B-text places Faustus in 'Wittenberg', which invites the connection to Luther's writings on equivocation, but the 1604 A-text's references to 'Wertenburg' alternatively associate Faustus with a radical puritanism that is equally apt. See Leah S. Marcus, *Unediting the Renaissance: Shakespeare, Marlowe, Milton* (London and New York, 1996), pp. 41–54.
86. Thomas Nashe, *The Terrors of the Night*, in Nashe, *Works*, I, p. 367.
87. *The Geneva Bible: A Facsimile of the 1560 Edition*, ed. Lloyd E. Berry (Peabody, Mass., 2007).
88. 'The Thirty-Nine Articles', in David Scott Kastan (ed.), *Doctor Faustus* (New York and London, 2005), p. 244; Christopher Marlowe, *Doctor Faustus* ed. Roma Gill (London, 1965), p. xxv.
89. See R.M. Cornelius, *Christopher Marlowe's Use of the Bible* (New York, 1984), pp. 11–12, 237.
90. Thomas Nashe, *Christs teares over Jerusalem* in Nashe, *Works*, II, pp. 39–40.
91. William Charke, *An answere to a seditious pamphlet* (London, 1581; STC 5006), Sig. C5v.
92. Robert Parsons, *A briefe censure uppon two bookes* (Pyrton, 1581; STC 19393), Sig. B5r; *A defence of the censure* (Rouen, 1582; STC 19401), Sig. E6r.
93. *Doctor Faustus*, RSC, Swan Theatre, Stratford-upon-Avon, 1989, dir. Barry Kyle; *Doctor Faustus*, Shakespeare's Globe, London, 2011, dir. Matthew Dunster.
94. Charke, *Answere*, Sig. E5v.
95. Nathaniel Woodes, *The conflict of conscience* (London, 1581; STC 25966); Kirsten Poole, *Radical Religion from Shakespeare to Milton: Figures of Nonconformity in Early Modern England* (Cambridge, 2000), pp. 74–103.
96. Quoted by Jennifer Loach, 'Reformation Controversies', in James McConica (ed.), *The History of the University of Oxford*, 5 vols, III: *The Collegiate University* (Oxford, 1986), p. 389.
97. U.M. Ellis-Fermor, *Christopher Marlowe* (London, 1927), p. 12.
98. Anthony Munday, *The English Romayne lyfe* (London, 1582; STC 18272), Sig. F4v; William Barlow, *An answer to a Catholike English-Man* (London, 1609; STC 1446.5), Sig. A3v.
99. See Gordon Braden, *The Classics and English Renaissance Poetry: Three Case Studies* (New Haven and London, 1978), pp. 7, 124–8.
100. Malcolm Kelsall, *Christopher Marlowe* (Leiden, 1981), pp. 19–25.

101. *Hero and Leander*, in Cedric Whitman (trans.) and Thomas Gelzer (ed.), Callimachus and Musaeus, *'Fragments' and 'Hero and Leander'*, Loeb Classical Library (Cambridge, Mass., 1975), l. 141.
102. John Lyly, *Campaspe*, in Carter A. Daniel (ed.), *The Plays of John Lyly* (Lewisburg and London, 1988), pp. 29–64.
103. Thomas Lodge and Robert Greene, *A Looking-Glass for London and England*, Malone Society (Oxford, 1932).
104. *OED*, 'sophister', *n.* 2.
105. William Fulke, *Two treatises written against the papistes* (London, 1577; STC 11458), Sig. EE5v; Barlow, *Answer*, Sig. F3v.
106. Harry Levin, *Christopher Marlowe: The Overreacher* (London, 1953), p. 37; Patrick Cheney, *Marlowe's Counterfeit Profession: Ovid, Spenser, Counter-Nationhood* (Toronto, Buffalo and London, 1997), pp. 246–7.
107. William Cecil, Lord Burghley, *The Execution of Justice in England*, in *'Execution' and 'Defense'*, ed. Kingdom, p. 3.
108. *A Treatise of Equivocation*, ed. David Jardine (London, 1851), p. 49.
109. 'The Confession of Leonard Romseye delivered unto me Thomas Barwicke minister with his owne hand', in Joan Dietz Moss, 'Variations on a Theme: The Family of Love in Renaissance England', *RenQ* 31 (1978), p. 191.
110. Charke, *Answere*, Sig. B2v.
111. See Perez Zagorin, *Ways of Lying: Dissimulation, Persecution, and Conformity in Early Modern Europe* (Cambridge, Mass., and London, 1990), p. 17.
112. *The Jew of Malta*, RSC, Swan Theatre, Stratford-upon-Avon, 1987, dir. Barry Kyle.
113. Thomas Heywood, *The Golden Age*, in *Dramatic Works*, 6 vols (New York, 1964), III, pp. 1–79.
114. See Zagorin, *Ways of Lying*, pp. 168–72; Martín de Azpilcueta, *Enchiridion* (Moguntiae, 1603), York, Borthwick Institute for Archives, Mirfield Collection 1603 AZP, Sig. M4r.
115. Martín de Azpilcueta, *Commenterius in cap. Humanae Aures*, in D. Martini ab Azpilcueta, *Navarri. I.V.D. Praeclarissimi Commentaria*, 3 vols (Venice, 1588), I, Sig. OO2v–OO4r.
116. See Christopher Marlowe, *'Doctor Faustus' and Other Plays*, ed. David Bevington and Eric Rasmussen (Oxford, 1995), p. 462.
117. See for example Théodore de Bèze, *Du Droit des Magistrats*, ed. Robert M. Kingdom (Genève, 1970), p. 22; Stephanus Junius Brutus [pseud.], *Vindiciae, Contra Tyrannos*, ed. George Garnett (Cambridge, 1994), pp. 56–7.
118. Richard Verstegan, *The copy of a letter lately written by a Spanishe gentleman* (Antwerp, 1589; STC 1038), Sig. C2r–C3r.
119. *Treatise of Equivocation*, p. 48.
120. Ibid., p. 50.
121. Raphael Holinshed, *The Third volume of Chronicles* (London, 1586; STC 13569), Sig. KK1r.
122. John Stow, *The chronicles of England* (London, 1592; STC 23333), Sig. Z3r.

123. Thomas Nashe, *An Almond for a Parrat*, in Nashe, *Works*, III, p. 355.
124. David Riggs, *The World of Christopher Marlowe* (London, 2004), p. 155.
125. John Warren, *Elizabeth I: Religion and Foreign Affairs*, 2nd edn (London, 2002), p. 141.

2: FALSE CONVERSION AND CONFORMITY

126. Christopher Haigh, *English Reformations: Religion, Politics, and Society under the Tudors* (Oxford, 1993, rpt. with revisions 1995), p. 295.
127. Alexandra Walsham, *Church Papists: Catholicism, Conformity and Confessional Polemic in Early Modern England* (Woodbridge, Sussex, 1993), pp. 1–12.
128. Ramie Targoff, *Common Prayer: The Language of Public Devotion in Early Modern England* (Chicago and London, 2001), pp. 4–12.
129. William Allen, *The copie of a letter written by M. Doctor Allen: concerning the yeelding up of the citie of Daventrie* (Antwerp, 1587; STC 370), Sig. A8v; Robert Parsons, *A brief discours contayning certayne reasons why Catholiques refuse to goe to church* (East Ham, 1580; STC 19394).
130. William Perkins, *A reformed Catholic* (Cambridge, 1598; STC 19736), Sig. A5r; John Greenwood, *An answere to George Giffords pretended defence* (Dordrecht, 1590; STC 12339), Sig. A2v, E3v.
131. Parsons, *Brief discours*, Sig. B7v.
132. William Allen, *An apologie and true declaration of the institution and endevours of the two English colleges* (Rheims, 1581; STC 369), Sig. N6v; Parsons, *Brief discours*, Sig. F4v–F5r.
133. Henry Ainsworth, *An apologie or defence of such true Christians as are commonly (but unjustly) called Brownists* (Amsterdam, 1604; STC 239), Sig. B2r; *Correspondence of Matthew Parker*, ed. John Bruce and Thomas T. Perowne (Cambridge, 1853), p 391.
134. Walsham, *Church Papists*, p. 1, pp. 43–4; George Gifford, *A dialogue betweene a papist and a Protestant* (London, 1582; STC 11849), Sig. A1v.
135. *Recusants in the Exchequer Pipe Rolls 1581–1592*, ed. Dom Hugh Bowler and Timothy J. McGann, *Catholic Record Society* 71 (1986), pp. 76, 186; David Riggs, *The World of Christopher Marlowe* (London, 2004), p. 129.
136. Emily C. Bartels, *Spectacles of Strangeness: Imperialism, Alienation, and Marlowe* (Philadelphia, 1993), p. 94. In the diocesan returns for 1577, recusants listed include Edmund Standon and his wife, 'valued at twoe hundred poundes by the yeere'; Thomas Barnes, 'valued at fiftie poundes in gooddes'; and Thomas Bray, 'a wicked fellow, but nothing worth'. *Miscellanea XII, Catholic Record Society* 22 (1921), pp. 45–6.
137. Christopher Marlowe, *The Complete Works of Christopher Marlowe*, ed. Roma Gill, 5 vols. (Oxford, 1995), IV, p. xiii.
138. See John J. LaRocca, 'Popery and Pounds: The Effect of the Jesuit Mission on Penal Legislation', in Thomas M. McCoog (ed.), *The Reckoned Expense: Edmund Campion and the Early English Jesuits*, 2nd edn (Rome, 2007), p. 339.

139. See also Dena Goldberg, 'Sacrifice in Marlowe's *The Jew of Malta*', *SEL* 32 (1992), p. 242.
140. See Michael C. Questier, *Conversion, Politics and Religion in England, 1580–1625* (Cambridge, 1996), p. 104 for a full discussion of the submission process.
141. John Florio, *Queen Anna's new world of words* (London, 1611; STC 11099), Sig. Bb6v.
142. William Rainolds, *A refutation of sundry reprehensions* (Paris, 1583; STC 20632), Sig. T5v; Zachary Lesser, *Renaissance Drama and the Politics of Publication: Readings in the English Book Trade* (Cambridge, 2004), pp. 86–9.
143. Robert Wilson, *The Three Ladies of London*, in Lloyd Edward Kermode (ed.), *Three Renaissance Usury Plays* (Manchester, 2009), pp. 79–163.
144. Questier, *Conversion*, p. 113.
145. Thomas Heywood, *The Captives*, Malone Society (Oxford, 1953); John Earle, *Micro-cosmographie* (London, 1628; STC 7441), Sig. C7r.
146. Parsons, *Brief discours*, Sig. A5v–A6r; Alban Langdale, *Reasons Why Catholics May Go to Church* (1580), in *Early Modern Catholicism: An Anthology of Primary Sources*, ed. Robert S. Miola (Oxford, 2007), p. 73.
147. Bartels, *Spectacles of Strangeness*, p. 98.
148. *The Jew of Malta*, RSC, Swan Theatre, 1987, dir. Barry Kyle.
149. See Mark Hutchings, '"In Thrace: Brought up in Arabia": *The Jew of Malta*, II.iii.131', *Notes and Queries* 47 (2000), pp. 428–30.
150. See Godfrey Goodwin, *The Janissaries* (London, 1994), pp. 32–53.
151. George Gascoigne, 'Gascoignes devise of a maske for the right honorable Viscount Mountacute', in George Gascoigne, *A hundreth sundrie flowres* (London, 1573; STC 11635), Sig. Bb2r; Giovanni Botero, *The travellers breviat* (London, 1601; STC 3398), Sig. G1r.
152. Jonathan Burton, *Traffic and Turning: Islam and English Drama, 1579–1624* (Newark, 2005), p. 13.
153. Thomas Kyd, *Soliman and Perseda*, in Frederick S. Boas (ed.), *The Works of Thomas Kyd*, 2nd edn (Oxford, 1955), pp. 161–230. See also Nabil Matar, *Islam in Britain 1558–1685* (Cambridge, 1998) pp. 52–63.
154. Thomas Heywood, *The Fair Maid of the West, Parts I and II*, ed. Robert K. Turner (London, 1968). Early modern sources often stressed the significance of circumcision as an indicator of Islamic faith: see Daniel Vitkus, *Turning Turk: English Theater and the Multicultural Mediterranean, 1570–1630* (New York and Basingstoke, 2003), pp. 111–25.
155. Robert Parsons, *A discoverie of J. Nicols minister* (Pyrton, 1581; STC 19402), Sig. M9v.
156. 'Richard Baines' Written Recantation of 1583', trans. Christopher Upton, in Roy Kendall, 'Richard Baines and Christopher Marlowe's Milieu', *ELR* 24 (1994), pp. 543–6.
157. Alan Haynes, *Invisible Power: The Elizabethan Secret Services, 1570–1603* (Stroud, 1992), p. 79.

158. See Paul Kocher, *Christopher Marlowe: A Study of his Thought, Learning, and Character* (New York, 1962), p. 293.
159. Jean Boucher, *La Vie et Faits Notables de Henry de Valois*, ed. Keith Cameron (Paris, 2003), pp. 81–2.
160 . See for example Niccolò Machiavelli, *The Prince*, ed. Quentin Skinner and Russell Price (Cambridge, 1988), p. 80.
161. Julia Briggs, 'Marlowe's *Massacre at Paris*: A Reconsideration', *RES* 34 (1983), p. 265.
162. Sara Munson Deats, 'Marlowe's Interrogative Drama: *Dido*, *Tamburlaine*, *Faustus* and *Edward II*', in Sara Munson Deats and Robert A. Logan (eds), *Marlowe's Empery: Expanding His Critical Contexts* (Newark, 2002), p. 203.
163. Sir Francis Bacon, *The Essays or Counsels Civil and Moral*, ed. Brian Vickers, Oxford World's Classics (Oxford, 1999), p. 32.
164. Lisa Ferraro Parmelee, *Good Newes from Fraunce: French Anti-League Propaganda in Late Elizabethan England* (Rochester, New York and Woodbridge, Sussex, 1996), pp. 95–6.
165. Briggs, '*Massacre*', p. 271.
166. See for example David Potter, 'Marlowe's *Massacre at Paris* and the Reputation of Henri III of France', in Darryll Grantley and Peter Roberts (eds), *Christopher Marlowe and English Renaissance Culture* (Aldershot, 1996), p. 74.
167. Briggs, '*Massacre*', p. 271.
168. *Calendar of State Papers, Foreign Series: Of the Reign of Elizabeth I*, Public Record Office, 23 (London: HMSO, 1950), pp. 405–6. Noted by Briggs, '*Massacre*', pp. 271–2, n. 38.
169. John Michael Archer, *Sovereignty and Intelligence: Spying and Court Culture in the English Renaissance* (Stanford, 1993), p. 70.
170. Edward Aggas, *A discourse uppon a question of the estate of this time* (London: John Wolfe, 1591; STC 6910), Sig. A2r.
171. Penny Roberts, 'Marlowe's *The Massacre at Paris*: a Historical Perspective', *Renaissance Studies* 9 (1995), p. 439.

3: OATH-TAKING AND OATH-BREAKING

172. William Allen, *An admonition to the nobility* (Antwerp, 1588; STC 368), Sig. C7v.
173. John Knox, 'Summary of the Second Blast of the Trumpet', in Roger A. Mason (ed.), *John Knox: On Rebellion* (Cambridge, 1994), p. 128.
174. Martin Marprelate [pseud.], *Oh read over D. John Bridges . . . Or an Epitome*, in Joseph L. Black (ed.), *The Martin Marprelate Tracts: A Modernized and Annotated Edition* (Cambridge, 2008), p. 53.
175. Thomas Nashe, *An Almond for a Parrat*, in Nashe, *Works*, III, p. 342.
176. Richard Bancroft, *Daungerous positions and proceedings* (London, 1593; STC 1344.5), Sig. B1v–B3r.
177. William Cecil, Lord Burghley[?], *The copie of a letter sent out of England to*

Don Bernardin Mendoza (London, 1588; STC 15412), Sig. D1v. Although ostensibly written by an English Catholic this letter was almost certainly produced by either Lord Burghley or one of his secretaries.

178. Anthony Munday, *A discoverie of Edmund Campion* (London, 1582; STC 18270), Sig. E8v.
179. Machiavelli argued that 'forced agreements will be kept neither by a prince nor by a republic'. *The Discourses*, trans. Leslie J. Walker, ed. Bernard Crick (London, 1970 rpt. with revisions 2003), p. 258.
180. Richard Wilson, 'Visible Bullets: Tamburlaine the Great and Ivan the Terrible', in *Christopher Marlowe and English Renaissance Culture*, ed. Darryll Grantley and Peter Roberts (Aldershot, 1996), pp. 51–69; Luke Wilson, *Theaters of Intention: Drama and the Law in Early Modern England* (Stanford, 2000), pp. 184–215.
181. Ovid, *Heroides and Amores*, trans. Grant Showerman, ed. G.P. Goold, 2nd edn, Loeb Classical Library (Cambridge, Mass., 1977), 2.8.7.
182. Ovid, *Amores*, 2.8.19. The alternative printing of 'selfe oathes' in the 1603 edition seems to reflect a fairly straightforward confusion of s/f by the compositor, but coincidentally and aptly gestures towards the selfish nature of the speaker's perjury. See Christopher Marlowe, *Ovid's elegies* (London, 1603[?]; STC 18931), Sig. C5v.
183. Otto van Veen, *Amorum emblemata*, trans. Richard Verstegan (Antwerp, 1608; STC 24627.a.9), Sig. S2v–S3r; Donna B. Hamilton, 'Richard Verstegan and Catholic Resistance: the Encoding of Antiquarianism and Love', in Richard Dutton, Alison Findlay and Richard Wilson (eds), *Theatre and Religion: Lancastrian Shakespeare* (Manchester and New York, 2003), pp. 97–101.
184. See Sara Munson Deats, 'Marlowe's Interrogative Drama: *Dido*, *Tamburlaine*, *Faustus* and *Edward II*', in Sara Munson Deats and Robert A. Logan (eds), *Marlowe's Empery: Expanding His Critical Contexts* (Newark, 2002), pp. 109–10; Diana E. Henderson, *Passion Made Public: Elizabethan Lyric, Gender, and Performance* (Urbana and Chicago, 1995), p. 148.
185. Donald Stump, 'Marlowe's Travesty of Virgil: Dido and Elizabethan Dreams of Empire', *Comparative Drama* 34.1 (2000), pp. 81–4; Lisa Hopkins, *Christopher Marlowe, Renaissance Dramatist* (Edinburgh, 2008), p. 131.
186. William Gager, *Dido Tragoedia*, ed. Adrianne Roberts-Baytop, in *Dido, Queen of Infinite Literary Variety: The English Renaissance Borrowings and Influences*, (Salzburg, 1974). All future translations are from this edition.
187. See for example Stump, 'Marlowe's Travesty', pp. 79–107.
188. Virgil, *'Eclogues'*, *'Georgics'*, *'Aeneid I–VI'*, trans. H. Rushton Fairclough, ed. G.P. Goold, Loeb Classical Library, 3rd edn (Cambridge, Mass., 1999).
189. Virgil, *Certain bokes of Virgiles Aeneis*, trans. Henry Howard, Earl of Surrey (London, 1557; STC 24798), Sig. E1v–E2r; Virgil, *Thee first foure bookes of Virgil his Aeneis*, trans. Richard Stanyhurst (Leiden, 1582; STC 24806), Sig. L1r; Virgil, *The nyne fyrst bookes of the Eneidos of Virgil*, trans. by Thomas Phaer (London, 1562; STC 24800), Sig. *3v, Sig. I2r–I2v.

190. See Nashe's preface to Robert Greene's *Menaphon* (London, 1589; STC 12272), Sig. **4v–A1r.
191. See Martin Ingram, *Church Courts, Sex and Marriage in England, 1570–1640* (Cambridge, 1987), pp. 189–90.
192. *Dido Queen of Carthage*, National Theatre, London, 2009, dir. James MacDonald.
193. See Sir John Baker (ed.), *The Oxford History of the Laws of England*, 12 vols (Oxford, 2003), VI, 862–8.
194. P.S. Atiyah, *Promises, Morals, and Law* (Oxford, 1981), p. 170.
195. Virgil, *Aeneid*, 4.324, 339; Phaer, *Eneidos*, Sig. I4v.
196. See William Urry, *Christopher Marlowe and Canterbury*, ed. Andrew Butcher (London, 1988), pp. 26–7.
197. John Lydgate, *The auncient historie and onely trewe and syncere cronicle of the warres betwixte the Grecians and the Troyans* (*Troy Book*) (London, 1555; STC 5580), Sig. Aa2r; William Alexander, *Julius Caesar*, in *The Monarchicke Tragedies* (London, 1607; STC 344). See Lisa Hopkins, *The Cultural Uses of the Caesars on the English Renaissance Stage* (Aldershot, 2008), pp. 117–18.
198. François Hotman, *Francogallia*, trans. J.H.M. Salmon with Ralph E. Giesey (Cambridge, 1972), pp. 254–7; Stephanus Junius Brutus [pseud.], *Vindiciae, Contra Tyrannos*, ed. George Garnett (Cambridge, 1994), pp. 113–14.
199. 'L'obligation de mariage compare au devoir du sujet à son superieur . . . Si par les canons ecclesiastiques une femme ne pouvant estre en seurté de sa personne avec un mari, ne peut estre contrainte d'habiter avec lui, pourquoi ne sera-il loisible à un Magistrat inferieur de se pourvoir et aux siens, et avoir recours aux Estats contre un Tyran tout manifeste?' Théodore de Bèze, *Du Droit des Magistrats*, ed. Robert M. Kingdom (Genève, 1970), p. 51.
200. Matthew Dimmock, *New Turkes: Dramatizing Islam and the Ottomans in Early Modern England* (Aldershot, 2005), pp. 17–18.
201. See *OED*, 'protest', *v.* 1a.
202. William Allen, *A True, Sincere and Modest Defence of English Catholics*, in *'Execution' and 'Defense'*, ed. Kingdom, pp. 78, 168.
203. Compare Niccolò Machiavelli, *The Prince*, ed. Quentin Skinner and Russell Price (Cambridge, 1988), p. 62.
204. *The contre-Guyse* (London, 1589; STC 12506), Sig. E4v–F1r.
205. Allen, *Admonition*, Sig. C5v.
206. Quoted by John Warren, *Elizabeth I: Religion and Foreign Affairs* (London, 1993), p. 140.
207. John Foxe, *Actes and monuments* (London, 1583; STC 11225), Sig. SS4r.
208. Allen, *Admonition*, Sig. A7r, D2r.
209. See Lisa Hopkins, *Christopher Marlowe: A Literary Life* (Basingstoke, 2000), pp. 8–12.

4: FROM REBELLION TO REGICIDE

210. Mark Hutchings, 'Marlowe's "Scourge of God"', *Notes and Queries* 51 (2004), pp. 244–7; see also Richard Levin, 'The Contemporary Perception of Marlowe's Tamburlaine', *Medieval and Renaissance Drama in England*, 1 (1984), pp. 51–70.
211. Robert Greene, *Perimedes the blacke-smith* (London, 1588; STC 12295), Sig. A3r
212. Thomas Lodge, *The Wounds of Civil War*, ed. Joseph W. Houppert (London, 1970); Anonymous, *The Tragical Reign of Selimus*, Malone Society (Oxford, 1908). See James Shapiro, *Rival Playwrights: Marlowe, Jonson, Shakespeare* (New York, 1991), pp. 33–7.
213. George Peele, *The Battle of Alcazar*, ed. John Yoklavich, in Peele, *Works*, II, pp. 213–373.
214. *Tamburlaine*, Old Vic, London, 1951, dir. Tyrone Guthrie; *Tamburlaine*, RSC, Swan Theatre, Stratford-upon-Avon, 1992, dir. Terry Hands.
215. Lawrence Danson, 'Christopher Marlowe: The Questioner', *ELR* 12 (1982), p. 13.
216. Pope Sixtus V [drawn up by William Allen], *A declaration of the sentence and deposition of Elizabeth* (Antwerp, 1588; STC 22590), Sig. A1r.
217. William Warner, *Albions England* (London, 1586; STC 25079), Sig. A4v.
218. Thomas Heywood, *The Golden Age*, in *Dramatic Works*, 6 vols (New York, 1964), III, pp. 1–79.
219. *OED*, 'doting, doating', *vbl. n.* 1. The term may also imply 'the bestowal of foolish affection', though the first date given for this usage in the *OED* is 1622 (*vbl. n.* 2).
220. William Allen, *The copie of a letter written by M. Doctor Allen: concerning the yeelding up of the citie of Daventrie* (Antwerp, 1587; STC 370), Sig. B3r.
221. William Allen, *An admonition to the nobility* (Antwerp, 1588; STC 368), Sig. B8r.
222. '*Il a esté loisible à David de se defendre contre la tyrannie de Saül*'. Théodore de Bèze, *Du Droit des Magistrats*, ed. Robert M. Kingdom (Genève, 1970), p. 31.
223. 'An Homilie against Disobedience and Wylfull Rebellion (1570)', in '*Certain Sermons or Homilies*' *and 'A Homily against Disobedience and Wilful Rebellion*', ed. Ronald B. Bond (Toronto, Buffalo and London, 1987), pp. 219–23.
224. C.L. Barber, *Creating Elizabethan Tragedy: The Theater of Marlowe and Kyd*, ed. Richard P. Wheeler (Chicago and London, 1988), pp. 82–4; Samuel Rowlands, *Hell's broke loose* (London, 1605; STC 21385), Sig. D3v.
225. Thomas Nashe, *The Unfortunate Traveller*, in Nashe, *Works*, II, pp. 232–41.
226. John Foxe, *Actes and monuments* (London, 1583; STC 11225), Sig. SS4r; Pedro Mexía, *The Forest*, trans. Thomas Fortescue (London, 1576; STC 17850), Sig. S2r. Thomas Fortescue is identified as the author of this translation in accordance with common critical practice.

227. Fortescue, *The Forest*, Sig. I3r–I3v.
228. Paul Whitfield White, 'Marlowe and the Politics of Religion', in *The Cambridge Companion to Christopher Marlowe*, ed. Patrick Cheney (Cambridge, 2004), p. 72; Daniel Vitkus, *Turning Turk: English Theater and the Multicultural Mediterranean, 1570–1630* (New York and Basingstoke, 2003), p. 47.
229. See *OED*, 'term', *v.* 2.
230. Allen, *Admonition*, Sig. A3v, D3r.
231. William Allen, *A True, Sincere, and Modest Defense of English Catholics*, in *'Execution' and 'Defense'*, ed. Kingdom, pp. 216–17.
232. Stephanus Junius Brutus [pseud.], *Vindiciae, Contra Tyrannos*, ed. George Garnett (Cambridge, 1994), p. 15, pp. 148–9.
233. Nicholas Tempe, 'Julius II as Second Caesar', in *Julius Caesar in Western Culture*, ed. Maria Wyke (Malden, Mass., and Oxford, 2006), p. 113; Lisa Hopkins, *The Cultural Uses of the Caesars on the English Renaissance Stage* (Aldershot, 2008), pp. 3–5; John E. Curran Jr., *Roman Invasions: The British History, Protestant Anti-Romanism and the Historical Imagination in England, 1530–1660* (Newark and London, 2002), pp. 153–78.
234. John Bakeless, *Christopher Marlowe* (London, 1938), p. 299.
235. Sir Philip Sidney, *An Apology for Poetry*, ed. Geoffrey Shepherd, 2nd edn (Manchester, 1973), p. 112. Noted by Edward Paleit, 'The "Caesarist" Reader and Lucan's *Bellum Civile*, *C.A.* 1590 to 1610', *RES* (2010), p. 212.
236. John Henderson, 'Lucan/The Word at War', *Ramus: Critical Studies in Greek and Roman Literature* 16 (1987), p. 124.
237. Paleit, 'The "Caesarist" Reader', pp. 215–22.
238. Bèze, *Droit*, p. 12; Patrick Cheney, *Marlowe's Republican Authorship: Lucan, Liberty, and the Sublime* (Basingstoke, 2009), pp. 143–4.
239. Lucan, *Lucans Pharsalia*, trans. Sir Arthur Gorges (London, 1614; STC 16884), Sig. H6r. Noted by David Norbrook, *Writing the English Republic: Poetry, Rhetoric and Politics, 1627–1660* (Cambridge, 1999), p. 41.
240. Norbrook, *English Republic*, pp. 39–41. See Agrippa d'Aubigné, *Les Tragiques*, ed. I.D. McFarlane (London, 1970), esp. Book VII.
241. Norbrook, *English Republic*, p. 41.
242. See Paleit, 'The "Caesarist" Reader', pp. 226–7.
243. Roma Gill, 'Marlowe, Lucan, and Sulpitius', *RES* 24 (1973), p. 401.
244. 'The narrow bounds of the Asylum pitted its owners one against the other.' Lucan, *The Civil War*, trans. and ed. J.D. Duff, Loeb Classical Library (Cambridge, Mass., 1928), 1.97.
245. See for example Allen, *Admonition*, Sig. A6v.
246. Richard Verstegan, *The copy of a letter lately written by a Spanishe gentleman* (Antwerp, 1589; STC 1038), Sig. A2v.
247. See for example Martin Marprelate [pseud.], *The Protestation of Martin Marprelate*, in *The Martin Marprelate Tracts: A Modernized and Annotated Edition*, ed. Joseph L. Black (Cambridge, 2008), p. 202.
248. See for example William Rainolds, *Calvino-Turcismus* (Antwerp, 1597);

Christopher Tyerman, *England and the Crusades 1095–1588* (Chicago and London, 1988), pp. 343–70.
249. Raphael Holinshed, *The first and second volumes of Chronicles* (London, 1586; STC 13569), Sig. 6B5r. Noted by Tyerman, *Crusades*, p. 363.
250. John Ponet, *A shorte treatise of politike power* (Strasbourg, 1556; STC 20178), Sig. G3r.
251. Robert Parsons, *An advertisement written to a secretarie of my L. Treasurers* (Antwerp, 1592; STC 19885), Sig. E1v.
252. Park Honan, *Christopher Marlowe: Poet and Spy* (Oxford, 2005), p. 273.
253. George Whetstone, *The English myrror* (London, 1586; STC 25336), Sig. F8r; Anonymous, *The contre-Guyse* (London, 1589; STC 12506), Sig. C4r, D4v.
254. *Contre-Guyse*, Sig. I2v.
255. Anonymous, *The Tragical Reign of Selimus*, Malone Society (London, 1908).
256. Julia Briggs, 'Marlowe's *Massacre at Paris*: A Reconsideration', *RES* 34 (1983), p. 270.
257. Compare Niccolò Machiavelli, *The Prince*, ed. Quentin Skinner and Russell Price (Cambridge, 1988), pp. 85–7.
258. See Bèze, *Droit*, p. 63, pp. 66–7; Quentin Skinner, *The Foundations of Modern Political Thought*, 2 vols. (Cambridge, 1978), II, pp. 302–9.
259. Brutus, *Vindiciae*, p. 185, p. 187.
260. Richard Bancroft, *A sermon preached at Paules Crosse* (London, 1588; STC 1347), pp. 74–9.
261. Robert Parsons, *A brief censure uppon two bookes* (Pyrton, 1581; STC 19393), Sig. E1v.
262. Ponet, *Treatise*, Sig. H1r–H3r.
263. John Warren, *Elizabeth I: Religion and Foreign Affairs* (London, 1993), p. 140.
264. Allen, *Admonition*, Sig. C5r.
265. William Kempe, *A dutiful invectiue* (London, 1587; STC 14925), §3v; Richard Wilson, 'Introduction: a torturing hour – Shakespeare and the martyrs', in Richard Dutton, Alison Findlay, and Richard Wilson (eds), *Theatre and Religion: Lancastrian Shakespeare* (Manchester and New York, 2003), p. 7.
266. George Whetstone, *The censure of a loyall subject* (London, 1587; STC 25334a), Sig. D2r.
267. I am grateful to Austen Saunders for bringing this tract to my attention.
268. Quoted in J.E. Neale, *Elizabeth I and her Parliaments 1584–1601* (London, 1957), p. 127.
269. See *A Treatise of Equivocation*, ed. David Jardine (London, 1851), p. 50.
270. Thomas Nashe, *Pierce Penilesse his Supplication*, in Nashe, *Works*, I, p. 186.
271. Martin Wiggins, *Journeymen in Murder: The Assassin in English Renaissance Drama* (Oxford, 1991), pp. 49–52.
272. François Hotman, *A True and Plain Report of the Furious Outrages of France* (London, 1573; STC 13847), Sig. E2r.

273. See Christopher Marlowe, *'Dido Queen of Carthage' and 'The Massacre at Paris'*, ed. H.J. Oliver (London, 1968), liv–lv.
274. '*Autres tiennent que la Royne mere dit en partant, à Henry de Valois, Allez hardiment, mon Fils, vous n'y serez pas long-temps; . . . Quoy qu'il en soit, le Roy Charles a esté empoisonné.*' Jean Boucher, *La Vie et Faits Notables de Henry de Valois*, ed. Keith Cameron (Paris, 2003), pp. 51–2.
275. Antony Colynet, *The true history of the civill warres of France* (London, 1591; STC 5590), Sig. Dd1r–Dd2r.
276. Foxe, *Actes*, Sig. Y2v.

5: 'DOCTOR FAUSTUS': A CRISIS OF CONSCIENCE?

277. Barnabe Barnes, *The Devil's Charter*, ed. Jim C. Pogue (London, 1980).
278. Frederick S. Boas, 'Introduction to *The Tragical History of Doctor Faustus* (London, 1932), pp. 36–7; *The Tragical History of Doctor Faustus*, Theatre Laboratory, 1963, dir. Jerzy Grotowski.
279. *Doctor Faustus*, Shakespeare's Globe, London, 2011, dir. Matthew Dunster.
280. Thomas Nashe, *Christs teares over Jerusalem*, in Nashe, *Works*, II, p. 91.
281. 'An Homilie against Disobedience and Wylfull Rebellion (1570)', in '*Certain Sermons or Homilie' and 'A Homily against Disobedience and Wilful Rebellion'*, ed. Ronald B. Bond (Toronto, Buffalo and London, 1987), pp. 210–11.
282. See for example John D. Cox, *The Devil and the Sacred in English Drama, 1350–1642* (Cambridge, 2000), pp. 111–13.
283. Lucretius, *De Rerum Natura*, trans. W.H.D. Rouse, ed. Martin Ferguson Smith, Loeb Classical Library (Cambridge, Mass., 1975), 3.798–9.
284. Thomas Beard, *The theatre of Gods judgements* (London, 1597; STC 1659), Sig. K1r.
285. See Nicholas Davidson, 'Unbelief and Atheism in Italy, 1500–1700', in *Atheism from the Reformation to the Enlightenment*, ed. Michael Hunter and David Wootton (Oxford, 1992), p. 64.
286. Lucretius, *De Rerum*, 1.55–7.
287. Ibid., 1.79.
288. Anonymous, *The Tragical Reign of Selimus*, Malone Society (London, 1908).
289. Anthony Munday, *An Edition of Anthony Munday's 'John A Kent and John A Cumber'*, ed. Arthur E. Pennell (New York and London, 1980).
290. Anthony Munday, *The English Romayne life* (London, 1582; STC 18272), Sig. G3v–G4r.
291. See Christopher Marlowe, *Doctor Faustus: A- and B-texts* (*1604*, *1616*), ed. David Bevington and Eric Rasmussen (Manchester and New York, 1993), pp. 399–413.
292. Robert Parsons, *An advertisement written to a secretarie of my L. Treasurers* (Antwerp: 1592; STC 19885), Sig. B1v.
293. Leah S. Marcus, *Unediting the Renaissance: Shakespeare, Marlowe, Milton* (London and New York, 1996), p. 58; Stephen Orgel, *The Authentic*

Shakespeare and Other Problems of the Early Modern Stage (New York, 2002), pp. 225–6.

294. Gabriel Harvey, *Pierces supererogation* (London, 1593; STC 12903), Sig. R3r.
295. *The English Faust Book: A Critical Edition Based on the Text of 1592*, ed. John Henry Jones (Cambridge, 1994), p. 92.
296. Simon Shepherd, *Marlowe and the politics of Elizabethan theatre* (Brighton, 1986), p. 135; David Riggs, *The World of Christopher Marlowe* (London, 2004), p. 241.
297. See David Zaret, *The Heavenly Contract: Ideology and Organization in Pre-revolutionary Puritanism* (Chicago and London, 1985), pp. 163–98, for a fuller discussion of commercial metaphor, the heavenly contract and the concept of spiritual ownership in early modern puritan preaching.
298. 'The Thirty-Nine Articles', in *Doctor Faustus*, ed. David Scott Kastan (New York and London, 2005), p. 247.
299. *The Geneva Bible: A Facsimile of the 1560 Edition*, ed. Lloyd E. Berry (Peabody, Mass., 2007); John Foxe, *Actes and Monuments* (London, 1583; STC. 11225), especially Volume 1.
300. Thomas Newhouse, *A learned and fruitfull sermon* (London, 1612; STC 18494), Sig. C1v.
301. *EFB*, pp. 95–7.
302. Niccolò Machiavelli, *The Discourses*, trans. Leslie J. Walker, ed. Bernard Crick (London, 1970, rpt. with revisions 2003), p. 409.
303. Machiavelli wrote that 'not only are forced promises not observed by princes when the force in question is no longer operative; but we also find that all other promises are broken when the reasons which caused such promises to be made no longer hold good'. Machiavelli, *Discourses*, p. 516.
304. Christopher St German, *Doctor and Student*, ed. T.F.T. Plucknett and J.L. Barton, *Selden Society* 91 (1974), p. 117.
305. Luke Wilson, *Theaters of Intention: Drama and the Law in Early Modern England* (Stanford, 2000), p. 207.
306. Barbara Howard Traister, *Heavenly Necromancers: The Magician in English Renaissance Drama* (Columbia, 1984), pp. 100–1.
307. Lisa Hopkins, *Christopher Marlowe: Renaissance Dramatist* (Edinburgh, 2008), p. 164.
308. Robert Parsons, *A brief censure upon two bookes* (Pyrton, 1581; STC 19393), Sig. D8r.
309. Nathaniel Woodes, *The conflict of conscience* (London, 1581; STC 25966).
310. *Tamburlaine*, RSC, Swan Theatre, Stratford-upon-Avon, 1992, dir. Terry Hands.

CODA: MARLOWE'S LEGACY

311. See J.A.I. Champion, *The Pillars of Priestcraft Shaken: The Church of England and its Enemies, 1660–1730* (Cambridge, 1992), p. 181.

312. See William M. Hamlin, 'Misbelief, False Profession, and *The Jew of Malta*', in *Placing the Plays of Christopher Marlowe: Fresh Cultural Contexts*, ed. Sara Munson Deats and Robert A. Logan (Aldershot, 2008), pp. 156–64.
313. Hugh Grady, *Shakespeare, Machiavelli, and Montaigne: Power and Subjectivity from 'Richard II' to 'Hamlet'* (Oxford, 2002), p. 26; John Roe, *Shakespeare and Machiavelli* (Cambridge, 2002), p. 1.
314. Cf. *A Treatise of Equivocation*, ed. David Jardine (London, 1851), p. 48.
315. See Peter Lake with Michael Questier, *The Antichrist's Lewd Hat: Protestants, Papists and Players in Post-Reformation England* (New Haven and London, 2002), p. 387; Garry Wills, *Witches and Jesuits: Shakespeare's 'Macbeth'* (Oxford, 1995), pp. 93–105; Arthur F. Kinney, *Lies Like Truth: Shakespeare, Macbeth, and the Cultural Moment* (Detroit, 2001), pp. 103–5.
316. Ben Jonson, *Mortimer his Fall*, in *Ben Jonson*, ed. C.H. Herford and Percy Simpson, 11 vols (Oxford, 1941), VII, pp. 51–62.
317. Ben Jonson, *Catiline*, ed W.F. Bolton and Jane F. Gardner (London, 1973).
318. John Michael Archer, *Sovereignty and Intelligence: Spying and Court Culture in the English Renaissance* (Stanford, 1993), pp. 115–17.
319. See for example Thomas Heywood, *The Captives*, Malone Society (Oxford, 1953), ll. 3206–11; Thomas Heywood, *The Fair Maid of the West, Parts I and II*, ed. Robert K. Turner (London, 1968), *Part II*, 3.3.139–69.
320. John Milton, *Paradise Lost*, ed. Gordon Teskey (New York and London, 2005); Stanley Fish, *Surprised by Sin: The Reader in 'Paradise Lost'*, 2nd edn (Basingstoke, 1997), pp. ix–x. For Fish's rebuttal see for instance pp. 57–91; Fish's emphasis on God's 'pure' and plain language itself relates intriguingly to the linguistic strategies used by Mephistopheles.
321. See Lawrence W. Hyman, 'Belief and Disbelief in *Lycidas*', *College English* 33 (1972), pp. 532–42.
322. John Toland, *Nazarenus: or, Jewish, Gentile, and Mahometan Christianity* (London, 1718; STC T139629), Sig. B8v. See Champion, *Pillars*, pp. 126–7; Thomas Hobbes, *Leviathan*, ed. J.C.A. Gaskin (Oxford, 1996), esp. pp. 330–3.
323. Charles Blount, *Religio laici* (London, 1683; Wing/B3314), Sig. A10v–A11r, B2r; Charles Gildon, 'Preface', in *Religio laici* (London, 1683), Sig. B4r.
324. Charles Gildon, 'Preface', Sig. B4r–B4v.
325. See Jonathan I. Israel, *Radical Enlightenment: Philosophy and the Making of Modernity 1650–1750* (Oxford, 2001), esp. pp. 329–43.

SELECT BIBLIOGRAPHY

A Treatise of Equivocation, ed. David Jardine (London, 1851)

Ainsworth, Henry, *An apologie or defence of such true Christians as are commonly (but unjustly) called Brownists* (Amsterdam, 1604; STC 239)

Allen, William, *A True, Sincere and Modest Defence of English Catholics*, in *'The Execution of Justice in England' by William Cecil and 'A True, Sincere and Modest Defense of English Catholics' by William Allen*, ed. Robert M. Kingdom (Ithaca, 1965), pp. 51–268

———, *An admonition to the nobility* (Antwerp, 1588; STC 368)

———, *An apologie and true declaration of the institution and endevours of the two English colleges* (Rheims, 1581; STC 369)

———, *The copie of a letter written by M. Doctor Allen: concerning the yeelding up of the citie of Daventrie* (Antwerp, 1587; STC 370))

Anonymous, *The contre-Guyse* (London, 1589; STC 12506)

Anonymous, *The Tragical Reign of Selimus*, Malone Society (Oxford, 1908)

Archer, John Michael, *Sovereignty and Intelligence: Spying and Court Culture in the English Renaissance* (Stanford, 1993)

Atiyah, P.S., *Promises, Morals, and Law* (Oxford, 1981)

Aylmer, G.E, 'Unbelief in Seventeenth-Century England', in *Puritans and Revolutionaries: Essays in Seventeenth-Century History presented to Christopher Hill*, ed. Donald Pennington and Keith Thomas (Oxford, 1982), pp. 22–46

Azpilcueta, Martín de, *Commenterius in cap. Humanae Aures*, in D. Martini ab Azpilcueta, *Navarri*, i.*V.D.*, *Praeclarissimi Commentaria*, in 3 vols (Venice, 1588), I

———, *Enchiridion* (Moguntiae, 1603), York, Borthwick Institute for Archives, Mirfield Collection (1603; AZP)

Babb, Howard S., 'Policy in Marlowe's *The Jew of Malta*', *English Literary History* 24 (1957), pp. 85–94

Bacon, Sir Francis, *The Essays or Counsels Civil and Moral*, ed. Brian Vickers (Oxford, 1999)

Baines, Richard, 'A note containing the opinion of on[e] Christopher Marly', MSS BL Harleian 6848, in Park Honan, *Christopher Marlowe: Poet and Spy* (Oxford, 2005), p. 374

Baker, Sir John (ed.), *The Oxford History of the Laws of England*, 12 vols (Oxford, 2003), VI

Bancroft, Richard, *A sermon preached at Paules Crosse* (London, 1588; STC 1347)

———, *Daungerous positions and proceedings* (London, 1593; STC 1344.5)

Barber, C.L., *Creating Elizabethan Tragedy: The Theater of Marlowe and Kyd*, ed. Richard P. Wheeler (Chicago and London, 1988)

Barlow, William, *An answer to a Catholike English-Man* (London, 1609; STC 1446.5)

Barnes, Barnabe, *The Devil's Charter*, ed. Jim C. Pogue (London, 1980)

Bartels, Emily C, *Spectacles of Strangeness: Imperialism, Alienation, and Marlowe* (Philadelphia, 1993)

Bawcutt, N.W., 'The "Myth of Gentillet" Reconsidered: An Aspect of Elizabethan Machiavellianism', *Modern Language Review* 99 (2004), pp. 863–74

Beard, Thomas, *The theatre of Gods judgements* (London, 1597; STC 1659)

Berry, Lloyd E. (ed.), *The Geneva Bible: A Facsimile of the 1560 Edition* (Peabody, Mass., 2007)

Bèze, Théodore de, *Du Droit des Magistrats*, ed. Robert M. Kingdom (Genève, 1970)

Bilson, Thomas, *The true difference betweene Christian subjection and unchristian rebellion* (Oxford, 1585; STC 3071)

Blount, Charles, *Religio laici* (London, 1683; Wing / B3314)

Boucher, Jean. *La Vie et Faits Notables de Henry de Valois*, ed. Keith Cameron (Paris, 2003)

Braden, Gordon, *The Classics and English Renaissance Poetry: Three Case Studies* (New Haven and London, 1978)

Briggs, Julia, 'Marlowe's *Massacre at Paris*: A Reconsideration', *Review of English Studies* 34 (1983), pp. 257–78

Brutus, Stephanus Junius [pseud.] *Vindiciae, Contra Tyrannos*, ed. George Garnett (Cambridge, 1994)

Burton, Jonathan, *Traffic and Turning: Islam and English Drama, 1579–1624* (Newark, 2005)

Cecil, William, Lord Burghley[?], *The copie of a letter sent out of England to Don Bernardin Mendoza* (London, 1588; STC 15412)

Cecil, William, Lord Burghley, *The Execution of Justice in England*, in *'The Execution of Justice in England' by William Cecil and 'A True, Sincere and Modest Defense of English Catholics' by William Allen*, ed. Robert M. Kingdom (Ithaca, 1965)

Champion, J.A.I., *The Pillars of Priestcraft Shaken: The Church of England and its Enemies, 1660–1730* (Cambridge, 1992), pp. 1–41

Charke, William, *An answere to a seditious pamphlet* (London, 1581; STC 5006)

Cheney, Patrick. *Marlowe's Counterfeit Profession: Ovid, Spenser, Counter-Nationhood* (Toronto, Buffalo and London, 1997)

————, *Marlowe's Republican Authorship: Lucan, Liberty, and the Sublime* (Basingstoke, 2009)

————, *The Cambridge Companion to Christopher Marlowe* (Cambridge, 2004)

Colynet, Antony, *The true history of the civill warres of France* (London, 1591; STC 5590)

Cornelius, R.M., *Christopher Marlowe's Use of the Bible* (New York, 1984)

Cox, John D., *The Devil and the Sacred in English Drama, 1350–1642* (Cambridge, 2000)

Curran, John E. Jr. *Roman Invasions: The British History, Protestant Anti-Romanism and The Historical Imagination in England, 1530–1660* (Newark and London, 2002)

Danson, Lawrence, 'Christopher Marlowe: The Questioner', *English Literary Renaissance* 12 (1982), pp. 3–29

Davidson, Nicholas, 'Christopher Marlowe and Atheism', in Darryll Grantley and Peter Roberts (eds), *Christopher Marlowe and English Renaissance Culture* (Aldershot, 1996), pp. 129–47

————, 'Unbelief and Atheism in Italy, 1500–1700', in Michael Hunter and David Wootton (eds), *Atheism from the Reformation to the Enlightenment*, (Oxford, 1992) pp. 55–86

Davies, Sir John, *Sir Martin Mar-people* (London, 1590; STC 6363)

Deats, Sara Munson, and Robert A. Logan (eds), *Marlowe's Empery: Expanding His Critical Contexts* (Newark, 2002)

————, *Placing the Plays of Christopher Marlowe: Fresh Cultural Contexts* (Aldershot, 2008)

Deats, Sara Munson, 'Marlowe's Interrogative Drama: *Dido*, *Tamburlaine*, *Faustus* and *Edward II*', in Sara Munson Deats and Robert A. Logan (eds), *Marlowe's Empery: Expanding His Critical Contexts* (Newark, 2002), pp. 107–30

————,' "Mark this show": Magic and Theater in Marlowe's *Doctor Faustus*', in Sara Munson Deats and Robert A. Logan (eds), *Placing the Plays of Christopher Marlowe: Fresh Cultural Contexts* (Aldershot, 2008), pp. 13–24

Dimmock, Matthew. *New Turkes: Dramatizing Islam and the Ottomans in Early Modern England* (Aldershot, 2005)

Downie, J.A. and J.T. Parnell (eds), *Constructing Christopher Marlowe* (Cambridge, 2000)

Dutton, Richard, Alison Findlay and Richard Wilson (eds), *Theatre and Religion: Lancastrian Shakespeare* (Manchester and New York, 2003)

Earle, John, *Micro-cosmographie* (London, 1628; STC 7441)

Febrve, Lucien, *The Problem of Unbelief in the Sixteenth Century: The Religion of Rabelais*, trans. Beatrice Gottlieb (Cambridge, Mass., and London, 1982)

Fielde, John, *A caveat for Parsons Howlet* (London, 1581; STC 10844)

Foxe, John, *Actes and Monuments* (London, 1583; STC 11225)

Fulke, William, *Two treatises written against the papists* (London, 1577; STC 11458)

Gager, William, *Dido Tragoedia*, in Adrianne Roberts-Baytop (ed.), *Dido, Queen of Infinite Literary Variety: The English Renaissance Borrowings and Influences* (Salzburg, 1974)

Gifford, George, *A dialogue betweene a papist and a Protestant* (London, 1582; STC 11849)

Gill, Roma, 'Marlowe, Lucan, and Sulpitius', *Review of English Studies* 24 (1973), pp. 401–13

Goldberg, Dena, 'Sacrifice in Marlowe's *The Jew of Malta*', *Studies in English Literature* 32 (1992), pp. 233–45

Grady, Hugh, *Shakespeare, Machiavelli, and Montaigne: Power and Subjectivity from 'Richard II' to 'Hamlet'* (Oxford, 2002)

Graham, Kenneth J.E., *The Performance of Conviction: Plainness and Rhetoric in the Early English Renaissance* (Ithaca and London, 1994)

Grantley, Darryll, and Peter Roberts (eds), *Christopher Marlowe and English Renaissance Culture* (Aldershot, 1996)

Greene, Robert, *Alphonsus King of Aragon*, Malone Society (Oxford, 1926)

———, *Greenes, groats-worth of witte* (London, 1592; STC 12245)

———, *Perimedes the blacke-smith* (London, 1588; STC 12295)

Greenwood, John, *An answere to George Giffords pretended defence* (Dordrecht, 1590; STC 12339)

Haigh, Christopher, *English Reformations: Religion, Politics, and Society under the Tudors* (Oxford, 1993, rpt. with revisions 1995)

Hamlin, William M. 'Misbelief, False Profession, and *The Jew of Malta*', in Sara Munson Deats and Robert A. Logan (eds), *Placing the Plays of Christopher Marlowe: Fresh Cultural Contexts* (Aldershot, 2008), pp. 156–64

———, *Tragedy and Scepticism in Shakespeare's England* (Basingstoke, 2005)

Harsnett, Samuel, *A declaration of egregious popish impostures* (London, 1603; STC 12880)

Harvey, Gabriel, *Pierces supererogation* (London, 1593; STC 12903)

Hattaway, Michael, 'Christopher Marlowe: Ideology and Subversion', in Darryll Grantley and Peter Roberts (eds), *Christopher Marlowe and English Renaissance Culture* (Aldershot, 1996), pp. 198–223

Hayes, Douglas W., *Rhetorical Subversion in Early English Dram* (New York, 2004)

Henderson, John, 'Lucan/The Word at War', *Ramus: Critical Studies in Greek and Roman Literature* 16 (1987), pp. 122–64

Heywood, Thomas, *The Captives*, Malone Society (Oxford, 1953)

———, *The Fair Maid of the West, Parts I and II*, ed. Robert K. Turner (London, 1968)

———, *The Golden Age*, in *Dramatic Works*, 6 vols (New York, 1964), III

Hobbes, Thomas. *Leviathan*, ed. J.C.A. Gaskin (Oxford, 1996)

Honan, Park, *Christopher Marlowe: Poet and Spy* (Oxford, 2005)

Hooker, Richard. *Of the Laws of Ecclesiastical Polity: Book V*, in *The Folger Library Edition of the Works of Richard Hooker*, ed. W. Speed Hill, 7 vols (Cambridge, Mass., and London, 1977), II

Hopkins, Lisa. *Christopher Marlowe, Renaissance Dramatist* (Edinburgh, 2008)

———, *Christopher Marlowe: A Literary Life* (Basingstoke, 2000)

———, *The Cultural Uses of the Caesars on the English Renaissance Stage* (Aldershot, 2008)

Hotman, François, *A True and Plain Report of the Furious Outrages of France* (London, 1573; STC 13847)

———, *Francogallia*, trans. J.H.M. Salmon with Ralph E. Giesey (Cambridge, 1972)

Hunter, Michael, and David Wootton (eds), *Atheism from the Reformation to the Enlightenment* (Oxford, 1992)

Hutchings, Mark, '"In Thrace: Brought up in Arabia": *The Jew of Malta*, II.iii.131', *Notes and Queries* 47 (2000), pp. 428–30

———, 'Marlowe's "Scourge of God"', *Notes and Queries* 51 (2004), pp. 244–7

Ingram, Martin, *Church Courts, Sex and Marriage in England, 1570–1640* (Cambridge, 1987)

Israel, Jonathan I., *Radical Enlightenment: Philosophy and the Making of Modernity 1650–1750* (Oxford, 2001)

Jones, John Henry (ed.), *The English Faust Book A critical edition based on the text of 1592* (Cambridge, 1994)

Jonson, Ben, *Catiline*, ed. W.F. Bolton and Jane F. Gardner (London, 1973)

———, *Mortimer his Fall*, in C.H. Herford and Percy Simpson (eds), *Ben Jonson*, 11 vols (Oxford, 1941), VII, pp. 51–62

Kempe, William, *A dutiful invectiue* (London, 1587; STC 14925)

Kendall, Roy, 'Richard Baines and Christopher Marlowe's Milieu', *English Literary Renaissance* 24 (1994), pp. 507–52

Kocher, Paul. *Christopher Marlowe: A Study of his Thought, Learning, and Character* (New York, 1962)

Kyd, Thomas, 'Unsigned Note to Puckering', BL Harleian MS 6849, in Park Honan, *Christopher Marlowe: Poet and Spy* (Oxford, 2005), p. 381

———, *Soliman and Perseda*, in *The Works of Thomas Kyd*, ed. Frederick S. Boas , 2nd edition (Oxford, 1955), pp. 161–230

Lake, Peter, with Michael Questier, *The Antichrist's Lewd Hat: Protestants, Papists and Players in Post-Reformation England* (New Haven and London, 2002)

Leslie[?], John, *A treatise of treasons* (Louvain, 1572; STC 7601)

Lesser, Zachary, *Renaissance Drama and the Politics of Publication: Readings in the English Book Trade* (Cambridge, 2004)

Levin, Harry, *Christopher Marlowe: The Overreacher* (London, 1953)

Lodge, Thomas, and Robert Greene, *A Looking-Glass for London and England*, Malone Society (Oxford, 1932)

Lodge, Thomas, in Joseph W. Houppert (ed.), *The Wounds of Civil War* (London, 1970)

Lunney, Ruth, *Marlowe and the Popular Tradition: Innovation in the English Drama before 1595* (Manchester, 2002)

Machiavelli, Niccolò, *The Discourses*, trans. by Leslie J. Walker, ed. Bernard Crick (London, 1970; rpt. with revisions 2003)

———, *The Prince*, ed. Quentin Skinner and Russell Price (Cambridge, 1988)

Marcus, Leah S., *Unediting the Renaissance: Shakespeare, Marlowe, Milton* (London and New York, 1996)

Marprelate, Martin [pseud.] *Oh read over D. John Bridges . . . Or an Epitome*, in *The Martin Marprelate Tracts: A Modernized and Annotated Edition*, ed. Joseph L. Black (Cambridge, 2008), pp. 49–86

———, *The Protestation of Martin Marprelate*, in *The Martin Marprelate Tracts: A Modernized and Annotated Edition*, ed. Joseph L. Black (Cambridge, 2008), pp. 193–207

Matar, Nabil, *Islam in Britain 1558–1685* (Cambridge, 1998)

McCoog, Thomas M. (ed.), *The Reckoned Expense: Edmund Campion and the Early English Jesuits*, 2nd edn (Rome, 2007)

More, Sir Thomas, *The second parte of the confutacion* (London, 1553; STC 18080)

Mornay, Philippe de, *A woorke concerning the trewnesse of the Christian religion* (London, 1587; STC 18149)

Moss, Joan Dietz, 'Variations on a Theme: The Family of Love in Renaissance England', *Renaissance Quarterly* 31 (1978), pp. 186–95

Munday, Anthony, *A discoverie of Edmund Campion* (London, 1582; STC 18270)

———, *The English Romayne life* (London, 1582; STC 18272)

Nashe, Thomas, *An Almond for a Parrat*, in R.B. McKerrow and F.P. Wilson (eds), *The Works of Thomas Nashe*, 3 vols (Oxford, 1958), III

———, *Christs teares over Jerusalem*, in R.B. McKerrow and F.P. Wilson (eds), *The Works of Thomas Nashe*, 3 vols (Oxford, 1958), II

———, *Have with you to Saffron-Walden*, in R.B. McKerrow and F.P. Wilson (eds), *The Works of Thomas Nashe*, 3 vols (Oxford, 1958), III

———, *Pierce Penilesse his Supplication*, in R.B. McKerrow and F.P. Wilson (eds), *The Works of Thomas Nashe*, 3 vols (Oxford, 1958), I

———, *The Terrors of the Night*, in R.B. McKerrow and F.P. Wilson (eds), *The Works of Thomas Nashe*, 3 vols (Oxford, 1958), I

———, *The Unfortunate Traveller*, in R.B. McKerrow and F. P. Wilson (eds), *The Works of Thomas Nashe*, 3 vols (Oxford, 1958) II

Newhouse, Thomas, *A learned and fruitfull sermon* (London, 1612; STC 18494)

Nicholl, Charles, *The Reckoning: The Murder of Christopher Marlowe*, 2nd edn (London, 1992)

Norbrook, David, *Writing the English Republic: Poetry, Rhetoric and Politics, 1627–1660* (Cambridge, 1999)

Orgel, Stephen, *The Authentic Shakespeare and Other Problems of the Early Modern Stage* (New York, 2002)

Paleit, Edward, 'The "Caesarist" Reader and Lucan's *Bellum Civile, C.A.* 1590 to 1610', *Review of English Studies* (2010), pp. 212–40

Parmelee, Lisa Ferraro, *Good Newes from Fraunce: French Anti-League Propaganda in Late Elizabethan England* (Rochester, New York and Woodbridge, Sussex, 1996)

Parsons, Robert, *A brief censure uppon two books* (Pyrton, 1581; STC 19393)

———, *A brief discours contayning certayne reasons why Catholiques refuse to goe to church* (East Ham, 1580; STC 19394)

———, *A defence of the censure* (Rouen, 1582; STC 19401)

———, *A discoverie of J. Nicols minister* (Pyrton, 1581; STC 19402)

———, *An advertisement written to a secretarie of my L. Treasurers* (Antwerp, 1592; STC 19885)

Peacham, Henry, *The Garden of Eloquence*, ed. William G. Crane (Ann Arbor, Mich., 1977)

Peele, George, *The Araygnement of Paris*, in R. Mark Benbow (ed.), *The Dramatic Works of George Peele* (New Haven and London, 1961), III, pp. 1–131.

———, *The Battle of Alcazar*, in John Yoklavich (ed.), *The Dramatic Works of George Peele* (New Haven and London, 1961), II, pp. 213–373

Pennington, Donald, and Keith Thomas, *Puritans and Revolutionaries: Essays in Seventeenth-Century History Presented to Christopher Hill* (Oxford, 1982)

Perkins, William, *A reformed Catholic* (Cambridge, 1598; STC 19736)

Ponet, John, *A shorte treatise of politike power* (Strasbourg, 1556; STC 20178)

Poole, Kirsten, *Radical Religion from Shakespeare to Milton: Figures of Non-conformity in Early Modern England* (Cambridge, 2000)

Popkin, Richard H., *The History of Scepticism: From Savonarola to Bayle* (Oxford and New York, 1960, rpt with revisions 2003)

Questier, Michael C., *Conversion, politics and religion in England, 1580–1625* (Cambridge, 1996)

Rainolds, William, *A refutation of sundry reprehensions* (Paris, 1583; STC 20632)

Recusants in the Exchequer Pipe Rolls 1581–1592, ed. Dom Hugh Bowler and Timothy J. McGann, *Catholic Record Society*, 71 (1986)

Riggs, David, 'Marlowe's Quarrel with God', in Paul Whitfield White (ed.) *Marlowe, History, and Sexuality: New Critical Essays on Christopher Marlowe* (New York, 1998), pp. 15–38

———, 'The Poet in the Play: Life and Art in *Tamburlaine* and *The Jew of Malta*', in Takashi Kozuka and J.R. Mulryne (eds), *Shakespeare, Marlowe, Jonson: New Directions in Biography* (Aldershot, 2006), pp. 205–24

———, *The World of Christopher Marlowe* (London, 2004)

Roberts, Gareth, 'Marlowe and the Metaphysics of Magicians', in J.A. Downie and J.T. Parnell (eds), *Constructing Christopher Marlowe* (Cambridge, 2000), pp. 55–73

Roe, John, *Shakespeare and Machiavelli* (Cambridge, 2002)

Rowlands, Samuel, *Hell's broke loose* (London, 1605; STC 21385)

Seneca, *Hercules Furens*, in *Seneca: Six Tragedies*, trans. Emily Watson (Oxford, 2010), pp. 139–77

Shepherd, Simon. *Marlowe and the Politics of Elizabethan Theatre* (Brighton, 1986)

Shuger, Debora Kuller, *Habits of Thought in the English Renaissance: Religion Politics, and the Dominant Culture* (Berkeley, Los Angeles and London, 1990)

Sidney, Sir Philip, *An Apology for Poetry*, ed. Geoffrey Shepherd, 2nd edn (Manchester, 1973)

Skinner, Quentin, *The Foundations of Modern Political Thought*, 2 vols (Cambridge, 1978)

Southwell, Robert, *An epistle of comfort* (London, 1587[?]; STC 22946)

———, *An humble supplication to her Majestie* (England, 1595 (printed 1600); STC 22949.5)

St. German, Christopher, *Doctor and Student*, in T.F.T. Plucknett and J.L. Barton (eds), *Selden Society* (1974), p. 91

Stow, John, *The chronicles of England* (London, 1592; STC 23333)

Strohm, Paul, *Politique: Languages of Statecraft between Chaucer and Shakespeare* (Notre Dame, Ind., 2005)

Stump, Donald, 'Marlowe's Travesty of Virgil: Dido and Elizabethan Dreams of Empire', *Comparative Drama* 34.1 (2000), pp. 79–107

Targoff, Ramie, *Common Prayer: The Language of Public Devotion in Early Modern England* (Chicago and London, 2001)

Toland, John, *Nazarenus: or, Jewish, Gentile, and Mahometan Christianity* (London, 1718; STC T139629)

Traister, Barbara Howard, *Heavenly Necromancers: The Magician in English Renaissance Drama* (Columbia, 1984)

Tyerman, Christopher, *England and the Crusades 1095–1588* (Chicago and London, 1988)

Urry, William, *Christopher Marlowe and Canterbury*, ed. Andrew Butcher (London, 1988)

Verstegan, Richard, *The copy of a letter lately written by a Spanishe gentleman* (Antwerp, 1589; STC 1038)

Vitkus, Daniel, *Turning Turk: English Theater and the Multicultural Mediterranean, 1570–1630* (New York and Basingstoke, 2003)

Walsham, Alexandra, *Church Papists: Catholicism, Conformity and Confessional Polemic in Early Modern England* (Woodbridge, Sussex, 1993)

Warner, William, *Albions England* (London, 1586; STC 25079)

Warren, John, *Elizabeth I: Religion and Foreign Affairs* (London, 1993)

Whetstone, George, *The censure of a loyall subject* (London, 1587; STC 25334a)

————, *The English mirror* (London, 1586; STC 25336)

White, Paul Whitfield (ed.), *Marlowe, History, and Sexuality: New Critical Essays on Christopher Marlowe* (New York, 1998)

————, 'Marlowe and the Politics of Religion', in Patrick Cheney (ed.), *The Cambridge Companion to Christopher Marlowe* (Cambridge, 2004) pp. 70–89

Wiggins, Martin, 'When Did Marlowe Write *Dido, Queen of Carthage*?', *Review of English Studies* 59 (2008), pp. 521–41

————, *Journeymen in Murder: The Assassin in English Renaissance Drama* (Oxford, 1991)

Wilson, Luke, *Theaters of Intention: Drama and the Law in Early Modern England* (Stanford, 2000)

Wilson, Richard, 'Visible Bullets: Tamburlaine the Great and Ivan the Terrible', in Darryll Grantley and Peter Roberts (eds), *Christopher Marlowe and English Renaissance Culture* (Aldershot, 1996), pp. 51–69

Wilson, Robert, *The Three Ladies of London*, in Lloyd Edward Kermode (ed.), *Three Renaissance Usury Plays* (Manchester and New York, 2009), pp. 79–163

Wilson, Thomas, *The arte of rhetorique* (London, 1553; STC 25799)

Woodes, Nathaniel, *The conflict of conscience* (London, 1581; STC 25966)

Zagorin, Pere, *Ways of Lying: Dissimulation, Persecution, and Conformity in Early Modern Europe* (Cambridge, Mass., and London, 1990)

Zaret, David, *The Heavenly Contract: Ideology and Organization in Pre-revolutionary Puritanism* (Chicago and London, 1985)

INDEX